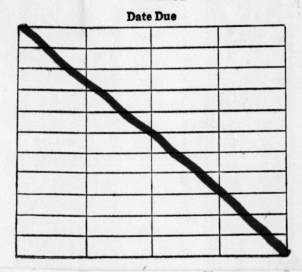

THREE TICKETS TO TIMBUKTU

THREE TICKETS

Halla Linker

TO TIMBUKTU

G. P. Putnam's Sons
New York

Contents

Illustrations appear after page 126.

THREE TICKETS TO TIMBUKTU

I

Green Iceland Is Not Icy Greenland

MUFFLED drums awakened me from a restless sleep in our mud-walled hut in a mountain village in northern Ethiopia. I tucked my thin army blanket more snugly about me and tried to still the chattering of my teeth. The village of Lalibela has an altitude of almost 10,000 feet, and the midnight air was icy, even though I slept fully dressed.

For a moment I thought I had only dreamed I heard the drums. But then a wailing chant joined the ominous, slow beat and I realized that this was no nightmare but the real thing.

I gasped and sat up. My husband, a few feet away on his own flimsy canvas cot, was instantly awake. "What is it, Halla?" he asked. I could hear him draw from its holster the small-calibered pistol he carried for emergencies.

"I'm sorry, Hal-minn." I spoke softly so as not to awaken our ten-year-old son David who slept on a cot between ours. "Those drums—and that chanting. At first I thought I was having a bad dream."

Hal chuckled. "It's all right, elskan-min," he said, using an Icelandic expression of endearment he had learned from

9

me before we were married. His strong hand grasped mine, and I immediately felt safer.

"But it sounds so savage, so threatening. Ethiopians are Christians. I thought only primitive tribes used drums."

"No, elskan-min. The priests of the Coptic Christian sect here use drums in their religious rites. They start at midnight and continue until dawn."

He paused and we listened to the cadence of the drums and the chant as it swelled and faded in the night.

"What you are hearing now," he continued, "is a religious ceremony that basically has not changed for thousands of years. It was adapted to Christianity sixteen hundred years ago. As a matter of fact, the Queen of Sheba once lived within a few miles of here. She would probably have felt right at home with that chanting and drumming. So go back to sleep, my Queen of Iceland, and dream of the Queen of Sheba!"

In the darkness I could not make out his expression but I knew he must be grinning as he slyly reminded me that I dream whenever I sleep, sometimes in color, even when I doze off into a catnap. When I first learned that not everyone shared this "talent," I had been astonished.

As I lay back on my rickety cot I started to tremble again but this time from the cold. Even in my discomfort I found myself smiling. Here I was, a native of Iceland, shivering in the mountains of Ethiopia, almost on the blazing Equator.

I began to recall some of the many adventures and travels I have shared with Hal during more than a dozen years of wonderful married life. Ours was more than just a marriage; it was also a delightful partnership in adventures that were colorful, fascinating and sometimes hazardous as we roamed the globe, filming material for our television travel-adventure series, *Wonders of the World*.

We had faced death on the Amazon and visited the Hairy Ainu of Japan, the fierce Gurkhas of Nepal and the gentle Samoans of Pago Pago. We had lived in the finest hotels on the Riviera, in Paris and Hong Kong, and in a camp in the wilds of Mozambique while on safari. We had become acquainted with native chieftains, dictators, kings and presidents. And now within three days we were to have an audience with one of the two remaining emperors on the face of the earth—His Imperial Majesty Haile Selassie, Emperor of Ethiopia, Conquering Lion of the Tribe of Judah.

I turned restlessly, wondering how one addresses an emperor.

"Try to sleep, Halla-min," my husband whispered. "Tomorrow will be a busy day."

"I'll try, dear."

Hal grunted and resettled himself. His cot sounded a warning as the rotting old canvas began to rip. I held my breath, but the ripping noise stopped. When the three of us retired, Hal had chosen the most dilapidated of the cots, with heroic resignation stating that if anyone had to wind up on the cold dirt floor, he might as well be the victim.

I stared up into the blackness of our hut. Sleep seemed further away than ever. Somewhere close by a rooster began to crow, and only my basically cheerful and optimistic nature prevented my brooding over the old Icelandic superstition that when a rooster crows throughout the night someone will die.

Then a new and entirely earthly worry entered my thoughts. The evening before, our hostess, the owner of the hut, a charming Ethiopian villager named Angwace, had taken us behind the hut and pointed out a shallow, newly excavated hole. Her meaning had been unmistakable. This was to be our very special and private water closet. But while convenient to the hut, it stood directly in front of three neighboring huts. Hal, David and I had agreed that it would be tactful to avail ourselves of this "convenience" only under cover of darkness.

I remembered that during my school days in Iceland I used to visit relatives who lived on a farm deep in the remote interior. Because I was a young lady from the big city of Hafnarfördur (with a population of 5,000), I had looked with disdain at the wooden outhouses behind the farm dwellings. Now, as the rays of a late, full moon sifted through a crack in our wooden door, I found myself wishing for the privacy they had provided.

The moonlight reminded me of an old American song I had learned in Iceland long before I met Hal. I began to hum "Shine On, Harvest Moon." And then I found myself wishing that I could think of a song calculated to make the moon *go away*. After a while sleep finally stole over me.

But not for long.

I gradually became aware that I was twisting and turning and violently clawing myself about the waist. An allergy? Or was it the wool blanket? But no—the itching became too acute. I suddenly realized that I was being attacked by fleas. Once more wide awake, I sat bolt upright.

In the darkness I could hear Hal scratching himself in his sleep. David, huddled between us, breathed evenly. The insects were probably devouring both of them but neither seemed disturbed.

I reached into my cosmetic case for the can of DDT which was as important as my toilet articles, and released what I hoped was a death-dealing cloud of spray. Alas, the fleas were buried too deeply within my clothing, and the DDT had no effect. I could only huddle on my cot in abject misery. During my childhood in Iceland I had rarely encountered bothersome insects and it was only after many trips through jungles, deserts and tropical countries that I had come to accept the insect world with any degree of calm.

Now an instinctive dread of having bugs in my hair came flooding back. I pulled a silk kerchief from a pocket of my bush jacket and tied it firmly around my hair. I realized that the kerchief could stop a flea invasion about as well as a fishing net could hold back a mountain stream, but at least it made me *feel* better.

The bitter cold and the attacking fleas combined with the

din of the rooster, the chanting priests and worshipers and the thumping drums to drive sleep further away than ever. Nevertheless, in the midst of all my discomfort I found myself happily reflecting on my extremely good fortune. Despite the occasional hardships and discomforts of travel, I still considered myself the luckiest woman in the world to be part of such a closely knit family team. Whether working abroad or in our home in Los Angeles, we were always together.

It had all begun in Reykjavík, Iceland, one August evening in 1950 when a young stranger leaned over my table in the restaurant of the Hotel Borg and spoke to me in a foreign language.

It was just three weeks after my graduation from the Menntaskolinn College in Reykjavík. With my closest girl friend and our dates, I had gone out for an evening of dining and dancing.

As my date held a chair for me at the table, I happened to glance across the room and met the fixed gaze of a foreigner who sat staring at me, holding his coffee cup in mid-air. I found myself disconcerted by his stare and haunted by a strange sense of familiarity.

My escort, noticing this, eyed the man and remarked that he was not an Icelander.

I picked up the menu. "I wish he wouldn't stare at me so."

I felt myself blushing when the others laughed. Then they grew quiet and looked over my shoulder. I turned and found the stranger at my elbow.

Close up, his features seemed more familiar than ever. While I racked my brain trying to recall where I had seen him, he spoke.

For a moment I was confused, and then it dawned on me that he was speaking English. While I had studied the language for several years and was considered rather good at it by my teachers and fellow students, I had never spoken English with anyone who used it as his native tongue. Although I had occasionally overheard visiting Americans or Englishmen on the streets or in the theaters of Reykjavík, they generally spoke with rapid-fire speed and with accents I simply could not understand. But now, to my utter amazement, I understood everything the stranger said.

"I beg your pardon," he began, "please forgive me for speaking to you without an introduction but"—he hesitated—"but do you happen to speak English?"

At that moment everything in my training should have led me to shake my head and dismiss him by turning my attention back to my companions. But I heard myself say, "Yes, I do."

A wide smile spread over his face. "Wonderful!" And then his expression grew serious. "I wonder if I might speak with you for a moment—on a very important business matter."

Had I obeyed my instinct and sent him on his way, my life would have continued in its placid Icelandic pattern. I did not know it at the moment, but my next words were to decide my entire future.

All I said was "Of course." But that impulsive decision was like a magic key to portals of happiness and high adventure all over the world.

When we were seated at his table, he wasted no time. "Please excuse me for approaching you in this way but, you see, you're just the person I've been looking for and . . ." He paused. "My name is Hal Linker. I'm an American and I'm in Iceland to make a color film for my travel-adventure lecture series in the United States."

Now I knew why his face had seemed familiar. "Of course. I read about your arrival and saw your photograph in the Reykjavík newspapers several weeks ago."

"Thank goodness for that. I've been looking high and low for the right person to pose in the beautiful national costume so many Icelandic women wear. The moment I saw you I said to myself, Ah—there's the person for my film." He paused again. "Do you *have* such a costume?"

"My mother has one that fits me."

"Then you wouldn't mind posing for me?" He glanced to where my friends sat watching us. "Provided your fiancé—or husband—wouldn't object?"

"The man with me is just a school chum, Mr. Linker."

His relief was only partially disguised. An unaccountable inner excitement grew in me, but I made myself say, in businesslike tones, "Mr. Linker, even though you've introduced yourself and I've read about you in the newspapers, I couldn't possibly work with you—unless, that is, someone from—from the government, shall we say—would—" I found myself groping for the proper word.

"Vouch for me?"

I nodded.

His forehead wrinkled in thought, and then: "How about Thordur Einarsson of the tourist office? After all, I'm the guest of your government. Surely his word—"

"I've heard of Einarsson, although I've never met him." I must have sounded dubious because a look of concern came over his face. "But why don't you ask him to get in touch with me?" I added quickly. "He'd come along with us during the filming, wouldn't he?"

His face lit up. "Oh yes. Absolutely. I'll ask him to call you. If the weather's good we can start filming tomorrow. Okay?"

I gazed at him. That typical American expression seemed so appropriate. "Okay." And I smiled.

He started to lead me back to my table when he suddenly stopped short. "I don't know what's gotten into me," he exclaimed, producing a pen and notebook. "I don't even know your name."

"Halla," I said.

His pen was poised in mid-air. "Er—would you please spell it?"

When I spelled my first name as H-a-l-l-a he looked puzzled. "But you pronounced it as though it had a d. It sounded like *Hodla*. There isn't a *d* in the spelling?"

"It's the Icelandic pronunciation, Mr. Linker. In Icelandic the double l happens to be pronounced as though it were dl."

And your last name?"

"Gudmundsdóttir."

He looked perplexed.

I went on, "It tells you that my father's first name was Gudmund. Since I'm his daughter, I take his name and add '*dóttir*' to it. Gudmunds-*dóttir*, you see. If I had a brother his last name would be Gudmund*son*."

When we rejoined my friends, he smiled at them, held my chair for me, and then excused himself.

My companions leaned forward in their seats. "Who in heaven's name was *that?*" my girl friend Sossa asked.

"Oh, he's that American who is making a travel film of Iceland," I replied. "Don't you remember? The *Morgunbladid* had a story about him and his work."

My friends laughed. "Come now," said Sossa's date, "Why, I'll bet that ever since that story appeared every American working at the airport at Keflavík has been masquerading under his name, trying to make a hit with our girls!"

"I suppose," my escort added, "he told you he's from Hollywood and wants to put you in a movie."

"Well, now that you mention it he *did* say he wanted me to appear in his film."

"Halla!" Sossa stared at me. "You didn't fall for *that,* did you?"

I felt a sudden spark of resentment but I said evenly, "Well, there's something about him that I trust."

The rest of the evening passed pleasantly enough, and I enjoyed the dinner and dancing. But I felt my excitement growing, and when I finally got home and to bed it was quite a while before I was able to fall asleep.

The next morning the telephone rang. It was Thordur Einarsson of the Icelandic Tourist Office. He was quite genial. "Mr. Linker and I will be at your place with an official car in an hour. He wants to pose you by the Hafnarfjördur Lava Field. Can you be ready that soon?"

"Oh yes," I said.

"Excellent."

The first day was interesting but busy. Hal Linker filmed me at the famous greenhouses in the little town of Hveragerdi, where roses, carnations, bananas, tomatoes and corn are grown with the aid of heat piped directly from the natural hot springs. He filmed me in close-up scenes and at a distance, amid clusters of grapes and cornstalks, surrounded by flowers and strolling along rows of growing plants.

To my unpracticed eyes, his camera equipment seemed fearfully complicated, and I began to feel a sense of pride in the way he went about the filming. The hours passed like minutes and I was disappointed when the sun went down.

By the time we were on the way back to my home, we were on a first-name basis. Hal said there would be more to film and asked if I was willing to continue posing. Of course I agreed.

The days passed quickly. Between film sequences Hal spoke freely about himself, and we were soon strolling hand in hand and exchanging thoughts. Little by little, the liking we had instantly felt for each other grew stronger.

As we spent more time together I was thrilled to learn that Hal had already filmed in many parts of Iceland and that he was well acquainted with the lore and history of my country. I listened delightedly, feeling as though I were hearing our island country's familiar history for the first time as he talked of Ingolfur Arnarson, who first settled Iceland with a group of Norwegian Viking colonists in 874 A.D.

Hal spoke of the founding of the world's oldest existing parliament, the Althing, which had been established in 930 on the plains of Thingvellir about thirty-five miles from Reykjavík. It is still in operation as the Parliament of the Republic of Iceland. I marveled that Hal knew that Iceland had been independent for about 300 years before it fell under the rule of Norway for around a hundred years and under the domination of Denmark for another five centuries. He remembered that complete independence had come in 1944 and Iceland had become a republic with Sveinn Björnsson as president. Hal had recently photographed Mr. and Mrs. Björnsson at the President's residence in Bessastadir.

Hal praised the *Sagas* and knew that they were written in Iceland and was aware that Leif Ericson, who had visited the New World almost 500 years before Columbus, had been an Icelander. Every Icelander knows this but it was gratifying that a foreigner also knew of the Viking explorer's origin. Hal told me that he had traveled all over my country to places even I hadn't visited—to the north to Akureyri, to Myvatn, with its fascinating lake, to Námasgard and the desolate lava fields and even to Siglufjördur, where he had filmed the herring industry. Most of all I was surprised to find that he completely understood the difference between Iceland and Greenland. He knew that Iceland has no Eskimos and has never had any and that it is not one massive sheet of ice like Greenland.

When I asked him how he managed not to get my country mixed up with Greenland, he replied airily, "Oh, it's easy. I just remember that Iceland is green and Greenland is icy!"

Together we visited the active volcano Mount Hekla, which had erupted two years earlier and still gave off clouds of steam. We traveled inland to the hot-springs area where we saw the great Geysir erupt. I reminded Hal that Geysir had given its name—which means "the gusher" in Icelandic—to erupting hot springs throughout the world.

"But it's your *language* that intrigues me," he told me while we were at Geysir. "It's obviously Scandinavian. Is it like Danish?"

"Oh no," I answered proudly. "You might say Danish is like Icelandic. You see, the language we speak today is the language of the Vikings of a thousand years ago. When the Vikings settled Iceland, they brought their language with them, and because of our isolation, it has remained almost unchanged. In the rest of Scandinavia, it developed into Swedish, Norwegian and Danish through the people's contact with other languages. You could say that Icelanders speak the mother tongue of Scandinavia."

"Can another Scandinavian understand Icelandic?"

"Not unless he has studied Old Norse. Our language has remained so unchanged that every schoolchild in Iceland can read the ancient *Sagas,* which were written in the 12th and 13th centuries."

Hal was curious about me, and I told him that I had been born in Reykjavík and had spent my entire twenty years in Iceland.

"My father Gudmund was lost at sea several years ago," I told him. "I'm looking forward to having you meet my mother and my stepfather."

There was a long silence and I could see that Hal was worried about that encounter.

Finally he began to tell me about himself. Born in New York City, he had lived in many parts of the United States as a child. He told me how he also had lost his father while still a child and how he had pitched in to help his mother. He had worked his way through the School of Foreign Service at Georgetown University in Washington, D.C., training for the diplomatic and consular service.

After he graduated with a degree in foreign service and with the highest honors in his class, World War II intervened and Hal volunteered for service in the United States Navy. He had been sent to the Japanese Language School at Boulder, Colorado, where he had trained as an interpreter.

As he spoke he painted a vivid picture of the war in the Pacific. He had been an amphibious forces intelligence officer and had participated in the landings on Iwo Jima and Okinawa.

He said that photography had always been his prime hobby, almost a passion, and he had won several awards before the war. Upon learning of this, the Navy gave him a motion pic-

ture camera and made him Fleet Photographer in addition to his other duties.

When the war ended, Hal decided to use his varied experience and abilities to become a travel-adventure film producer and lecturer, and had made his home in Hollywood.

Only the year before we met he had made a trip around the world, filming for a forthcoming lecture engagement in the United States. "In fact," he added, "my being here is the result of a terrible London fog. What we Americans would call a fluke."

I looked puzzled. "But isn't a fluke a part of a whale?"

Hal chuckled. "Well I'm hoping to go out on an Icelandic whaling expedition before I leave, but by fluke I mean a quirk of fate."

He described how, the previous November in Copenhagen, on the last leg of his global journey, he had happened to meet a representative of Icelandic Airlines, Ásbjörn Magnússon.

Ásbjörn had invited him to come to Iceland and shoot a final section of his round-the-world film. Arrangements had been completed for Hal to fly from Copenhagen to London, where he was to board an Icelandic Airlines plane for Reykjavík.

"But it wasn't in the cards. Our London-bound transport ran into one of the worst fogs England had ever seen. We landed miles from London, and I missed the plane I was to take for Iceland." Hal smiled. "So I flew to the United States instead and postponed my visit until this year when I sailed from New York on the tiny Icelandic ship, the *Tröllafoss,* as a guest of your government's tourist office and"—he shrugged —"here I am."

A fluke or a quirk of fate! I realized that had it not been for that fog the year before, Hal would have flown to Reykjavík in November, taken his films and left, and we would never have met; I was then in college busily preparing for final examinations.

When I mentioned this he looked shocked. He stared at

me for a long moment. "I'm probably the first person ever to say, 'Thank heaven for that wonderful English fog!' " We both laughed.

A familiar voice boomed out behind us. It was Thordur Einarsson. "There you are," he said affably, nodding to me and putting his hand on Hal's shoulder. "I've been looking high and low for you, Mr. Linker."

"What is it, Thordur?" Hal asked.

"I've arranged for you to go on that whaling expedition. It should provide wonderful adventure shots for your picture."

"When?" Hal asked, gazing at me.

"Tomorrow morning—at the crack of dawn!"

2

Adventure Bride

HAL was gone for three days. On the last a terrible storm raged. All day I kept myself busy so I wouldn't worry. Finally the phone rang and I nervously picked up the receiver.

"I'm back!" Hal's words came tumbling out. "I know it's late but I simply *must* see you. It's something terribly important—" He paused. I stood as though transfixed. "Are you still there, Halla?" His voice seemed filled with alarm.

"I'm here, Hal." I felt warm and marvelously alive. "I'm here. Of course I'll see you."

"Could you meet me in the dining room of the Hotel Borg? I just got off the whaling ship and I can get there in about an hour and a half."

"I'll be there, Hal," I said.

When I saw him he was unshaven and haggard. "Is everything all right?" I asked anxiously.

"What's that? Oh, *this* you mean." He laughed, fingering his chin. "The weather was so bad I couldn't shave for the entire three days."

"No, I mean with the filming," I replied. "Did it go well?"

"Oh, the filming. It was fine. I got some unusual shots." He was very casual about it. (He did not know that the spectacular color film he had taken on that whaling expedition

22

would soon be leased from him for use in the Academy Award-winning film *The Sea Around Us*.)

"But you look so worried, so preoccupied," I insisted.

"I really am worried. Out on that whaling ship I had a lot of time to think and I realized that you're the girl I've been looking for all my life. Halla, will you marry me?"

I hesitated only a moment. "Yes, Hal, I'll marry you."

His worried expression changed into a smile as he leaned across the table and kissed me, oblivious to the raised eyebrows all around us.

"I only had time to stop at a store Thordur told me about. That's why I had no chance to shave." He took a small jewel box out of his pocket.

"See—I just *had* to take a chance that you'd say yes." There were two wedding rings in it.

"Thordur told me all about your Icelandic custom of double rings." Hal picked up the smaller of the two rings and reached for my left hand. As he slipped it onto my finger I noted his name engraved inside it, in the Icelandic manner. "I ordered them before I left," he said. "I sort of guessed at your size."

Now it was my turn to play a part in this impromptu ritual. I took the larger ring and placed it on the ring finger of his left hand. My name had been engraved in it.

After the wedding the rings would be transferred to our right hands—the Icelandic custom.

I was now engaged but my happiness was tempered with a slight uneasiness. Marrying Hal would mean leaving Iceland to live in a strange land far from my parents and friends—perhaps never seeing them again.

While in school I had studied the history of the United States and was aware of its immense size, wealth and power. And while I had grown accustomed to the presence of the small colony of Americans in Reykjavík and at the airport at Keflavík, my viewpoint had been that of an Icelander toward a mere handful of guests within my own country. Now the prospect of crossing the ocean and actually becoming a resident of the United States was somewhat frightening. How would the Americans there—Hal's friends and relatives in particular—take to me, an Icelander barely twenty years old. And how would my parents like Hal?

But I needn't have worried about that. From the moment he stepped through the doorway of our home, my American seemed to hit it off with my mother and stepfather despite the fact that the "conversation" was partly carried on by means of gestures and partly through me as interpreter. My parents spoke no English and Hal spoke no Icelandic.

Later when I left Hal with my stepfather in the parlor and joined my mother in the kitchen, she paused in the middle of preparing coffee and grasped me by the shoulders, looking straight into my eyes. I inwardly braced myself. Her expression was serious.

"Halla," she said, "I think you've found the right man."

After a moment I managed to reply, "Of course I have, Mama. But I wanted you to be sure, too."

She looked searchingly at me again and then smiled. "Good. You're truly happy. It will be a good marriage for you, Halla. I know. I'm glad."

My eyes misted. I was tremendously proud of my mother, realizing how she felt about losing her only child to a perfect stranger.

Concealing my emotion, I said, "You sound so positive, Mama. Is it the Isafjördur gift or feminine intuition?" I knew that women from her home town, Isafjördur, away up in the north, were supposed to have occult powers and to be able to foretell the future.

"Perhaps both, Halla-min." She smiled. "Perhaps both."

It was Hal's idea for me to follow him to America after completing the preliminary paperwork required for entrance into the United States. He would come from California to meet me in New York City and we would be married.

I went with him to the American Embassy in Reykjavík to learn what each of us must do before a visa could be issued. Our time together flew by all too quickly, and soon he was finished with his filming.

Almost before I knew it, I found myself at the Reykjavík Airport where, after embracing me, Hal boarded the Loftleidir Icelandic Airlines plane that was to carry him to New York.

After the DC-4 had become a speck in the sky, I was assailed by a feeling of loneliness which was not lifted by the good-natured teasing of my friends.

"Oh, you know those Americans," they said. "Once they get back to their homes, they forget all their promises." I knew better than to take such bantering seriously. Still, when more than a week passed without word, I found myself lying awake at night, wondering.

And then the documents arrived—bank statements, letters of recommendation, affidavits of responsibility. I obtained my American visa with them and, almost in a daze, found myself saying farewell to my parents and friends at the foot of the stairs that led to the cabin of a big American airliner at Keflavík Airport. Ingibjörg Pálmadóttir, one of my classmates, was accompanying me on the long transocean flight. She had received a scholarship to study at Macalester College in St. Paul, Minnesota, and had arranged to take the same plane so that we could share the journey.

I recall sitting with my nose pressed against the vibrating window and staring down at my native land, momentarily overcome by a feeling of sadness. And then as the island disappeared behind the wings, a sense of anticipation began to warm me.

Hours later when we approached America the sun was past its zenith. The earth below was a deep purple, crisscrossed by innumerable lakes and streams that reflected the lowering sun with eye-dazzling brightness. Ingibjörg and I had both been peering down at this strange new country, wondering where all the skyscrapers were. A stewardess told us that we were still flying down the Maine coast and that New York was some minutes away. I felt a thrill of excitement. Somewhere down there, almost two miles below, was the land of "Vinland" which Leif Ericson had seen in the year 1000.

When I mentioned this to my companion, she nodded. "What a contrast between Leif the Lucky with his dragon boat, which must have taken weeks, and we two, flying on metal wings and reaching 'Vinland' in a matter of hours!"

From the air, New York City was breathtaking, more stupendous than I had anticipated, even after Hal's descriptions.

When we stepped from the cabin door of the plane at the old International Airport, I noticed a concrete barrier that separated the field from the parking area and buildings. To my amazement, I saw a man's head bobbing up and down behind it.

"Look, Ingibjörg, there's someone behind that fence, jumping up and down. What on earth do you suppose he's doing?"

Ingibjörg squinted. "Maybe he's exercising on a trampoline. I've heard Americans are fanatics about physical culture."

It was a strange sight. The two of us stopped spellbound, but the stewardess came up behind us and pleasantly but firmly insisted that we clear the passageway.

We filed down the steps to the ground, and laden with packages and coats, straggled into a small building with the other passengers. My first official hosts, uniformed representatives of the United States Federal Government, were politely aloof. They scanned our documents, asked a few questions, managed slight, stereotyped smiles and then nodded. It was hard to believe. We were actually here—in America. We left the customs area and entered a hall. There waiting for us, was Hal, looking very relieved.

As a typical Icelander with an aversion to public display of any emotion, I ran true to type in my greetings. I am afraid

Hal thought me somewhat aloof at first, although that could not have been further from the truth.

After being introduced to Ingibjörg, Hal took us to the airport coffee shop, where we could relax until our baggage was finally brought from the customs area where it had been inspected.

For a long moment there was an awkward silence. Hal searched my face and then asked, "Are you all right?"

I nodded. "Of course. Why shouldn't I be?"

"Then you didn't know about the trouble with your plane?"

"Trouble?" Ingibjörg and I exchanged startled glances. "Our flight was smooth. What trouble, Hal-minn?"

He smiled. Later he told me that my spontaneous Icelandic term of endearment had reassured him.

"Why, your plane was unreported for more than ten hours. As far as anyone knew, it had been lost and possibly had gone down at sea!"

We stared at him in astonishment.

He paused and shook his head. "It's been a hellish ten hours for me and the others who waited."

Hal's story was incredible. There had been a breakdown of communication somewhere along the line. That same day Pan American Airways had taken over all American Overseas Airways flights. The airlines authorities in New York had not been told that our takeoff from Keflavík had been delayed for ten hours for minor repairs. What with new schedules and heavy traffic, no one had even bothered to verify whether we had left Keflavík on time or had disappeared in mid-Atlantic.

"The plane just didn't arrive when it was supposed to," Hal had been told.

"Planes kept landing and discharging passengers. I kept watch on each one because I had no idea which one you might be on. And the fence was so high that I had to keep jumping up and down to see who was getting off."

Ingibjörg and I looked at one another again and burst into

peals of laughter. "So that was *you* who was jumping up and down when we arrived!"

I could see Hal blush beneath his tan. "Let's be on our way to town, it's getting late," he said.

The hotel room that Hal had reserved for Ingibjörg and me drove all thoughts of sleep from my mind. It was on the 34th floor and the panorama of Manhattan spread out below was incredible. It was hours before I could fall asleep.

During the next few days Hal took us through the stone canyons of Wall Street, to the top of the Empire State Building, to the Aquarium at the famed Battery and to the Statue of Liberty.

The more impressed I was, the more I determined to hide my feelings. I didn't want Hal to think I was unsophisticated. After all, Hafnarfjördur *was* the third largest town in Iceland, with its 5,000 population, and our capital Reykjavík did have almost 60,000 residents. The natural Icelandic tendency to hide one's emotions was still strong within me. Hal began to watch me with a somewhat worried expression.

His question, "Is anything wrong, Halla?" became more frequent as the sight-seeing expeditions continued.

He would give me a dubious look when I answered, "Oh no. Everything is fine. I'm enjoying myself tremendously."

More exciting days passed as Hal doggedly took Ingibjörg and me to virtually every fascinating nook and cranny of New York. Then Ingibjörg left for St. Paul.

That same day Hal confronted me with a rather glum expression. He took my hands and looked anxiously into my eyes. "Elskan-min, are you *sure* you want to marry me?"

My heart pounded. Had I done something to offend him? "Why of course I do!" I tried to sound casual. "Why do you ask?"

He hesitated, then shrugged slightly. "Well, it's only that—I mean, ever since you arrived you've been so restrained, so casual about your trip and about being here." His voice quickened. "Why haven't you once asked when we'll be married and where the wedding will take place?"

"Please don't let that worry you," I answered. "It's just my natural Icelandic reserve, I guess. We are brought up to not show our emotions."

A look of comprehension came over his face. His grasp tightened on my hands.

"Truly, Hal-minn, I've been thrilled beyond belief by the flight and by this marvelous city. As for our getting married, I just took it for granted that you'd complete all the arrangements and set the time. I'm ready to marry you whenever you're ready and wherever you decide."

Hal's relief was obvious. As for the place, he decided that we would be married in New Haven, Connecticut, where a married cousin of his lived.

"It won't be a formal wedding," he explained, "but I just don't like the idea of getting married in this hectic city."

Because his lecture season was scheduled to begin within a few weeks, it would be necessary for us to leave for our new home in California immediately after the ceremony. The thought of the trip there made me even more excited than I had been.

"As soon as we're married, we'll take the train to Washington for a short honeymoon. Then we'll fly to Hollywood. I do want you to know something about your new nation." He paused. "How does that sound?"

I searched my mind for words to express how excited and thrilled I was. Instead, all I could summon up was, "Wonderful elskan-min, just wonderful!"

The two days we spent in Washington after our simple wedding in New Haven were unforgettable. We rode to the top of the Washington Monument, strolled through the Lincoln Memorial, and sat in awe during sessions of the Supreme Court and Congress.

But perhaps nothing brought home to me the incredible

size and splendor of my adopted country as much as our flight from Washington to Los Angeles. I sat close against the window of the plane and watched fertile fields and sprawling cities slowly pass beneath us. Presently I grew drowsy and fell asleep, my head resting on Hal's shoulder. When I awakened hours later it was dark. We were still flying. Cities, now shimmering gems of light, were still parading beneath us. The United States of America seemed endless, even more than the stretch of ocean that separates Iceland from North America.

And when we finally circled over that vast metropolis called Los Angeles which to me was to be home from then on, I was literally speechless with amazement. Not even New York City and its skyscrapers could match that almost unending vista of twinkling lights from buildings, homes and automobiles that spread to all sides as far as the eye could see.

Hollywood was a gift box of surprises, both pleasant and bizarre, from the moment Hal romantically carried me across the threshold of the tiny apartment that was our new home.

The weather itself was a source of delight. We had been married on October seventh with winter just around the corner, yet the days were warm, and to my way of thinking, amazingly long. I was accustomed to a native land located on the edge of the Arctic Circle, and when I heard my new friends and neighbors complain of an occasional overcast day, I thought of Iceland's long winters with their daily average of four hours of melancholy daylight.

For years I had read of Hollywood's garish architecture and its habit of turning night into day, and much of this I had taken with a grain of salt. But directly across from our apartment on Vine Street was the huge, sprawling Hollywood Ranch Market, with strange decorations and gaudy signs which boasted that it was open twenty-four hours a day, every day of the year—a fact emphasized by the unending din of cars coming and going in the always jammed parking lot.

To my inexperienced Icelandic eyes, the market itself was fantastic. At home, shopping was a half-day task that meant visiting separate shops for vegetables, meats, poultry or fish. But here under one immense roof was a treasure trove of all kinds of commodities. I enjoyed pushing a gleaming metal basket on wheels slowly through the labyrinth of brightly lighted aisles between rows of every conceivable kind of food and household necessity and devouring everything with my eyes, whether or not I bought it.

My first experience with a supermarket such as this one emphasized, more than anything else, the fact that my newly adopted country was indeed a land of plenty.

And today when we return from a filming trip in other less-fortunate lands where hardship, poverty and famine are often the rule rather than the exception, I revisit my neighborhood supermarket to realize once again how plentiful is the bounty of this land of ours and how fortunate we are to be living here.

Our little apartment was crammed with Hal's camera equipment, motion picture film-editing apparatus, containers of film and volume upon volume of books and magazines describing almost every corner of the world.

Hal explained that the equipment and stacks of canned film represented thousands of dollars' worth of "frozen assets," although we had little actual money.

"But when I get more bookings to show these films and give lectures, all this"—he waved—"will someday become a gold mine, elskan-min!"

What I didn't learn until later was the fact that his lecture-booking agent had tried to discourage Hal from getting married, explaining that lecturers' marriages often broke up because they must be away from home so often. But Hal had other ideas and he saw to it that our marriage had no such problem.

Lecturing was hard work. After deducting the expenses of transportation, hotels and meals and the 25- or 30-percent commission demanded by his agents, we wound up with less than half the usual $150 fee. At least a hundred bookings were necessary before he started making money, since actual filming expenses were also borne solely by the lecturer, as were the costs of advertising brochures. I remember how excited Hal was when his agent booked him for his first lecture before the National Geographic Society in Washington, D.C.

It was during the height of his seasonal bookings on the Pacific Coast, but the prestige of an appearance before this famous society in the East would be an invaluable investment in our future.

For the first time since our marriage, Hal was to go flying off by himself and leave me behind in the apartment. He sat down and did some arithmetic to show me why. His fee for the lecture in the capital was to be an apparently substantial $300. The agent immediately deducted $90 for his service. (This was the agent who took 30 percent; our West Coast agent took only 25 percent.) The air fare to and from Washington came to $275. Staring us in the face was a net loss of $65, even if Hal traveled alone. I assured him that I understood—besides, he was to be gone only one day.

He filled a lecture engagement in a Los Angeles suburb the evening of his departure. At midnight he boarded a plane to Washington, and after an all-night flight (this was long before jets) and no sleep to speak of, made his appearance before the National Geographic Society the next night and returned to Los Angeles on another overnight flight, to fill another lecture engagement in Los Angeles the very next day.

He had gone without sleep for nearly three nights but his decision proved sound. The National Geographic Society has invited him to appear several times, but now the lectures are always arranged for times when we are traveling near Washington. Hal's reputation as a lecturer soared that season, and he was soon listed as one of the best in the travel-adventure field.

But now a new situation had to be faced. "Elskan-min," I asked him casually one evening a few months after we were married, "do you like children?"

"Oh I suppose so. I can take them or leave them."

"I hope you'll like ours," I replied, searching his face anxiously.

Hal jumped to his feet, yelling, "You're going to have a baby? That's wonderful!"

"But we have to travel so much and take pictures and—and—"

"And we'll continue to travel together and do our filming together—"

"With a baby, Hal-minn?"

"With twins or even triplets if we're that fortunate!" He laughed and began to whirl me around the room in an exuberant dance.

According to our doctor's calculations, the baby could be expected by mid-August. This of course compounded the overall problem, since Hal lectured from autumn to spring and had to work during the summer months on putting together a new film lecture each year.

I worried about the situation for days, but Hal came through as I could always depend on him to do.

He rushed into the apartment one evening with his eyes dancing. "I've arranged everything. We'll fly to England at the end of May. We'll film all over that country and in Wales. Then we'll hop over to Finland and make another film." He looked into my eyes. "And now for the *big* surprise—after we've finished with Finland, we'll fly to Iceland, where you can have the baby with your parents nearby!"

For a long moment I couldn't speak. Then as the full realization of my good fortune sank in, my Icelandic reserve melted and I cried with happiness.

3
Three Passports

OUR trip started on a wing and a prayer, financially speaking. Hal had invested most of our working "capital" in raw-film stock and equipment. Herman Ramo of the Finnish National Travel Office in New York was prepared to provide a round trip for one person from the United States to Helsinki. His government was greatly interested in a filming in Finland, but could see no reason to provide transportation for a wife. But Hal had worked out my passage by arranging with his Finnish hosts to take two one-way tickets rather than one round trip. To reach Finland meant traversing Britain, and he planned to have us stop off there first, then go on to Helsinki.

"Once we finish in Finland, we'll get to Iceland somehow," Hal explained. "I'm taking along the lecture film I made there, and I'll show it in Iceland and lecture with it. With any luck, I'll make enough money for our return flight home."

Despite the possibility that showing a color film of Iceland to Icelanders might be like carrying coals to Newcastle my optimism and happiness matched his.

Our flight from New York to Glasgow, where we were to connect with a London-bound plane, was tediously long and turbulent because of storm conditions and head winds. But while other passengers complained, I was still in a state of euphoria over the opportunity to visit new lands and see my parents again.

The fact that our cash supply, regardless of how economical we were, was slowly dwindling did not disturb us. We had $50 to our name, but our optimism was boundless. All we had to do for reassurance was to touch one another, to exchange understanding glances.

If the flight across the Atlantic had been rough, the hop in a small DC-3 of World War II vintage from Scotland to London was much more uncomfortable. It was accomplished at night during a May ice storm, and the ship accumulated ice on its wings at an alarming rate.

I huddled in my seat and told myself that the crackling and banging of ice fragments flung against the fuselage from wings and propellers meant nothing. Several times during the flight the engineer popped out of the cockpit to check the wings with a flashlight. Each time he did so Hal asked him if everything was okay. The man, a dour-looking Scot, would nod and go back to the cockpit. And when Hal tightened his arm around my shoulder and peered at my face, I pretended to be sound asleep, even as the ice crashed, the engines rumbled unevenly, and the plane shuddered as though the wings had fallen off.

But memories of that flight passed quickly when we landed at London and began to drive through England's lovely countryside in a tiny car donated by the Victor Britain car rental company.

The Lake Country, Salisbury and Stonehenge, York with its street called Shambles, the beautiful Welsh country with its castles at Harlech and Caernarvon, its coal and slate mines, the Welsh National Eisteddfod, with its singing and poetry, all passed before my wondering eyes.

I was feeling quite fit during our first expedition together although I was nearing the seventh month of my pregnancy. We finally finished our filming in England and Wales, during which we drove 2,000 miles and stayed at the Trust Houses hotels as their guests.

A short flight brought us to Finland, where we traveled the length and breadth of that courageous country, riding all sorts of conveyances from small planes to mail buses on the dirt highways of the north. Ivalo, Inari, Rovaniemi, Kemi and Tornio were all visited and photographed. My admiration for the stalwart Finns has remained undiminished from my first contact with these admirable people.

On our return to Helsinki from the north, Hal decided to film the unique Children's Castle which is actually a modern children's hospital and nurses' training school built by the late Baron von Mannerheim and his wife, Baroness Sophie.

While Hal busied himself filming, I was examined by a pleasant young woman obstetrician. Hal had insisted on this checkup as a precaution although I assured him that I felt fine. I was then nearing my ninth month. The doctor agreed with me and smiled her approval.

As a token of his appreciation, Hal had the idea of giving a lecture and showing his film on Iceland as a means of raising funds for the hospital. It was a great success. The newspapers in Helsinki devoted considerable space to his hour-long color film, *Sunny Iceland, Land of the Vikings.*

We were prevailed upon to stage a second showing. The newspapers were more than enthusiastic. Reporters looked on me as a sort of oddity: it was hard for them to believe that this was really my first venture as my husband's traveling companion, since I took my pregnancy so much as a matter of course. One of the reporters, an elderly journalist, kept asking if I had been to the Orient or South America or Africa.

"Not yet," I laughingly tried to explain, "but I hope to."

"I was wondering if you had ever visited Timbuktu!" he said, disappointed. "I've never met anyone who has."

I turned to Hal. "Timbuktu? Hal-minn is there such a place?"

"Indeed there is," he answered. "It's in the southern Sahara

Desert in French West Africa. It has come to symbolize the end of the earth to most people. In fact, a great many people think it doesn't even really exist."

Timbuktu! What a romantic sound it has, I thought.

The name was to pop up again and again as people we met throughout the world, on hearing of our extensive travels, would time and again ask wistfully, "Have you ever been to Timbuktu?"

How could I have known that there in Finland, at that very moment, Hal secretly made up his mind to take me and our soon-to-be-born child to Timbuktu someday. But that was to be many miles and almost a hundred countries later.

The atmosphere at the United States Consulate in Reykjavík was quite formal, and the office of Robert J. Gibbons, the Vice-Consul, was quiet. I held our tiny son in my arms. Hal stood by us.

Mr. Gibbons' twinkling eyes belied the air of solemnity surrounding us. I felt that we were old friends. He had arranged my immigration papers when I had set forth to marry Hal. And then his wife had given birth to her own son a few doors from me in the hospital in Reykjavík on the same day that David Thor was born. Now Mr. Gibbons was about to issue an American passport to our baby!

Although I was still an Icelandic citizen and David was born in Iceland, we had learned that United States law specifies that a child born abroad to a family with at least one American parent, while they are temporarily residing abroad, can claim United States citizenship. We had decided to do so, since I planned to become an American citizen myself as soon as possible. Interestingly enough, our son, under Icelandic law, will be able to claim Icelandic citizenship when he becomes twenty-one years of age if he wishes, because he was born in Iceland and one of his parents was an Icelandic citizen at that time.

Mr. Gibbons cleared his throat. "Now let's see. We have his

name—David Thor Linker [I had chosen David and Hal had chosen Thor]. Age, seven weeks. And his description"—he beamed at David—"husky should do it."

With a straight face he produced a tape measure, stepped from behind his ornate desk, and gravely measured David. "Height, one foot six inches. And his weight?"

"Four kilos one hundred sixty-two grams," I answered proudly.

Mr. Gibbons' brow furrowed, and he muttered to himself, "Let's see now; there are two point two pounds in a kilo and one thousand grams in a kilo—" He took out a piece of paper and did some rapid figuring. "Say, that's nine pounds three ounces," he exclaimed admiringly. "He really *is* husky."

I smiled proudly.

He made a note. "And let's see—description." He looked dubious. "His hair is fuzzy and blondish now but that doesn't mean anything; and his eyes seem blue." He peered at Hal and me. "You're blond, Mrs. Linker, and your husband is brunet, so let's guess that your son's hair will be light brown and he'll continue to have your blue eyes." He entered these prophetic data, unaware that David would really grow up to have hazel eyes and dark blond hair.

David yawned in my arms.

"This is a serious matter, young man," Mr. Gibbons said, with mock severity. "Do you realize that you're going to be one of the youngest holders of an American passport?"

He looked at Hal and me. "Of course, the United States Government requires full information about David Thor Linker's past activities. I think we can forego the required letters of reference. I'll vouch for him. But can you assure me, Mr. Linker, that he has never been convicted of a major crime or advocated the overthrow of the United States Government?"

Hal grinned. "You have our word, Mr. Gibbons."

"Well, then, we'll need a photo to attach to his passport."

"I have one right here." Hal reached into his wallet and

produced a snapshot taken when David was only a week old.

Mr. Gibbons nodded with approval.

Finally it was done. Passport No. 233 was formally and officially issued to David Thor Linker, aged seven weeks. We now had the three passports which later turned out to be three passports to adventure.

Hal's lectures in Iceland had proved amazingly successful. He had shown his color film ten times and we had almost $1,000 all our own. We flew back to Los Angeles in style.

Since that ceremony in Mr. Gibbons' office in Reykjavík almost fifteen years ago, David has traveled all over the world with us, more than 300,000 miles—farther than the distance from the earth to the moon. He has celebrated his birthday in a different country every year, since we always travel abroad to make films during the summer and his birthday is on July 27th. He has ridden in almost every kind of conveyance, with the exception of a submarine or a space ship, and who knows but that he may even count a trip to the moon or to Mars among his travel memories by the time he reaches his twenties?

David's first international journey, when he was only ten weeks old, was the 6,000-mile flight from Iceland to our home in Hollywood. But once there we found ourselves on the road more than in our little apartment. Bookings for lectures were increasing and the three of us traveled by car, plane and train from one city to another all over the United States and Canada.

It was a hectic existence. Some of the American wives I met looked on making hotels and motels one's home and living out of suitcases with a degree of horror, but I felt that this constant traveling was infinitely preferable to waiting at home alone while Hal crisscrossed the continent on lecture assignments. Besides, David seemed to enjoy being carried about in a special portable bed with handles; in fact, he thrived on it.

Hal's professional reputation continued to grow, and the

months that followed were wonderfully exciting as we went to the far corners of my new country.

David was only ten months old when Hal told me, one night after a lecture in Kansas City, that he was hoping to make a film in far-off Pakistan. The government of that country also wanted him to make a tourist promotional film, and an airline had asked him to make commercial films in India and Israel. Explaining that this would mean a trip completely around the world, he looked at me anxiously. "Can you handle it, elskanmin? It means taking our young son with us to the Orient and the Middle East before he's a year old."

"Of course," I assured him. "I'll take care of David, you take care of business, and we'll make out all right."

Hal breathed a sigh of relief. "That's a load off my mind. Now I can tell you the *real* news."

"You mean there's something more than the trip around the world?"

"I've also arranged for us to go back to Iceland again before we return to the United States. How would you like to show your parents how big David has grown?"

I couldn't answer a word, but I'm sure Hal could tell how wonderful I thought he was.

Around the world with a ten-month-old baby! I marvel now that I felt so confident. Of course, I always had the utmost trust in Hal and never doubted that he would be able to get us out of any predicament. But what about our child and the diseases we might encounter? Our pediatrician regretfully informed us that David was too young to get most of the inoculations against typhoid and typhus, not to mention cholera, the scourge of the Orient.

"But," she assured me, "children that young have a natural immunity to most exotic diseases." She gave her approval of the trip but I must confess I would have made it anyway. I belonged with my husband.

Our baggage problem was a serious one. We couldn't trust the food we might find in remote parts of the world, so we decided that, regardless of cost, we would take along all the canned baby food and milk David could possibly use. It had to last until we returned to the Western World. To make sure that our son would not pick up any diseases from cribs we might rent in the Orient, we carried a collapsible wooden one that could also serve as a playpen. It was about four feet square when fully open and had a foam-rubber mattress. David slept in this every night. We also bought a collapsible aluminum stroller that folded into a compact package when not in use.

Fortunately the previous lecture season had been a good one and money was now available for these needs, as well as for diapers, bottles, baby powders, and so on. (All of this weighed about 150 pounds and shocked the airline clerks everywhere.) But when Hal had bought the film needed for the trip, we found our resources drained again. We would have to travel on a tight budget, as we had often done before. Hal was sustained by the knowledge that we would have funds coming in again once the commercial films for the airline and the Pakistan Government were completed.

Our big transport first took us to Hawaii. We stopped there for several days, as I fell in love with those beautiful islands. I can still recall the thrill I felt as the three of us sat on the beach at Waikiki and bathed in the warm waters. And even today, after several visits there, I still delight in hearing Hawaiian music and watching the graceful undulations of the hula.

I seemed to be dreaming as I absorbed the sights and sounds of Manila, with the sad yet noble remains of Intramuros, the shattered inner city. Darting "jeepney" taxis, converted from World War II jeeps, made crossing the streets a constant challenge. And how charming the young ladies of the Philippines looked in their filmy lace dresses with their puffed sleeves.

But Hong Kong, our next stop, really made the greatest impact, since it was my first experience with the mysterious East. The strangeness of its teeming streets jammed with col-

orfully costumed jostling crowds and lined with shops advertising heaven-knows-what in Chinese characters really frightened me at first. I dreaded having Hal out of my sight for
even a minute when he wandered off to film some scene he
had spotted from a distance. But gradually, after a few days,
this nervousness wore off when I saw that the people around
me were going about their everyday business and had their
worries the same as we had. Soon the strange odors of the
Orient no longer shocked me as we passed food shops where
dried octopus and shark fins hung alongside mysterious foods
which I couldn't possibly even identify. Since that first contact with the pungent odors of the Orient, I can truthfully
say that I have become so accustomed to them that I hardly
notice them.

We filmed Hong Kong from Victoria Peak, which we
reached after a climb on a cogwheel railway to an altitude
of about 1,200 feet. Hal's cameras also focussed on Aberdeen, the Chinese fishing village, and Kowloon, with its teeming apartment houses for the refugees from Red China. All
too soon we had to leave.

We stopped for a while in Calcutta, since at that time this
was on the only route by which we could enter East Pakistan,
which Hal wanted to film first.

This was my first contact with India and I felt like the
Vikings of old must have felt when they rowed the seas and
came upon new and strange lands. Cremation Ghats of the
Hooghly River, Jain Temples, the Black Hole of Calcutta and
the sight of sacred cattle wandering in the streets are engraved
on my memory from that visit. On we went to the Ganges
near Dacca, and to Chittagong, in East Pakistan, where we
saw the jute industry in operation. When British India
achieved independence in 1947, the Moslem areas of the
country insisted on forming their own Moslem nation. It
turned out that while the largest Moslem population lived in
the western part of the country near the Indus River, a large
number of Moslems also lived along the eastern border near

the Ganges. And so it was that the Moslem nation of Pakistan was formed with one segment in the east, with Dacca as its provincial capital, while the other was a thousand miles to the west, separated by India itself. And so when we finished filming in the humid heat of East Pakistan, we flew across India to West Pakistan, where we encountered the dry heat of the deserts.

During our weeks in West Pakistan we filmed in all parts of Karachi, then the capital, the nearby Sind Desert, Hyderabad, Lahore and even as far north as the Khyber Pass at Peshawar. We saw snake charmers and mongooses. Tribal dancers and musicians performed for us, and the Khyber Rifles paraded before our cameras. We steeped ourselves in the lore of the country.

Hal's film lecture on that country was to prove a great success. It was the first one made after Pakistan's independence, and I remember how the Consul-General hugged Hal with excitement after seeing the premiere of the film at the San Francisco Town Hall the following autumn.

After leaving Pakistan, we arrived in Israel and filmed a short subject for the airline. I was thrilled by the modern aspects of this new country—a drastic contrast to our sojourn in remote parts of the Orient. But most of all I remember how pleased I was to find that they had real laundromats in Tel Aviv, and for the first time in two months I could have David's diapers laundered by machine instead of doing them myself by hand. To assure ourselves of a supply of boiled water to mix with David's canned milk, we had bought a tiny electric stove that also served to heat water for washing diapers. Where there was no electric current, I had done them in cold water. Tel Aviv, Jerusalem, Nazareth, Acre and Haifa all became part of my memory.

Without realizing it, Hal had scheduled us to fly to Rome on July 27th, David's first birthday. And so that morning we had a little party in Tel Aviv for him on the balcony of our small hotel, and that evening, after a five-hour flight, we had another in Rome. We like to think that started him off early along the path of nonsectarian tolerance.

Our stay in Iceland seemed all too short, but I had no cause for complaint. We had now been married two years and I had already been back to Iceland twice.

The years of lecturing that followed were filled with excitement as we visited and filmed in new parts of the world each summer. No matter how many countries we added to our memories and our collection of films, we never became bored or lost our sense of adventure.

We celebrated David's second birthday in Cuba, where we were making our next lecture film. During our two-month stay there we met and photographed Major General Fulgencio Batista y Zaldivar, who had begun his rise to the presidency of the island nation in 1933 when, as a sergeant in the Cuban Army, he had led a revolt which overthrew the regime of the hated Dictator Machado. In 1944, Batista had retired but he returned in 1952 to take over as president once more in a bloodless coup.

When he heard that David was to celebrate his second birthday in Cuba, Batista gave our tiny son an amethyst ring bearing both his and David's initials.

After we had filmed in all parts of western Cuba from Havana to the Isle of Pines and from Pinar del Rio to Varadero, we flew to Santiago de Cuba on the eastern tip of the island to film the yearly fiesta of San Diego, the patron saint of the city. We had accommodations at a motel-like establishment called the Rancho Club, which not only overlooked Santiago but also gave us a view of the nearby Moncada military barracks.

The morning after our arrival I was awakened by muffled sounds that reminded me of the distant crackling of firecrackers. The fiesta's starting early, I thought, and dozed off again. A short while later when we were fully awake and had started a leisurely breakfast on the terrace, the firecrackers began again.

"Has the fiesta begun already, Hal-minn?" I asked.

He shook his head and peered toward the sounds. When he turned to me his expression was grim. "Those aren't fireworks, elskan-min," he said. "That's machine-gun fire. Something is going on at the Moncada barracks!"

The something was an attempt by a small group of revolutionaries to seize the barracks as the first step in an attempt to overthrow the Batista regime. The attempt failed, but almost a hundred men died in the fighting. The exact date was July 26, 1953. And the ringleader of the rebels, who was later captured and exiled, was a young student and lawyer named Fidel Castro. That date became a rallying symbol for Castro's revolutionary movement. Since martial law was immediately declared by Batista that day, David's birthday celebration the following day was a solemn affair, especially since every shop and building was closed and the memory of those who had fallen a few hundred yards from us was vivid.

In the years that followed our Caribbean experiences, we filmed all over Belgium and Japan, and came away with memories of Bruges and Ghent, Ostend and Antwerp, Brussels and Liège, all competing with those of Tokyo and Osaka, Kyoto and Hokkaido, Takarazuka, Kabuki dancers and Sumo wrestlers—and of Japan in general, from south to north. Because Hal had been trained as a Japanese interpreter in World War II, he enjoyed practicing up in that language as we made our way into remote areas of the country where no one spoke a word of English.

My first contact with Darkest Africa was to come when we traveled 10,000 miles through the Belgian Congo just before it achieved independence. We met and filmed the pygmies of the Ituri Forest, the Watusi Warriors of Ruanda-Urundi, the King of the Bakuba with his 400 wives, and the Mangbetu, who bind the heads of their children to force the heads into the elongated shape which gives them prestige. We filmed native troops being trained by the Belgians, and so it was that years later when the Congo erupted into violence, we felt the tragedy of the situation more strongly than most people as we read of the destruction visited on Stanleyville, Bunia and Elisabethville and many of the other places we had visited.

From the Congo, our path took us to Egypt on our return home, and here we fulfilled one of my childhood dreams. I had always longed to visit Egypt, and our filming there was not a disappointment in any way. We took the pyramids and the Sphinx, the temples at Luxor and Karnak, the tombs of the Valley of the Kings and the magnificent treasures of King Tut's tomb. And when we returned to the United States and Hal's lecture series, I felt that I was truly becoming a world traveler with Cuba, Japan, Belgium, the Congo and Egypt added to the countries I had already visited.

But it was at our first newspaper interview in New York City after our return that it happened again.

"Mrs. Linker," said Ed Wallace, a well-known reporter for the New York *World-Telegram,* "those are certainly interesting places you've been visiting, but have you ever been to Timbuktu?"

This time I knew where Timbuktu was but I had to admit that we had never been there but had been near it when we landed at Kano, Nigeria, on our way down to Leopoldville. I could see that my answer disappointed him.

Oh well, no one else has been to Timbuktu, I thought, so I'll be satisfied with the glamorous places I've already visited. Little did I know what was in store for me.

Our life changed radically that year. Hal had several opportunities to make television appearances with his films, first in Detroit for the *World Adventure* series and then in Los Angeles as a guest on a travel adventure series whose host had never been abroad but delighted in presenting the films of those who had traveled.

And so it came about, after our return from Africa that Hal took me by the hand one evening and said, "Halla-min, now that we have added footage from Africa to our collection, I think we might have enough material for a television program of our own, using only the films I've made throughout the world. It will be unique—no other program limits itself to films made by the hosts."

"Hosts!" I gasped incredulously. "Does that mean that there will be more than just you on the program? Surely you can't mean that I will be on it, too?"

"Of course you will, Halla-min, and the viewers will love you, I *know* it."

I felt faint. "But, Hal-minn, you know how I hate to appear in front of an audience. It's the Icelander in me. You've always had to argue with me before you could get me to appear before a lecture audience of even a thousand people, and now there may be millions watching. What if I make a mistake in English? After all, I'm speaking a foreign language."

"They'll be crazy about you," Hal assured me. "You've been with me on all the trips and you'll give the woman's viewpoint on what you've seen."

I felt myself weakening. "But who'll take care of David while we're rehearsing and doing the program? He's only five."

"Oh," Hal replied casually, "David will be on the program with us. He's been everywhere with us, too!"

I must have turned pale because Hal asked, "Are you all right, Halla-min?"

"Yes—I guess so," I managed to get out. "How many programs will we have to do? I hope you're not thinking of more than four or five."

"Well, I've been talking to an advertising firm," Hal explained, "and they have agreed to try to get our program on the air. But they tell me that no station will even listen unless they are assured of at least thirteen weeks of programing."

"Thirteen weeks!" I gasped. "That's three months! Oh, Hal, can we do it?"

"I guess so," Hal said cautiously. "I think I can squeeze out thirteen programs, since this will be our one fling at television. Just think—if we make it, someday we'll be able to tell our friends that for *thirteen full weeks* we had our own television program. I just hope we can last that long."

The thirteen weeks went by like magic. Then we were successively renewed for another thirteen weeks, for twenty-six weeks, for a full year, for a second full year, for two years, and finally for two more. And as I write this we have just entered our tenth consecutive year on television with our weekly program *Wonders of the World* in color. But I never dreamed that all this would happen when a few weeks later the advertising agency notified us that they had signed a contract for us to appear on KCOP Channel 13 in Los Angeles for thirteen weeks, to start early the following year.

As the debut of our program approached I could hardly stand the mounting tension. What if I did something silly or entirely forgot what I was supposed to say? How terrible it would be if I disgraced my husband before such an uncounted multitude of viewers. But I was always sustained by Hal's assurance that after thirteen weeks he would probably be out of film and we would resume the less demanding existence of traveling about on his lecture circuit, and seeing him appear alone before small audiences. During the thirteen weeks Hal would continue his lectures because they were our primary business. This would mean many midnight plane flights, but he felt it was worth it for the duration of the television venture.

The day of our program's debut remains hazy in my mind. We went through the rehearsal but I was in a daze, finding myself almost hypnotized by the staring eye of the big camera so close to me in the absolute silence of the studio. The few times I had appeared on the stage to be introduced, at Hal's insistence, I had always been able to look out over a sea of faces without concentrating on any one person, and the murmur of the audience had always been a comfort; they seemed to react so sympathetically to the few words I said. Now in the frightening studio the technicians were so close and they stared so directly at me as I spoke, that the grotesque eye of the camera seemed to peer right through me.

As the program began I felt sure I could never make it. But Hal's reassuring squeeze of my hand sustained me as the little red light came on at the top of the camera, telling me that we were on the air.

Hal spoke first. "Hello, everyone. I'm Hal Linker. I make travel adventure films in intriguing and sometimes remote parts of the world. I believe that families should always try to remain together, and so everywhere I've gone I've taken my wife Halla and son David along with me."

At this point he walked over to where I stood, fluttering inside but trying to show a brave face to the world. David was standing by and hadn't come on camera yet. He was the calmest one on the set that night.

Hal continued: "I met Halla in her native Iceland when I was making a film there in 1950, and we have traveled everywhere together since we were married that year."

This was the moment I had dreaded—it was my turn to speak. To my amazement, Hal's calmness and confidence proved to be contagious. I found myself smiling easily and saying, "I had never been out of Iceland until I married Hal, and since then I've traveled with him to thirty-seven countries. I've often been asked which country I like best, but I find it impossible to decide, except that Iceland, of course, is my sentimental favorite." I turned to Hal again. What a wonderful feeling it was to know that I hadn't let my husband down!

I heard him continue. "I guess it would be difficult, Halla, to choose a favorite when they're all so fascinatingly different." Then he turned to the audience. "Everywhere we've traveled we've taken our son David with us. He is five and he's been all around the world. Here's Davey now."

And David entered exactly on cue, as he had been told to do, with a Congolese mask held before his face—a wooden Bakuba one in which the grinning mouth had a tooth missing.

Hal continued, "That's not Davey's real face but one they made for him in the Congo in honor of his missing tooth. [David took away his mask.] *Here's* Davey."

At this point I held my breath. Our five-year-old son was supposed to say something at this moment and he had never made a public appearance. But I needn't have worried.

David piped up on cue, "Hello, everyone. I hope I didn't scare you." And then when his father asked him, "Do you remember where you had your last birthday?" David replied casually, "Yes, in the Belgian Congo."

The rest of the first program was anticlimactic. Everything went smoothly as Hal and I divided the narration on one of the films we had made in the Congo. It was called "The Mysterious Congo Witch Dancers" and it was a tremendous success according to the reviewers. But my proudest moment came when we were told that my participation with David made the program far more enjoyable for the viewers and that I was an asset to the program. I was helping my husband in his career, at least in what I then thought of as his temporary television career. The date of that first program was January 16, 1957, and it opened up a new world for us.

From then on our filming grew more difficult and hectic than I could have imagined. Not only was it necessary for Hal to make sure that he got a lecture film made each summer, but he also had to be sure that we had enough new films of different areas to keep our program going for another thirteen or twenty-six weeks. Hal did all the filming and the still photography, while I took care of our basic needs and looked after the baggage and the health of our family. But now instead of filming in only one or two countries during the three months of summer, Hal had to film in ten or more in the same period, in order to get varied footage suitable for television. It was almost an impossibility but somehow he managed it as we filmed in Portugal and Spain, in Italy, where we attended the Palio festival at Siena, and filmed the Leaning Tower of Pisa, in Orvieto, in Florence and finally in one of my favorite places, Venice, where we played hooky from work and devoted a full day to just being romantic American tourists gliding through the canals in a gondola. David took a photo of Hal and me on that ride and I still keep it tacked inside the cupboard door in my kitchen, so I can see it every time I open the cupboard. We saw and filmed Tahiti, Fiji and Samoa, enjoying every moment of the South Seas. We visited Greece and Turkey, and even explored the length and breadth of the Soviet Union, entering from Odessa in the south and traveling through the entire country until we left by train for Helsinki. But it was when we started on our trip to South America that my mode of living and traveling changed completely, for then Hal taught me how to use our still cameras and keep his technical notes and I became a working assistant while still continuing my duties as "supervisor of health, morale and baggage."

4

Over the Andes to Iquitos

ALMOST from the moment we set foot in Lima, I was enthralled. A fascinating city in a land of chaotic color, with brooding highlands and the aura of mysterious, lost civilizations, Lima was for us—veterans of travel though we are—a treasure trove of things to do, and, more important, places to film.

Peru's capital is a mixture of the past and present with architectural hints of the future. Stately colonial Spanish buildings date back to the era of the viceroys. Overshadowing them are high-rise modern apartment houses, hotels and glittering new commercial buildings in the business sections.

The Jirón de la Unión, Lima's shopping center, is a woman's paradise. Commencing at the Plaza San Martín, with its statue of the 19th-century revolutionary in the center, the Jirón is lined with large and small shops that offer mouthwatering tea sets, dining services, jewelry, even toys, all made of silver, which Peru still has in abundance.

Wedged among silver shops are establishments that offer such things as leather goods, colonial antiques, Inca curios, fluffy llama slippers and fur rugs.

The Jirón spills into Lima's tremendous Plaza de Armas, flanked on one side by the gleaming white baroque Presidential Palace erected on the site of Francisco Pizarro's original *residencia*. Guarding the palace were stern-faced young Indian soldiers wearing ornate red-and-black uniforms and gleaming, plumed helmets.

We encountered a friendly young captain of the guards who was intrigued by our camera gear and stayed with us long enough to act as a temporary guide while we filmed the palace and its sentinels.

He took us to a patio and showed us a fig tree originally planted by Pizarro's men, which still bears fruit. After that he escorted us to the Torre Tagle Palace, now Peru's Foreign Ministry headquarters, which was erected by the Marquis Torre Tagle, Permanent Paymaster of His Majesty's Pacific Fleet during Spanish colonial days.

While we admired the beautiful structure with its overhanging balconies of carved cedar, our captain pointed out that the palace was probably the best-preserved example of Lima's golden age of colonial architecture.

"Even in those years this building must have been an expensive undertaking," Hal said when he had finished filming the palace.

The captain smiled. "Do not forget, Señor Linker, that the Marquis was paymaster for the fleet. He had absolute control of all the money. Who was there within five thousand miles to watch what he did with the royal payroll?"

He left us then, urging us not to forget to visit the Quinta Presa Palace at the edge of town.

We returned to the hotel, where we observed David's eighth birthday celebration. It was July 27th again. There were several other youngsters of various nationalities who were guests of the hotel and they eagerly accepted our invitation to attend the party. It turned out to be a heartwarming junior United Nations affair. That evening we filmed a recital by Yma Sumac, the famous Peruvian singer, who had just returned to her native land after years in the United States. When she learned of David's birthday, she sang "Happy Birthday" just for him to the obvious delight of her husband, Moises Vivanco and their own twelve-year-old son Charlie.

Fortunately our visit to Lima coincided with the celebration of the nation's Independence Day, July 28th. So we filmed the military parade past the monuments erected to Pizarro and José de San Martín, the patriot who liberated Peru from the Spanish yoke in 1812.

Remembering our impromptu guide's insistence that we visit the Quinta Presa, the 17th-century villa which is now a museum, we set out for its site in Bajo el Puente, a section of Lima that has changed little since the Spanish colonial era.

On the way we drove across the Puente de Piedra, an ornate bridge that spans the Rimac River. This bridge is supposedly the original of Thornton Wilder's famed *Bridge of San Luis Rey*. Wilder tells of Micaela Villegas, a beautiful Peruvian actress who was half Indian and half Spanish. She was known as La Perricholi (a word that I understand is an uncomplimentary epithet in Spanish) and was famous as the mistress of the Spanish Viceroy Manuel de Amat y Junit who ruled Peru autocratically during the late 1700's.

In order to reach the palace, which Don Manuel had erected as a trysting place for La Perricholi, we drove through streets with such colorful and descriptive names as the Avenue of the Barefoot Priests and the Promenade of Waters before finally drawing up to an 18th-century villa with a red-tiled roof.

Wandering through the grounds, we looked at the ornately decorated baroque coach which the viceroy had often dispatched for La Perricholi's use, and we climbed the stairs leading to the top of a tower where, according to legend, Don Manuel used to sit and observe the natural beauties of Lima— which included his mistress as she bathed in the pool below.

On the way back to our hotel we detoured some twenty miles south of the city to the mysterious pre-Inca ruins of Pachácamac. Dominating the rather desolate spot on the coast is the Temple of the Creator-God which predates the nearby

Inca Temple of the Sun by many centuries. The place is an archaeologists's paradise. No matter where one thrusts a shovel or pick into the soil, remains of forgotten races—bits of utensils, tools, artifacts, even human bones—are quickly unearthed.

Here we were confronted by a tantalizing mystery. The temples of the Creator-God and Sun strongly reminded us of the ziggurats (temple towers) of the ancient Babylonians. In fact, we learned that some authorities believe in more than a coincidental link between those who constructed these buildings and the Sumerians and Babylonians of biblical times.

As we strolled past walls that tower seventy feet tall, I found myself absorbed in the notion that the ancient people of Peru might actually have been descendants of biblical Semitic seafarers of fifty centuries ago who sailed all the way around the world on an eastward passage, finally to land on the west coast of South America.

If this is so, it means that the ancient people of the Middle East may have preceded my Viking ancestors to the New World by thousands of years!

Our trip to Iquitos required crossing the Andes in a nonpressurized DC-4, propeller-driven plane—a three-and-a-half-hour flight.

We took off just as the sun emerged from behind the purple ramparts of the Andes at 6 in the morning. The plane quivered and drummed as it struggled to reach a cruising altitude.

When we reached 10,000 feet, the stewardess passed out oxygen devices—wooden mouthpieces on long tubes. These were attached to special cabin wall openings, and from them a sustaining supply of oxygen could be inhaled by each passenger.

The awesome grandeur of the Andes took our minds off the discomfort of the rarefied air. The pilot invited us into the cockpit so that Hal could get better films of the thrilling scenery. We plugged ourselves in to the oxygen supply in the cockpit, and as Hal started to film, David and I stared out through the windshield.

The altimeter needles showed us to be at 17,500 feet, yet the peaks of the Andes towered above us on all sides. The pilot pointed out Huascaran, the highest mountain peak in the Peruvian part of the Andes. There it loomed above us to our left—an ice-crowned mass 22,205 feet above sea level. Our skipper informed us that Huascaran is only 600 feet lower than Aconcagua, the highest peak of all the Andes.

As for us, we were flying down an "alley" known as the Callejón de Huaylas between the Cordillera Blanca and Cordillera Negra (White Mountains and Black Mountains). Tremendous waves of granite rose on either side. They seemed to lean toward us, as though to reach out and crush our fragile, manmade flying insect whose noisy engines undoubtedly disturbed the sleep of ancient deities in peaks and crannies.

When the pilot volunteered the information that for years airmen had flown this treacherous passageway in single-engine, wood-and-fabric machines during foul weather and fair, I had to shudder and at the same time marvel at the cheerful abandon with which "Vikings," be they Scandinavian sea rovers of the Middle Ages or Peruvian pilots of Indian and Spanish descent, have always been ready to challenge the elements.

After two hours the Callejón de Huaylas opened out. Before us spread a seemingly limitless green carpet of vegetation. The Andes fell away abruptly and our pilot started a long, slow descent over the Selvas, a vast, lush, jungle-covered equatorial plain that rolls down toward the Amazon and the Brazilian border.

Our DC-4 lurched and wobbled in rising currents of heated air as it approached Iquitos, and the cabin began to grow noticeably warmer. We thankfully abandoned the oxygen devices as we passed the 10,000-foot level on our way down.

When we landed at Iquitos Airport and taxied to a stop

before the terminal, the humid, dense heat of the Amazon immediately enveloped us.

Our ears were popping after the long trip at high altitudes, but we could hear a din which made me think we had inadvertently entered the world's largest and most crowded zoo. The terminal had hundreds of caged creatures waiting to be flown to zoos in all parts of the world. The chattering of monkeys, yowling and snarling of jaguars, and shrieking and whistling of parrots and macaws were almost ear-shattering.

This was Amazon country, mysterious and remote. Or so I had been led to believe. But as we were driven in a fairly modern taxi to our hotel on the banks of the mighty Amazon itself, there ahead of us on the river was, of all things, a sizable ocean steamer.

"Look, Hal!" I exclaimed. "It must be a mirage. A huge liner here in the middle of South America!"

"It's no mirage, elskan-min." He laughed. "Iquitos is a seaport, believe it or not. Ships navigate from the South Atlantic Ocean, twenty-five hundred miles along the Amazon to Iquitos to pick up cargoes of crude rubber. The Amazon is navigable for a distance longer than that from New York to Iceland!"

By the time we reached our hotel the three of us were soaked with perspiration and thought back to the cold upper reaches of Andean air with a certain regretful nostalgia. Fortunately our accommodations were in the air-conditioned part of the building.

The final arrangements for our trip on the Amazon to an encampment of Yagua Indians where Hal was anxious to obtain footage depended on a meeting with a Chinese travel entrepreneur. This man not only had boats for hire but a place with "modern conveniences" for overnight visitors. Most important of all, he claimed a rapport with the Indians that would ensure their willingness to pose for us.

Unfortunately Mr. Wong couldn't be reached at the moment. To avoid wasting precious time, we dressed as lightly as possible and decided to explore the city despite the almost choking heat.

But stepping from our air-conditioned room into the sunshine was like entering a blast furnace. We strolled along the main thoroughfare, dabbing at rivulets of perspiration that stung our eyes and dampened our clothing. At close hand it was obvious that Iquitos, with a current population of 40,000, had fallen upon lean times. Hal explained that the city's heyday had been during the rubber boom of 1900 to 1910 and that when Oriental rubber from Malaya became available, the Iquitos monopoly was broken and the rubber trade gradually declined, although a considerable tonnage was still being shipped out of port.

Iquitos has a definite frontier atmosphere. And when we encountered an establishment called, of all things, The North Pole, it made me feel a little cooler. I managed to resist entering to ask for an Eskimo pie, especially since a small supermarket nearby actually did have them for sale!

Hal insisted on obtaining footage of me, an Icelander presumably accustomed to the frigid north, daintily mopping my brow as I stood before the North Pole sign. Several interested passers-by paused to watch our "location" shot. One of them suggested that we might go to the main square, where we would find an interesting building housing the Social Club.

"It was built, this *edificio,* in 1880 by none other than the famous, the great, the most celebrated Frenchman Alexandre Eiffel!" our informant proudly announced.

"The builder of the Eiffel Tower in Paris?" Hal asked.

The man beamed. "None other!"

This we had to see. When we reached the square, the building was easy to spot. Its beams and riveting vaguely reminded us of the Eiffel Tower, but after we had filmed it, we learned that Eiffel himself had not actually come to this out-of-the-way corner of the world. He had constructed the building in

France, then taken it apart and shipped it to Iquitos, where the proud citizens had put it together again.

During all this time the air had grown increasingly oppressive. Hal looked at the sky and saw dark, looming clouds that looked like an advancing range of mountains. We finished our filming and hurried back to the hotel.

Just as we reached our room the storm broke over Iquitos like a tidal wave. Blinding flashes of lightning accompanied by jarring thunderclaps shook our building. The rain was driven almost horizontally by near-hurricane winds. Our hotel actually vibrated. The noise was almost deafening and when the downpour momentarily slackened and we could see through the drenched windows, the surface of the Amazon was a churning, foaming maelstrom that had the anchored ships rocking and tugging at their moorings.

The storm abated as suddenly as it had come. Within minutes the sky was clear again and the turbulent surface of the mighty river was calm. When I remembered that we were going to travel on this same river in a small boat, I shuddered. What if a storm such as this overtook us while we were en route to the Yagua Indians!

David and I sweltered in the stern of the ancient wood-hulled motor launch as it struggled to make headway against a strong current. Hal and the thickset, scowling young native boatman, the mysterious Mr. Wong's assistant, were in conference in the bow.

The sun's rays beat down like heat from molten metal. The water of the Amazon, a mile wide above Iquitos, was still muddy as a result of the previous day's storm. Since our speed was hardly faster than a snail's pace, the motion of the boat caused no cooling breeze.

David and I shared space with half a dozen five-gallon drums of gasoline, our camera equipment, a small bag containing meager essentials and my ever-present carryall travel case. The passing scenery was spectacular, with thick jungle

growth literally spilling into the water on both sides. As our
engine hiccupped in the suffocating humidity, flocks of brilliantly plumaged birds rose from the foliage, swooped curiously over us, and then, with weird cries, returned to the
shores.

The journey had started off on the wrong foot through no
fault of ours. Mr. Wong had promised Hal that we would be
taken to his encampment in a "new, all-metal, modern boat."
However, when we arrived at the Wong landing in the comparative cool of early morning, we were met by our youthful
pilot who casually reported that Señor Wong had gone up to
the encampment himself in the new boat. Despite Hal's pre-
arrangements, which included partial payment in advance,
there was left for our use the old wooden scow in which we
now sat.

It was evident that the hull leaked, as an inch of water
sloshed about under the floorboards. And several holes had
rotted through the bow of the craft. This was disturbing,
since although not overloaded, the launch rode low in the
water. Should a storm such as the one we had witnessed the
day before come up, there was an excellent chance that we'd
founder in the first waves.

When we learned of Mr. Wong's double-dealing, Hal's annoyance verged on downright anger. However, arguing with
Wong's representative would have been worse than futile.
Our filming schedule demanded that we keep going at all
costs, at least until we could catch up with our Chinese friend
at the encampment near the Yaguas and straighten things out.

"The weather at least should hold out," Hal said to me
while the boatman stood by, staring blankly into the water.
"It'll be a slow trip—perhaps five or six hours. But eventually
we'll get there and I'll be able to get the footage."

"Well, if worst comes to worst and we should all fall in, at
least the water will be warm," I said laughingly.

There was a peculiar glint in Hal's eyes. He nodded and
helped David and me aboard. Much later he told me that

when I mentioned the warm water, the possibility of our encountering the ferocious, man-eating piranha fish had crossed his mind. These fierce little creatures, barely eighteen inches in length, travel in schools and infest stretches of the Amazon and its tributaries. With rows of razor-sharp teeth and insatiable appetites, they have been known to strip a full-grown cow to the bone within minutes. Fortunately I did not know this at the time. When we clambered into the decrepit launch, a piranha was the farthest thing from my mind.

And as we *putt-putted* away from Iquitos, Hal assured me that if a sudden squall should come up, we could easily make a landing on the shore and wait until the danger passed.

As I gingerly settled David and myself among the odoriferous gas cans, I asked why we had to carry so much extra fuel. Hal looked disgusted. "The engine is so ancient that it gulps fuel. And since we'll be struggling against the current, we'll need every drop."

Refueling, I quickly discovered, involved coming to a halt, stopping the engine, and drifting helplessly backward while the boatman, aided by my husband, filled the emptied tank.

Despite the inconvenience, disappointment and incredible heat, we found much that absorbed our interest and made us almost forget the seamy aspects of the trip. While Hal took color motion picture footage of life along the banks, I made copious notes, trying to keep perspiration from saturating the pages of my notebook. And when dugout canoes passed with their smiling, waving natives, the journey upriver did not seem so tedious.

Time passed fairly quickly. It must have been two hours after we had cast off—and two refueling interludes later—when an exclamation of dismay from our boatman made us look ahead. Bearing down on us was a huge, battleship-gray paddle-wheeled steamer. Even as we stared, the onrushing ship, monstrous in comparison to ours, let out an ear-shattering screech on its steam whistle.

Our pilot throttled back our decrepit engine. "Is anything wrong, Hal-minn?" I asked.

Hal queried our boatman in rapid-fire Spanish.

"The ship is a Peruvian Navy patrol called *Queen of the Amazon*. Jorge says that it won't slacken speed as it passes us. Its wake can be dangerous to this rickety boat." Then Hal added, "Chances are we'll come out of it okay if he keeps his bow headed into the waves."

The patrol ship swept past with a thrum of engines and a deluge of spray from its threshing paddle wheels. The wake formed billows of water that rushed toward us like miniature tidal waves. I gripped the gunwale with one hand and clutched David with the other. Our launch creaked as its bow rose high and then lurched. Water washed aboard and was added to the slosh that curled around our feet.

Hal and I rode it through quietly and grimly. David, however, thought it rare fun, and when crewmen aboard the receding ship waved, he insisted on waving back. Strangely enough, we didn't feel like joining him.

With an audible sigh of relief, Jorge pushed the throttle of our engine forward and once more we resumed our slow journey.

It was midafternoon when our pilot drew into the narrow Mayniti River, a tributary of the Amazon. We were, Jorge said with a surprisingly cheerful smile, quite near Wong's encampment which, of course, was next door to the Indian village, and so on, and so on. We listened without enthusiasm. By this time we were not prepared to believe anything we heard.

And sure enough, Jorge's notion of being "quite near" was illusory to say the least. It was almost dark when we finally reached Wong's campsite. By then we had resigned ourselves to expect the opposite of the "completely equipped campsite" that Wong had promised Hal. Although far from ideal and somewhat primitive, it did turn out to consist of a fairly substantial thatch-roofed structure on stilts which in a pinch could accommodate eight or ten people.

Along with mosquitoes and clouds of other insects of large and menacing shapes, we were greeted by the blandly smiling, moon-faced Mister Wong, who reminded me of an amateur actor stumbling through the role of Charlie Chan in a high school theatrical.

"Oh—so happy to see you made it," he bubbled.

Hal looked at him, glanced at the metal boat tied up nearby, and muttering something under his breath, turned without answering our host and began to unload equipment.

Mr. Wong was not dense (aside from running boats and maintaining encampments, he had a corner on the photographic business in Iquitos) and instantly sensed Hal's displeasure. Wong's technique was to pour on charm and be superhelpful. He insisted on helping David and me from our floating sieve to the dock, meanwhile barking staccato commands in Spanish to Jorge to "*ayudes al* Señor Linker."

The house was built on poles which supported the roof; the floor was several feet above the ground. I did not have to ask why. I suspected that this method of construction was used to discourage crawling intruders from the insect and reptile worlds. When Hal asked where our cots were, so that he could stow our equipment, Mr. Wong shrugged, sighed and piously rolled his eyes skyward.

"I forgot to mention, Señor Linker, that this camp is so new that we haven't had a chance to completely equip it for our guests. There is only one cot and I'm already using it. So"—he smiled—"I'll fix mattresses for you and your family on the floor."

My husband literally exploded. "You'll do nothing of the sort!" he exclaimed. "I'm paying you a hundred dollars a day for this trip. I was led to believe that the price also included transportation in a reasonably safe metal boat [Hal pointed toward our waterlogged craft] and not a rotten cockleshell apt to sink at any moment!"

During my husband's outburst I'd been watching Wong's face. At first he merely stared, lips slightly parted and round head bobbing, as though in complete agreement. But as Hal continued, his voice betraying mounting anger, Wong's expression went blank and his eyes became glazed. It was as though he had turned himself off.

"Very well, Mr. Linker, you can have the cot." Mr. Wong then continued his efforts to restore peace by suggesting that after dinner we all go out and hunt crocodiles.

I gazed toward the river which by now had blended into the blackness of the night. The notion of wandering through the dark jungle in search of crocodiles with questionable dispositions was somewhat chilling despite the thick, oppressive heat.

Hal and David settled matters by instantly and enthusiastically taking up our host's invitation. Mr. Wong beamed.

"But first we have dinner, no?" Wong rubbed his hands and began to shout at Jorge, who nodded and ambled off toward an end of the building that turned out to be a dining area of sorts.

As we followed him I was conscious of swarms of flying things, invisible in the gloom, that kept brushing my hair. But I disregarded these creatures as I did the dampness of my cotton slacks and bush jacket which were sopping wet with perspiration and clung to my body.

"Hal—how will we be able to see crocodiles in the dark?" I whispered.

"Their eyes shine in the night," he answered. "Especially when you beam a light at them."

"May I hold the light, Pabbi?" cried David, using his favorite Icelandic term for Daddy. (It's pronounced as though it were spelled Poppie.)

I absently slapped at a hungry and persistent bug. "But can you trust our"—I lowered my voice even more—"host after what has happened? Maybe he'll try—"

Hal patted my arm. "Don't worry. He'll be okay. After all,

he hasn't been paid in full yet and knows he won't be until we get back to Iquitos safe and sound."

Dinner consisted of fried fish and bananas. It was silently served by two expressionless Indian women who materialized from nowhere. The food was undoubtedly nourishing but was tasteless. We were really too hot to care. The mosquitoes came crowding in from the jungle and river and helped themselves to copious drafts, biting my thighs and knees through my slacks.

Our crocodile safari, Wong assured us, would not take long. Half an hour—an hour at the most. "They are everywhere," he explained as we cautiously made our way to the mooring.

We settled ourselves in the metal boat, and even in the nearly pitch blackness of the Amazon night, I could appreciate the vast difference between this boat and the wooden one we had used before.

When Jorge started the engine and we glided away from the shore, the sensation was eerie—as though we were suspended in a black void while the campsite's lights slowly faded behind us like a mirage at midnight.

The hunt was weird enough to be fascinating. We alternately *putt-putted* and drifted silently, with a flashlight directed toward the bank. Wong was correct. There were more crocodiles present than was comfortable. At first, to my unpracticed eye, they looked like logs. It was only when the flashlight's rays shone on their bulging eyes, gleaming like miniature automobile headlights, that I could realize they actually were crocodiles.

Most of them merely stared without moving. A few slithered into the river and disappeared beneath the surface. It was an exciting experience—in the category of one of those I'm-glad-I-did-it-once-but-never-again-thanks things.

When we turned back, Hal and I were convinced that Jorge had the eyes of a cat. He started the engine and headed briskly through the impenetrable darkness. We strained our eyes but could not see a thing. Finally when I was beginning to wonder whether we would ever sight the camp, Jorge eased back on the throttle and moved the tiller. The boat turned, and there, glimmering in the distance, were the oil lamps of the encampment.

When we finally felt ground underfoot, we were so tired that I knew we'd all sleep well in spite of any number of flying or crawling intruders.

David and I kissed Hal good night and went to the cot that we were to share.

I told David to get undressed, and absently reached for the mosquito netting. My hand froze in midair. Squatting on the netting, not more than six inches from my face, was a monstrous spider as big as my fist! For a long moment we stared at one another.

David came to my side. "What's the matter, Mama?"

I retreated silently, pulling him with me. "Hal!" My throat felt dry. "There's a—a big, hairy spider on my cot!"

My husband looked up from his sleeping bag. "I'll be darned," he cried, almost eagerly. "That's the biggest tarantula I've ever seen!"

He jumped to his feet. Looking about the floor, he spied a piece of firewood. "That ought to do it," he muttered, picking up the wood and advancing toward the tarantula.

"Wait, Hal-minn." He looked at me. "Before you kill it, why don't you film it?"

There was a quizzical look on his face. "Is this my Halla, my Icelandic Queen who cannot stand bugs?"

"This is your bug-hating Halla, all right," I answered; "but I also know that this—this monster should make interesting viewing for our audiences."

Keeping on the alert for interesting camera angles that Hal might happen to overlook had become almost second nature to me. In this case my "professional" instinct, reasserting itself, was a lifesaver for my nerves and took my mind off the menace of that hideous-looking creature.

Hal dragged out his portable battery-operated lights and camera.

"You stand back, David," he said and handed me the lights. "Shine this on our friend while I get some footage."

My grip was not too steady. The bright light wavered as I listened to the whir of Hal's camera. The tarantula seemed to crouch, as though annoyed by all the attention and ready to attack.

My fear and revulsion came crowding back. "That's enough, Hal-minn!" I gasped. "Please get rid of it now!"

He nodded and recranked the camera. "Here," he said, handing it to me. "You film it while I get him on the floor and make him move. Otherwise people may think we filmed a dead tarantula."

I could only nod. Hal took a small flashlight and poked the tarantula until it fell to the floor with a solid thump. It merely crouched down on its long, hairy legs and didn't move. Hal pushed it again. The creature stirred.

"Now!" Hal said excitedly. He gave the spider a determined poke. It scuttled several feet—fortunately away from me; I was able to keep my trembling finger on the camera's trigger.

"Got it?" Hal glanced toward me. "Good. Now we can get rid of it."

He raised the stick and I turned away. The sound of the blow made me feel queasy. Then I heard scraping sounds as Hal pushed the creature outside.

"*Qué pasó?* What goes on?" It was Wong, who had been attracted by the noise and bright light. When Hal finished explaining, our host stared at us. "*Madre de Dios!* You poked it with that flashlight?"

"It was all I had," Hal answered.

Wong shook his head. "Don't you know that these tarantulas can *jump!* And if they *bite—*" He squatted down and gazed outside at the dead creature. "I've nothing here for tarantula bite." Again he shook his head.

Hal and I exchanged looks. He swallowed once or twice. "Well, I guess we were lucky. He must have been sleepy or sick or something because he hardly moved."

Wong rose to his feet. "Well, Señor, the next time just remember that they jump."

"How far?" asked David.

"Far enough, *chico*," Wong replied.

Sleep after that was a long while coming. Since I always dream, the thought of meeting that tarantula in my sleep made me apprehensively wakeful. But gradually my eyelids grew heavy. I did not dream of the tarantula. Instead, I was driving a leaky wooden boat down Vine Street in Hollywood.

5
Amazon Adventure

T HE torrent of noise at dawn the next morning made me imagine I had somehow been transported from the Amazon to Bedlam. The sounds were a mixture of strange, shrill screeches and the trilling, silvery notes of mysterious birds. They seemed to come from all sides.

I awoke abruptly and became conscious of the diffused daylight sifting through the thatched roof. My shirt and slacks, the mattress, the mosquito netting and boots beside the cot, all exuded the sour odor of mildew typical of the equatorial jungle.

My watch told me I had slept six hours; it felt more like six fleeting minutes. I swung my legs over the side of the cot and then remembered the tarantula. I quickly tucked my legs under me and groped for my boots. I took each boot in turn, held it upside down and vigorously pounded the sole to dispossess any unwelcome lodger. Nothing fell out. I peered into each one to make sure. Even then I carefully, almost hesitantly, slipped my feet into the boots. Although the leather of the soles was already beginning to curl and had shrunk slightly from moisture, their blessed emptiness made me feel almost cheerful.

I shook off the last trace of drowsiness and walked to the

door. Hal and David stood nearby in a clearing. My husband had his camera aimed toward the green-topped columns of trees that comprise the incredible rain forest which stretches almost 3,000 miles along the Amazon basin to the Atlantic.

Gazing toward the forest "roof," which must have been nearly 200 feet high, I realized that the sun was shining brightly. The weak sunlight that reached us had been filtered through masses of thick branches, foliage and huge, climbing vines.

Although it was sultry it was not uncomfortable. Had we not been protected by the forest, the full strength of the sun would have been nearly unbearable.

Our campsite, with its long, unwalled sleeping quarters and mess hall, seemed deserted and completely cut off from the rest of the world. A path led from our building and abruptly disappeared into the forest which, even from a distance of a few yards, looked impenetrable. Actually a small village of "civilized" Indians who after a fashion looked after things for Wong was located a mere hundred feet away. But the trees were so thick that the presence of their huts was impossible to detect.

Looking about, I found the cause of the indescribable din that had awakened me. Monkeys, which we later learned are called guaribas (red howlers), were in competition with brilliantly plumaged parrots, macaws and caciques shrilling from lofty nests.

My husband and son came to my side. "Isn't this fantastic?" Hal said, his eyes gleaming with the photographer's lust to film everything in sight.

The mysterious Indian woman reappeared to serve breakfast, which once more consisted of fried bananas and tea. And again the legions of insects came to join us but by now my appetite had returned and I aggressively protected my plate.

While we ate, Hal told me of Mr. Wong's latest blunder. Although our so-called itinerary had called for an early departure to film upstream at the Yagua Indian village, Wong had instead decided to take both boats and sail downstream to a landing where he could get gasoline for the engines. It seemed he had underestimated the amount of fuel our rickety engines would eat up on the trip to the camp.

"But this is his camp and he comes here all the time," I said. "Surely by now you'd think he would know."

Hal shook his head. "He's either inept or the biggest liar I've ever met. No matter what, we're stuck until he returns."

It was a worrisome development. Our schedule was extremely tight: we had allowed only two days for the boat trip from Iquitos to the Yaguas and back; our plane for the flight over the Andes to Lima was scheduled to leave at 10:30 the following morning. Since there were only two flights a week out of Iquitos, if we did not reach the airport on time, we'd be stuck in Iquitos and lose precious hours that would rule out another important stop later on.

"We may have to go downriver at night to make our plane in time," Hal said.

The thought of gliding downstream in pitch-black darkness made me shiver in the humid air. Even so, I managed to say, "I wouldn't mind if we could use the metal boat."

"Don't worry," Hal said grimly. "I'll see to that."

Rather than sit around fuming and idly waiting for Wong's return, Hal persuaded Jorge to hire an Indian to guide us into the rain forest. We found a guide who spoke a few rudimentary words of Spanish. He was a gnarled old man incongruously equipped with a long, gleaming machete slung from one shoulder. His head constantly bobbed in agreement with anything we said and his lips wore a constant grin that revealed large, discolored teeth. However, he was an expert woodsman and as we followed he hacked at the undergrowth with his machete, to clear the way for us. He kept remarking —mostly in his own dialect—about the various trees and plants.

The floor of this vast ocean of foliage was like a soft, rich, beautifully colored mosaic carpet of aroids, orchids, fungi and ferns, with profuse mushrooms, all poisonous, growing all about.

The Indian paused by a tree, and by means of gestures and fragments of Spanish, described how the milky sap is used by his people for medicinal purposes. He made motions that could only indicate a headache, holding both palms to his temples, rolling his eyes and moaning. Then he cut a gash with his machete, took the sap and put it to his mouth. Immediately he beamed and removed his hands from his temples.

"*Ahh—dolor de cabeza,*" Hal said in Spanish. "And this cures it?"

"*Si, si!*" Our friend nodded. "*Medicina—medicina.*" He rubbed the sap with a finger. "*Tinga Maria—tinga Maria. Es muy bien, si!*"

A short time after that demonstration of a natural remedy, David, who had trotted on slightly ahead, darted toward a large tree that stood somewhat apart and looked quite different from the others, as though it were a stranger encircled by suspicious natives.

The Indian gave an exclamation and grabbed our son's arm. He began to scold the boy. When Hal questioned him, he pointed to the tree, and again with gestures and disjointed Spanish but now without smiling, explained that this tree's sap was a deadly poison. Natives use it to poison arrow tips. Should any of the sap get into one's eyes, blindness would result, he told us.

Chilled by this disclosure, I felt deeply grateful to this friendly Indian who had turned out to be a guardian angel as well as a guide. Following his instructions, we shielded our eyes in passing under that tree and others like it.

It had been barely 7 in the morning when we set out. We returned to the camp (without our friend, we'd have been hopelessly lost) toward noon. Wong still had not made an appearance.

The sunlight began to dim. It was hazy above us and a mountain of large, fleecy clouds loomed in the distance.

"Dammit, there's a storm coming up," Hal muttered. He looked at me. "That's all we need. A blow like the one at Iquitos would wipe out any chance of filming the Yaguas."

Not only that, I thought, but perhaps it would also keep us penned up in Wong's camp long enough to miss several Lima-bound planes. Navigating downriver in a storm, even in the metal boat, was of course out of the question.

When we reached the mooring, we saw that our Chinese host had returned from wherever he had gone. Both the metal craft and the rickety wooden one were tied up.

Wong, oozing geniality, approached us. "Just in time to go visit the Yaguas," he chirped. "I've got enough gas to get us to the village."

Hal's face reddened. His temper was beginning to boil over. "That's fine," he said carefully, "but how do we get back here from the village? And back to Iquitos after that?"

"Oh—plenty of gas—lots." Wong began to undo the line of the metal boat. "Let's hurry. We'll still have time to get there and back before dark if we start now."

I wondered why he was putting us in the metal boat and then remembered that he was coming with us.

The journey led up the Mayniti. Along both banks the jungle, alive with bird life, bordered the water.

For miles we saw not the slightest trace of a human being. When we heard a long, hearty shout from the river bank on the right, the three of us were startled.

"We're here," announced Wong. He headed toward shore where a stocky Indian waited, his face daubed with streaks of varicolored paint and wearing a colored skirt woven of raffia. This odd individual went about helping to secure the boat in a businesslike way.

Wong introduced all of us in what must have been the Yaguan's native tongue although it sounded like mere gibberish and the Indian seemed perplexed at times. However, we smiled at him and extended our hands. That was understandable to all concerned. His welcome was quite warm and he beckoned us to follow him.

A pathway, hardly visible to our unpracticed eyes, led us abruptly into the village where a group of Yaguas quickly surrounded our group. We noticed that the men wore tufts of raffia on their muscular upper arms and a woven chest device suspended by a cord around their necks. Several of them also boasted rather rakish, feather-bedecked raffia hats. The headgear, we learned, was for male Yaguans only; evidently millinery was taboo for the women. However, the women had decorative designs tattooed on their flat-cheeked, broad, copper faces. It was obvious that this "beautification" took place at an early age, because I noticed several girls who could hardly have been more than twelve or thirteen, perhaps even younger, who had designs all over their cheeks.

The villagers seemed friendly enough although most of the males were solemn-faced. The women, on the other hand, were frankly curious, especially about me. My blond hair and fair complexion seemed to intrigue them. In their own society they apparently occupy an inferior social position. I could sense their wonderment at the fact that I, a female, seemed to be treated as an equal by my husband. They watched us with sidelong glances. Whenever we caught their eyes, they would giggle among themselves, as though sharing an enormous jest at our expense.

The atmosphere was friendly enough, but as we roamed through the tiny community I remembered the things we had learned about them before we started on the trip. Not too long ago the Yaguas had been feared headhunters and displayed deadly hostility to visitors. As I strolled through the village, I could not entirely dismiss this memory and hoped we would not offend them and become targets for their poison-tipped arrows and blowgun darts.

The community itself consisted of small thatched huts. A few were rectangular, the majority conical.

Our host and guide turned out to be none other than the

chief. He was an obliging host; he not only consented to pose for Hal but he insisted that many of his warriors get into the act and demonstrate their skill with blowguns and bows, using a leaf target set up on a tree. They even showed David how to shoot a blowgun.

After being assured that there was no poison on David's darts, I left Hal to his filming and wandered to a circle of young women seated around large wooden trays, pounding some roots into a gluelike substance. Nearby were huge pots with their contents simmering over a fire. The women looked at me, giggled, whispered and went on about their work. There was something hauntingly familiar about this activity. It suddenly dawned on me. They were grinding manioc (known to us from the Congo as the cassava root) for food. This is a staple diet for many natives of Africa as well as of South America.

Since the South American manioc root is basically poisonous, it must first be boiled to eliminate its hydrocyanic acid. It is then kneaded and crushed into a paste that is either baked into a kind of bread or eaten plain.

I was shocked to see the girls frequently take a mouthful of manioc, chew it, and then spit it back into the pot! This stomach-turning procedure was new to me. They hadn't done this in the Congo.

I asked Wong about the strange procedure. He laughed. "It's how they make *cerveza*—beer!"

He explained that human saliva induces fermentation in the mashed manioc which is then set aside for a few weeks during which it transforms itself into a potent brew called *chibcha*.

I must have grimaced unconsciously. One of the women, misunderstanding my expression, poured some of the older, already-fermented concoction into a small gourd and offered it to me. I declined as tactfully as I could. But when Wong took the gourd and drained it with lip-smacking relish, I hurriedly made my escape back to Hal and David.

By the time my husband had finished filming, the sun was low and partly obscured by a bank of clouds and a light, misty drizzle had begun to sift down through the trees. We said our farewells to the Yaguas, striving to shorten the usual protracted ceremony of leave-taking as much as possible without giving offense, and hurried back to the boat.

Our downstream return was fairly swift. Within less than an hour Wong turned toward his campsite. By the time we arrived night had fallen, dark and wet, since the drizzle had become more than a mere mist.

"Dinner and a good night's sleep and then we go back to Iquitos in the morning," Wong said with expansive good humor.

"We pack and go to Iquitos immediately," Hal answered. "Our plane leaves for Lima in the morning and we simply have to be aboard."

In the dark I could not make out Wong's expression. For a moment he was silent, with the forest on both sides of the river alive with the mournful plaints of the toucans, the calls of perdiz (a sort of jungle quail) and of whippoorwills.

Finally: "Señor, I do not like to navigate the river after dark."

"Nor I," said Hal, "but it can't be helped. There's been too much time lost by your inefficiency, not ours. We agreed on a schedule before we started. I'm going to hold you to it."

Wong's resentment could be felt. *"Bueno,"* he snapped. "We will go, then!"

Hal, David and I went about assembling our own gear. Although our personal equipment was negligible, putting together the photographic equipment for safe transit was a complicated business.

When it was finally finished, Jorge, who had stood by restlessly, turned on his flashlight and guided us to the mooring. At the water's edge we found Wong standing near the rickety wooden boat. It was filled to capacity with fuel cans and our equipment.

Wong indicated the old tub. "Just get on board and follow us. Jorge will pilot you."

Hal was speechless with anger. Aside from the consideration of greater safety in the metal craft, we had the heavier load—not to mention the fact that we were paying the entire cost of the expedition. Since it was our only chance to reach Iquitos and get a few hours sleep, we had no time to lose.

If Hal had sprung at the Chinaman's throat I would not have blamed him. As it was, he displayed amazing self-control.

"Excellent, Wong," he said. "I wouldn't think of disturbing your arrangements. However, since I *am* concerned with the safety of my wife and son, I insist that you come with us in this old tub and let Jorge pilot the new boat!"

In the yellowish flashlight Wong's face began to twitch. His eyes rolled toward Jorge, who was having a hard time suppressing a grin.

Our Chinese "patron" muttered something in what I took to be Cantonese and gingerly stepped into the boat. We followed him and then cast off. The flickering lights of the encampment were almost immediately swallowed by the blackness of the night. A dull rumble of thunder and lightning flashes came from downriver.

When we neared the entrance to the Amazon itself, a native canoe carrying a man and woman materialized like a phantom. Jorge throttled back and engaged in rapid-fire conversation with the Indians. We drifted alongside the metal boat.

Wong called over, "*Qué pasó,* Jorge?"

Jorge turned. "They have just come from the big river, these two, and they say storm is ver' bad there and coming here quick!"

I visualized the furious storm that had hit Iquitos and remembered how the huge freighters had been rocked. I felt sure that our ancient wooden boat would come apart like tissue paper the moment we were hit by a storm.

Hal spoke up quickly. "Turn back to camp, Wong."

"Ah yes, yes, of course!" Wong beamed. "It is wise."

"We'll start out again the moment the storm passes," Hal added.

We had hardly reached the landing area of the camp when the storm broke over us, drenching us before we could run the few yards to the building. Our equipment was safe, though, in the camera cases.

Dinner was a depressing affair. We all sat around the wooden table and pecked at the bananas and fried fish. The downpour on the thatched roof was nearly as deafening as the ceaseless artillery of the thunder.

It was almost ten o'clock.

I gazed down at my plate. The cold, unappetizing meal had hardly been touched. David had tried one bite of his and given up. Only Wong and Jorge had cleaned their plates. Waves of weariness washed over me. I shook my head to clear the cobwebs.

"It'll take at least six hours to reach Iquĭtos, Hal-minn," I said. "If we're to be on that plane, we simply must leave here, storm or no storm!"

"Your safety and David's must come first," Hal replied quietly. With a shrug, he added, "If we're stormbound here, we'll drop one of our scheduled stops and wait over for the next plane to Lima."

Wong nodded. *"Bueno.* Good. That's logical, Señor Linker. I—"

Hal gave him a hard look and he subsided.

I touched David's shoulder. "To bed," I whispered and led him to our cot. For a moment I hesitated and then carefully looked it over, inside and out. No tarantulas. David climbed in and I joined him. We were asleep before our heads touched the mildewed pillow.

A gentle but persistent hand finally roused me from sleep. In the darkness I sensed rather than saw Hal bending over me.

"The storm's over, elskan-min," he whispered. "We can get going now."

I sat up and looked at the luminous face of my watch. It

was three in the morning. Although there were still ominous mutterings of thunder, they were faint and far away. I awakened David. Hal helped me get our son on his feet and together we groped our way from the building to the water's edge.

The dim light barely illuminated the metal boat which, to my surprise, contained all our equipment. Wong, yawning enormously, looked startled and then beckoned impatiently. "Well—*vamos, vamos pronto,* quick before another storm, she comes up!"

Before we boarded the craft I looked questioningly at Hal. "How did you manage the change to the aluminum boat, Hal-minn?"

"I got up before anyone else and simply loaded our things in it. Wong didn't have nerve enough to make me change, and now there's no time."

He helped me into the boat. I settled myself amidship and arranged some torn sheets and a tarpaulin into a makeshift shelter for David and myself. It was still at least two hours before dawn. With a sort of numb thankfulness that things were working out without further aggravation, I managed to doze off again, with David in my arms, almost before we got under way.

Daylight once more brought wakefulness. The already soaring temperature balefully foreshadowed what we would have to endure when the sun reached its zenith. David and I sat up and blinked at the river, which seemed to sweep us along at a fantastic speed. The water was churning and yellowed by mud washed away from the banks on either side by the torrential storm of the night before. Huge logs, and whole branches of trees ripped from the rain forest by the wind seemed to be floating everywhere.

Wong frequently had to throttle back and execute hard turns to left or right to avoid collisions. I pictured what could have happened to us had Hal not decided to turn back the night before. The old wooden boat could hardly have sur-

vived the turbulent water, not to mention a mid-river colli-
sion in the dark with those menacing floating objects.

When we reached Iquitos and Hal had paid Wong off, we
piled into a cab and rushed to the airport, where we boarded
our plane with only minutes to spare.

As we took off and began to climb through layers of turbulent air on the return flight over the Andes to Lima, the
DC-4 felt as luxurious and stable as the *Queen Elizabeth!*
Sometime later we learned that Wong's battered old wooden
boat had finally sunk a few hundred yards from the dock,
ducking Jorge in the muddy waters of the Amazon. Fortunately there were no piranha nearby.

Cuzco rests at an altitude of more than two miles high
in the Andes. Because it is surrounded by towering peaks on
all sides, the weather of the ancient Incan capital is brisk and
the air piercingly sharp and thin.

After the humidity and sultry density of the Amazon and
Lima's comparatively mild climate, we found ourselves gasping and shivering despite the blessed sweaters I had brought
along.

Our guide cautioned us to rest for a day or so in the hotel
and get our lungs adjusted to the thin air. But we declined,
explaining that such leisurely travel was for pleasure-seeking
tourists; we had a production schedule to follow.

A potpourri of Indian and Spanish colonial architecture,
the latter predominant, the beauty and grandeur of historic
Cuzco almost made us forget our physical discomfort as we
slowly strolled along its streets.

The cathedral on the Plaza de Armas has an altar of silver.
Inside the treasure room is a golden monstrance in which is
set a dragon carved from a single immense emerald. Despite
inquiries, we were unable to learn the significance of this
work of art.

The present cathedral, the Iglesia y Convento de Merced,

was fairly "new"—it had been erected in the late 17th century on the site of the original building destroyed by an earthquake in 1650.

Dominating the city of 50,000 souls is the towering fortress of Sacsahuaman, built by the Incas as an impregnable citadel more than a century before Pizarro's conquest.

Climbing the winding streets, mostly paved with cobblestones, to the entrance of the fortress was a heart-testing ordeal, but the discomfort was a small price to pay for what we found. The walls of the citadel are formed of huge stone blocks. The Indian builders put them together without mortar and so precisely that even now, after centuries of exposure, earthquakes and warfare, it is impossible to insert a knife blade between any two of the stones.

The ability of the Indians in architecture and engineering, as well as their knowledge of mathematics and astronomy, still confounds modern scientists. On a street with the improbable name of Jatunrumiyos, we filmed a twelve-sided stone that forms part of a tremendous wall and is fitted into it perfectly, without the slightest imperfection.

An open field with terraced, grassy banks was used as a stadium by Aymara Indian folk dancers and singers. I noted that the music and songs were startlingly similar to Chinese melodies we had heard in Hong Kong!

We were so impressed that Hal decided to make a full-scale production of folk dancing and singing within the walls of Sacsahuaman. He entrusted the arrangement of the details to our guide, Americo Luna. The filming was to be done on our return from Machu Picchu, the awesome "lost" mountaintop city of the Incas, two days later.

The "train" which was to take us from Cuzco to Machu Picchu was a tiny, diesel-powered bus resembling a Volkswagen and fitted with flanged wheels. The little vehicle sputtered over eighty-six winding miles of track, and as we rode along I began to notice that my breathing improved. Little wonder. Machu Picchu, although located on a mountain, is surrounded by a gorge bounded by much higher ground and has an altitude of but 6,000 feet—practically sea level compared with Cuzco's 11,444 feet.

Spanish conquistadores had never been able to locate this lost city built by the Incas as a secret last-resort retreat. It remained but a legend until 1911 when Hiram Bingham, a Yale professor who later became United States Senator from Connecticut, was led to the magnificent ruins by an Indian guide.

Spread out beneath us on an ascending triangular peak surrounded by frowning, ominous mountains, was an amazing sight. Terraces, temples, towers and mausoleums; palaces and simpler homes; guardian walls with battlements, and an altar to the sun god. There it was—Machu Picchu, the brooding, mystic last stronghold of the mysterious Incas. In the vast silence, disturbed only by a sighing wind, it was easy for my imagination to people the city once more with the ghosts of its inhabitants of the past.

Feeling like conspirators and gasping with shortness of breath and weariness, the three of us followed Señor Luna through a narrow doorway and down rickety stairs into a large room filled with about thirty dancers and singers.

We had returned to Cuzco that same evening from Machu Picchu, expecting to find arrangements completed for filming the performers at Sacsahuaman the next morning. Instead our guide told us that the Indians had absolutely refused to perform for the *"Norteamericanos!"*

When Hal asked why, Luna merely shrugged. It would have been so easy to forget about it and tumble into our hotel beds.

Instead Hal said, "May I talk with them and see if I can persuade them?"

"I don't think it will help, but"—the guide threw up his hands—"why not?"

Exhausted as he was, Hal pulled himself together. "You

and David might as well stay here," he mumbled in a tired monotone.

I shook my head.

A wan smile crossed his face. And so it was that a short while later we found ourselves surrounded by people whose coppery features, cloaked in shadow, seemed hostile, almost sinister to my imagination. It turned out that the "commissar" of their *"sindicato"* had harangued the performers against cooperating with the "yanqui imperialists!"

After the first surprise of our appearance had passed, one of the hostile orators resumed his impassioned appeal in Spanish. Hal listened intently. When the man paused for breath, my husband rose and quietly begged the audience's permission to say a word in explanation.

The Indians stirred. For a moment our opponents hesitated and then they stood aside while Hal faced the audience. In fluent Spanish, he managed to impress them with his sincerity. He told them that our films would present a true picture of Peru, their race, culture and heritage not only to American audiences but to people elsewhere, since our films frequently were shown in other countries of the world. (By that time our program was being shown in Hong Kong and Finland and in thirty American overseas bases.)

As he spoke I could see that the Indian listeners were becoming interested. And the "commisars" plainly showed their annoyance. After he had finished, with an apology for his schoolbook Spanish, the *sindicato* men began to speak—this time, in Indian dialect, so that Hal could not understand them.

The expressions on the faces of the audience, which had shown interest during Hal's piece, now became stolid as they listened to our opponents. Our guide, who could understand Quechua, the local dialect, whispered that there was nothing more to be done. The performers would take a vote and send word to us the following morning.

The night passed fitfully for Hal and me, but David had

become completely adjusted to the extreme altitude after a first-day dizzy spell, and slept soundly.

Headache and lack of appetite had plagued me for days. In the early morning, exhausted from sleeplessness and unable to bear even the thought of food, we decided to forget filming the dancers and instead push on to Bolivia, which meant a long, all-day railroad journey from Cuzco.

We were beginning to pack when there was a knock on our door. We opened it to find Mr. Luna, his face wreathed in smiles. "I don't know how you did it, Señor Linker," he said, "but the dancers voted to perform for you this afternoon!"

6

Riot in the City of Peace

T HERE are no superlatives in any language that can do
justice to the awesome grandeur of that immense spine of ice
and snowcapped mountains called the Andes which runs the
length of South America along its Pacific Coast.

The journey to Puno, on Lake Titicaca, en route to Bolivia,
was truly breathtaking. Our train negotiated hairpin curves
and skirted the edges of frightening precipices. And because
we were traveling at an altitude of more than 14,000 feet, we
suffered from lack of oxygen.

The previous afternoon when the Cuzco dancers in brilliant Andean costumes had whirled, leaped and sung to the
accompaniment of their strange melodies, I had marveled at
their liveliness and energy. Since they had lived in the rarefied
air all their lives, their lungs were accustomed to the meager
supply of oxygen. But Hal, for some reason, was having a
dreadful time of it—worse than David and I. Although we
assisted him in many ways, the actual burden of film production, which involved lugging our heavy gear and climbing
to difficult vantage points, was entirely his.

He never complained. He just suffered and pretended that
there was nothing wrong. The train carried us higher and

higher to an altitude of 14,172 feet above the village of La Raya, and at this elevation we were all gasping.

Uncomfortable as we felt, we were truly impressed by the dramatic grandeur of the scene. Far above the timberline, La Raya is dwarfed by soaring, jagged peaks that challenge the cold, cloudless sky in all directions. Hal painfully and with obvious effort recorded the dramatic scene with his cameras as I took a stroll near the station. It was strange for me to realize that I was actually walking at an altitude higher above sea level than many airliners had flown until just a few years ago.

Colorfully costumed Aymara Indian women hawked their native food to the native passengers while the Indian men offered llama-skin rugs and dolls at each train window. I wasn't in a shopping mood, what with the magnificent scenery on every side—scenery whose austere, treeless grandeur strangely reminded me of the interior of my native Iceland.

Our long, all-day train ride ended late that evening at a tiny port named Puno which is located on the Peruvian side of Lake Titicaca. Over 12,000 feet high in a valley surrounded by Andean peaks, Titicaca sprawls over some 3,500 square miles and is jointly owned by Peru and Bolivia.

It was a brilliant, briskly cold, star-filled night when we left the railroad station at Puno and made our way to the dock where we boarded the *Ollanta*, a 265-foot-long steam packet. This historic vessel accommodates sixty-six passengers, and we learned that it had been built by British shipwrights in 1929 and shipped to Lima, dismantled on the Pacific Coast and brought piecemeal by rail to Puno, where it was reassembled for use on Lake Titicaca.

The labor involved in this remarkable operation must have been formidable, even for huge-lunged Peruvians and Bolivians. But as Hal pointed out, it was really nothing compared to the labor and hardship involved in 1861 when the very first steamer, the *Yavary* was transported over the Andes on the backs of Indians and mules and reassembled that same year.

It operated for almost seventy years before being replaced by the *Ollanta*.

The night aboard ship was fitful. Hal had given up all idea of sleep long before dawn and was slowly pacing the deck. He felt better on his feet than lying down. After the sun came up at 5, he decided to film and called us to witness the magnificent sunrise as we were arriving at Guaqui, in Bolivia, on the other side of the lake.

"It is much better for me to drive you to La Paz in my Volkswagen bus than for you to take the train. Where I will take you is most interesting for a cinematographer, Señor Linker."

The speaker was Darius Morgan, a slender Rumanian expatriate who had emigrated to South America years before and finally settled in Bolivia as the proprietor of a travel service called Crillon Tours.

"Besides," he added with emphasis, "the train takes six hours to travel fifty miles and I will get you to La Paz in four, even if we stop at the lost city of Tihuanaco."

"A lost city here in Bolivia?" I asked.

Darius nodded and grabbed the wheel in time to keep the bus from coasting into the nearby lake. "Older than Machu Picchu," he said. "Much older. Its people developed engineering and architecture before the Incas. You will see!"

Tihuanaco turned out to be only a few miles from Guaqui. Although most of the structures have fallen into ruin, there remained enough to make us realize how magnificent the city must have been in its days of glory when more than a million souls lived there. Some archaeologists estimate that it reached its highest development two or three thousand years ago.

As with the stonework of Machu Picchu and the old Inca stronghold of Sacsahuaman, unique methods of construction had been employed here—blocks placed together without mortar to create buildings of brilliant mathematical precision. It is even believed that the Incas may have learned their skill from their predecessors at Tihuanaco. Actually not too much is known of the original Tihuanacans. When the city flourished, it was apparently at the very edge of Lake Titicaca itself. During the following centuries the lake receded and its present shoreline is miles away from the remains. At the ruined Palace of the Ten Doors there was enough left to indicate the high degree of architectural skill the vanished civilization had attained.

Adjacent to the palace is an archway called the Gateway of the Sun. Standing ten feet tall, it is carved out of a single block of stone now known as andesite. On top is the sculptured figure of a large sun god holding a scepter in each hand. Numerous smaller carved figures face this deity as if they were running toward him. Half of these smaller figures represent human beings; the bodies of the others are topped by the feathered heads and beaks of condors, those tremendous Andean birds of prey. The symbolic meaning of this archway mystified us, as it has puzzled archaeologists and anthropologists throughout the years.

In the Indian language, Tihuanaco actually means Place of the Dead. The name was given to the mysterious city after it had been abandoned by its original inhabitants. What disaster, natural or otherwise, caused the abandonment of Tihuanaco may never be known. But judging from the numerous carved stone figures of men five to six feet tall that are found in the area, it must have been dreadful. The expression on the face of each figure is one of tearful grief, and the secret of Tihuanaco may be locked forever behind their mournful, mysterious crying eyes.

Back in Darius' bus on the way to La Paz, it became harder to sustain our interest as the air became more and more rarefied. The route climbed toward a 15,000-foot ridge, and the little Volkswagen engine had a difficult time of it; even in low gear the tiny, air-cooled engine sputtered in protest.

Darius stopped at the very top of the ridge.

"Now here," he said cheerfully, "is a fine view to film."

"Can't see it," muttered Hal. "My eyes hurt. My head is splitting and the light is blinding me. I'm afraid this altitude's got me."

It was his first open complaint and it frightened me. Darius studied him and nodded like a doctor who has verified his own diagnosis.

"*Soroche*—mountain sickness," he said. "I've got just the thing for it!"

"An oxygen bottle?" Hal muttered hopefully.

"No." Darius smiled. "Something just as good—but it's at La Paz. We'll have to wait." He sighed. "Too bad you won't look at the view. One hundred miles of twenty-one-thousand-foot peaks!"

Hal groaned. "Don't tempt me."

But his photographer's instinct made him open his eyes. He gasped and then, over my protests, painfully crawled out of the bus and up a nearby rise to record the fabulous scene.

There, spread across the entire horizon, were at least fifteen visible jagged peaks towering over 21,000 feet in one long, panoramic scene. When Hal finished and slowly staggered back to the bus, Darius and I helped him put the equipment away. Hal slumped down in his seat, his face ashen. He hardly opened his eyes for the remainder of the trip down to La Paz, situated a mere 12,000 feet above sea level.

After Darius helped install us in our hotel, he left, promising to return in a few minutes with the wonderful cure for *soroche*.

Hal looked at David and me. He tried to grin but the result was a weak, sickly grimace. "I think the iron man has had it for a while, elskan-min. Guess I'd better lie down."

Darius returned shortly with a teapot and cup.

"Drink this right away," he said, pouring a hot liquid.

"What is it?" Hal asked.

Darius shrugged. "A special sort of tea."

My husband took the cup and sipped. He made a wry face. "Sure is funny-tasting tea," he said.

Darius watched quietly as Hal slowly finished the cup. "Now," he asked, "how do you feel?"

Hal smacked his lips. "I do feel much better!" He began to pour another cupful.

"Better you only drink one cup now—perhaps another one later."

"Just what kind of tea is it, Darius?" I asked.

"We-ell, it's brewed from coca leaves and—"

"Why—that's what cocaine is made of! How dare you drug my husband?" I almost shrieked.

Darius looked upset. "Please, madam. Actually everybody—that is, nearly everybody here—even natives, I mean—some of them anyway—like I say, they all use it when they exert themselves in the fields. Even the women. When they're working —women and men—they also chew the coca leaves. They're always hungry. They never have enough food because the land here is so barren, and—well, the coca leaves give them energy and at the same time keep them from feeling hungry."

"Just one experience won't turn me into an addict, elskanmin," Hal said with a smile. "S'matter of fact I'm beginning to come back to life. There's still plenty of sunlight. Why don't we go out and get some more footage?"

"You'll go right to bed and rest," I said firmly. "There'll be plenty of time for filming tomorrow. But now we'll all get some sleep."

"Of course," Darius nodded. "I'll call for you in the morning. Meanwhile I'll leave the rest of the tea—just in case—"

I picked up the pot and handed it to him without saying a word. He studied my expression, shrugged and departed.

"We'll have no more of *that*," I said, turning to Hal. He was sound asleep.

Whether it was my husband's recuperative powers or Darius' remedy, I'll never know. At any rate, after nearly fourteen hours of uninterrupted sleep, Hal awakened almost completely restored.

We felt like living people again rather than zombies now that we'd been able to get some rest.

When we explored La Paz the following morning, we were able to walk and film with hardly a trace of the *soroche* that had plagued Hal almost from the moment we left Cuzco. David, of course, had been his normal, agile self after the first day.

La Paz, with a population of about 400,000 is one of two capitals of Bolivia. It is the seat of the executive branch of the government and of Congress. The other and older capital, Sucre, some 250 miles away, is the seat of the nation's Supreme Court.

La Paz lies at the bottom of a deep narrow gorge, entirely surrounded by snowcapped mountains. The most prominent is Mt. Illimani, which resembles a gigantic, hooded warrior wearing a gleaming helmet. According to Darius, the Indians believe that Illimani watches over La Paz. No matter where we went, Illimani was there, peering over our shoulders. I found myself almost believing the native superstition.

Roaming the city by bus and afoot, we filmed churches that date back to the days of the Spanish Conquest and whole neighborhoods that bear the unmistakable stamp of the 17th and 18th centuries, the era of the viceroys when Bolivia was part of Peru.

We visited the airport, the highest commercial airfield in the world, at an altitude of more than 13,000 feet.

I found the shopping center along the Calle Comercio crowded with shops offering vicuña rugs and coats, alpaca, gold and silver jewelry and filigree. But we found the Sunday market on the Plaza San Francisco the most colorful. The stalls are operated by native women wearing the incongruous derbies adopted by the Andean Indian women about a century ago.

A slightly gnawing uneasiness I had begun to feel since coming to Bolivia came into sharper perspective when we visited the plaza. Standing before the cathedral was a lamp post flanked by two fully armed infantrymen.

Noticing our surprise, Darius explained that the lighting standard was a "national shrine."

"Shrine? To what?" Hal asked.

Darius shrugged. "To a former *presidente*. During one of our many revolutions in this country, a mob broke into the government *palacio*, seized the *presidente*, dragged him here and hanged him from this lamp post!"

The brilliant sunlight dappling the picturesque plaza seemed to dim.

"The present government is of the same party as was the martyred *presidente*," Darius went on. "As long as they are in power, they intend to keep this as a shrine."

"Evidently by force if necessary," Hal murmured.

"*Exactamente*," Darius answered with a nod.

David tugged at my arm. "Mommy, look!" He pointed to the roof of the cathedral.

I raised my eyes to receive the shock of my life. Staring back at me were the muzzles of two machine guns that protruded from openings in a pile of sandbags at each corner of the church. The fact that the gun crews lounged and idly chatted with one another did not reassure me. I mutely called my husband's attention to the weapons which appeared to me to be desecrating this place of worship.

Hal raised his camera. One of the "shrine" guards stirred.

Darius whispered nervously, "I would not advise that, Señor Linker!"

Hal hesitated, then filmed anyway. We managed a smile for the lamp-post sentries (which they did not return) and strolled from the scene with elaborate nonchalance. It took all the courage I could muster to turn my back on those bayoneted rifles held by the hard-eyed soldiers and the wicked muzzles of the rooftop machine guns.

Darius' attempt at conversation did not restore my peace of mind. "The people of Bolivia are very changeable," he said.

"Did you know that since 1825 there have been more than sixty revolutions, seventy *presidentes* and eleven constitutions?"

Hal laughed. "Thanks, that makes me feel much better. Let's be on our way!"

On one street we noticed a group of approaching marchers in nondescript khaki uniforms. All of them carried rifles and wore bandoliers of what looked like large firecrackers. They filled the street from one side to the other. Darius turned pale and shut off the motor with an air of resignation.

"They are the civilian militia—the *dinamiteros*," he whispered. "We wait here for them to pass."

Hal stepped out with his camera. He was halfway up the street toward the approaching militiamen before Darius realized what he was doing.

"Please stop him," Darius begged me. "They are unpredictable and dangerous. They are *communistas*—they hate foreigners, especially Americans. What they are carrying is dynamite. They might light a fuse—"

But it was already too late. Hal had quickly set up his camera and was about to film when we could see that he suddenly realized that the marchers were militia. He immediately decided to brazen it out rather than show fear and perhaps bring on an attack. I gasped as I watched him wave his hand in a friendly manner at the approaching marchers, smiling broadly at the same time; he repeated the gesture several times. I noticed that his other hand was on the shutter of the camera, and I knew that he was filming without putting his eye to the viewer. The marching men looked startled. A few made half-hearted movements toward the dynamite they carried, but then brought their hands up in the Communist salute, with clenched, upraised fists. As they swirled past our car I could see that many of them were drunk; they staggered as they tried to keep up with the others.

Suddenly they were gone and Darius breathed a sigh of relief. Hal returned to the car looking a bit shaken himself.

"A few weeks ago," Darius blurted out, to explain his nervousness, "a newspaperman from Uruguay was killed while riding into town from the airport with some of his colleagues. A rifle shot was fired at his car. Everyone knows it was done by a *dinamitero* but no investigation has been made because the authorities don't dare punish one of them—the others would riot."

"Ah, but now," he went on, brightening somewhat, "we'd better be on our way to the Campo de Mars."

We had arranged our trip so that we would be in the city on August 5th for the celebration of the independence of Bolivia, won from Spain by Simón Bolívar and José Sucre at the Battle of Ayacucho in 1824.

We found the streets jammed with Indians—men, women and children—some in contemporary dress, the majority in colorful native costumes. Most of the women had those incongruous derbies perched atop their raven-black hair, but some of them wore white straw sombreros with big brims.

"They are *mestizos*," Darius explained. "They speak Spanish, or claim they do!"

They were all headed toward the Campo de Mars, a tremendous military parade ground where the actual Independence Day ceremonies were to be held.

The narrow, winding streets became even more constricted by the swelling foot traffic. Meanwhile Darius had again begun to grow more nervous with each passing moment. Quite abruptly he twisted the steering wheel and headed for a parking space.

"It is just half a mile farther," he explained, "but it is impossible to drive through this crowd to the field. If we hit an Indian accidentally, they may attack us."

Hal and I exchanged glances. It had been this way in the Congo, too, and there we had been warned to flee from the scene of any accident and report it to the authorities later, because the natives would attack anyone involved in a mishap. Darius was obviously worried. We did not protest. Getting out of the little bus, we divided the camera equipment between us and became part of the slowly flowing stream of humanity.

As we walked we were jostled repeatedly. Men and women, especially the men, stared at me curiously. My fair skin, blond hair and blue eyes have always made me an object of curiosity to natives in jungle or veldt. This almost continuous appraisal did not bother me at first, but as we went on the jostling grew more noticeable, as though it were deliberate. At the same time a quite nauseating odor was becoming stronger. Hal, David and I identified the scent at the same split second. It was human excrement.

The Indians had been streaming in from all directions during the night. When their bodily functions grew demanding, they relieved themselves wherever they happened to be. Now we all walked with lowered heads, searching eyes and careful steps. The jostling continued and suddenly someone pawed me!

This was not the backside pat of a Parisian boulevardier or the impudent, sly pinch of a Roman. But the culprit, whoever he was, simply melted into the crowd and I could only stand there frustrated with rage.

"Someone just grabbed me," I whispered to Darius. "I'll tell Hal."

"No, please don't," begged Darius, his eyes fearfully darting toward the passing faces. "These people are—dangerous when excited. They can be violent. A fight—" He shuddered. "Just pretend nothing happened. I beg of you!"

I placed myself between him and David and continued to follow Hal, who was leading the way through the crowds, unaware of what had happened.

When we finally reached the Campo de Mars, there was a momentary improvement. The place was huge and the crowd began to spread out. Darius hurried us past lines of police and got us to a position near the ornately decorated reviewing stand that would be occupied by the president, his cabinet and high-ranking military and diplomatic officials.

As Hal set up his equipment I was still shaking inside but more in control of myself. Hal had begun to film the arriving dignitaries when he suddenly straightened up.

"I think it's foolhardy to be this close to the reviewing stand," he said. "Those dignitaries up there make tempting targets for an assassin. Let's set up our cameras a little farther away."

We gathered up our gear and hurried a few hundred feet away from the stand. The onlooking audience stared at us. When we resettled ourselves and placed the camera into position, I could almost feel the physical impact of their eyes staring at our backs.

And then the ceremonies began, ushered in by reverberating drum rolls and the flourish of trumpets. Then came the ground-shaking *pound, pound, pound* of booted feet. Regiment after regiment of troops, bayonets gleaming in the sun, came goose-stepping by. From their coal-scuttle steel helmets down, they seemed like a dark-skinned reincarnation of Hitler's *Reichswehr!*

I realized of course that this resemblance—the uniforms and equipment—was primarily due to the fact that the Bolivian Army had been trained by Germans before World War II. Although Bolivia actually joined the Allies in 1943 and declared war on the Axis, the uniforms, arms, maneuvers and tactics of its army were purely German. As I watched the swarthy, Oriental-looking features of the Indian troopers, shaded by the brims of their helmets which rattled from the impact of their heels, I wondered whether that Teutonic influence had also penetrated their minds. Military cadets, Air Force personnel, bazooka-armed suicide squads—all passed in review.

For an independence celebration, the ceremony had a grim aspect. We had been watching and filming this almost endless procession of military men for almost an hour when there was a pause. The procession came to a halt while the units ahead were maneuvered through the hordes of spectators to make room for the rest of the troops yet to come.

It was hot despite the altitude. Perhaps the solid wall of perspiring humanity behind us added to the sun's heat. After the pounding of marching boots and the cadence of drums and bugles, it was almost quiet—until I became aware of a mounting murmur from the spectators. I turned in time to see a shower of stones hurtling toward us from somewhere behind the front row. We ducked instinctively. As we turned to see where the missiles had come from, we found ourselves confronted by expressionless Indian faces staring back at us.

Hal turned to me. "The camera's okay. Nothing has hurt the lenses. Are you okay?" he added.

"Yes, Hal! No harm here."

And then David's voice, thin and wondering, said, "Mommy, look. I'm bleeding!"

I whirled. My child held his hands to his head; blood seeped between his fingers. Even as I gasped, temporarily paralyzed by utter shock, another shower of stones whirled about our ears. Several struck me but were deflected by my thick coat.

For a long moment everything seemed unreal. I remember a company of soldiers tramping toward us as though in slow motion. The roar of the crowd, the martial music, everything seemed to be far away. And then everything blurred as I grabbed David's hand and started to run blindly for a doctor.

"Halla—stop!"

It was Hal. His firmness and the tone of his voice brought me back to my senses.

I didn't intend to let go, but my body began to shake with convulsive sobs. "David's been hurt. We've got to get help."

"I'll take care of it." Hal calmly converted his handkerchief into a compress, removed David's gory hands from the wound, and put the folded linen on an ugly gash. "Here, David, press hard on the handkerchief. It'll stop the blood."

"Elskan-min." Hal's voice was steady. "We'll walk, not run, for help. This crowd is still under control but if we lose our heads and run, it can turn into a mob!"

His words brought me back to my senses.

"Follow me." Hal shouldered his camera and tripod and led the way toward an approaching platoon of helmeted soldiers. David and I stumbled behind him. Darius followed us, wringing his hands.

"Hundreds will be dead tonight," he muttered over and over—a prediction hardly calculated to quiet my fears. His prophecy was to prove unfounded but at the moment my only thought was to get David to a doctor.

Hal slipped us right into the ranks of the marching soldiers and off we marched to the obvious amazement of the troops, phlegmatic though Indians are.

By striding along in the midst of those goose-stepping infantrymen, we succeeded in deterring our assailants and the fickle mob. I daresay the sight must have been more than weird—three foreign civilian adults, one a woman, and a little boy marching along surrounded by startled soldiers in full parade regalia. Of course we didn't try to keep in step.

The whole situation was an absurd nightmare. But we were temporarily safe and Hal's strategy proved sound. In a short while he spotted a fluttering Red Cross banner.

"Thank God," Hal exclaimed. "We can get help at this first-aid station."

We slipped out of the ranks, doubtless to the relief of the soldiers and their stunned officers.

The Indian nurses in the aid station looked at David with dismay. They swept him into their arms and hearts as though he were their very own. Their remarks, in Spanish and Aymaran, could not be misunderstood, and the tones of their voices and the withering glares they cast on the spectators spoke for themselves.

"Savages!" they muttered as they clucked over David's

wound. They marveled, as I did, that he uttered no word of complaint. During the entire incident he hadn't cried once.

"Eg er afskaplega montin af thér. Thú hefur verith mjög hugrakkur," I whispered to him in Icelandic as I held him close, and got a proud smile in return. I have spoken to David in Icelandic almost exclusively ever since he was born, and he speaks that language fluently. So he had understood me when I told him, "I am very proud of you. You've been very brave."

Darius, pale and trembling, finally found a lane of escape around the crowd. We followed him to the car. The parade was no longer important; we wanted to get David to the hospital to find whether the injury was serious. Fortunately, it turned out to be merely a deep cut. But as we carefully honked our way through the fringes of the crowd, leaving the goose-stepping Indians soldiers behind, I heard Hal muttering to himself.

"What is it, Hal-minn?" I asked, hoping he hadn't forgotten a piece of equipment back in the threatening mob.

"What irony!" he blurted out. "In this country there is revolution after revolution, presidents killed and hung up by their heels from lamp posts, Communist militia carrying live dynamite across their chests. And now we get stoned by a mob. And all this in La Paz, which means the City of Peace!"

7

The Gold of South Africa

BY the time we returned to Los Angeles, the unpleasantness of altitude sickness had faded in our minds. The grim undertones of the stoning in Bolivia had been replaced by memories of the more pleasant aspects of that country.

We had ridden halfway around Lake Titicaca to the tiny town of Copacabana, site of a famous annual festival. In the clear air of the 12,500 foot altitude, we could see our destination for some time before we reached it, nestled on the shore near the Island of the Sun, legendary home of the gods in the middle of the lake.

At Copacabana (which, interestingly enough, gave its name to the famous Copacabana Beach in Rio de Janeiro rather than the other way around, as one would suppose), we saw the fascinating gyrations of the Devil Dancers of Bolivia, wearing their fearsome masks of papier-mâché with the features of demons.

When one of the dancers stopped for a moment, David approached him to examine his costume and after a few moments' close scrutiny, called out to me in Icelandic, "Mother, look. These big, staring eyes of the mask are made of old electric light bulbs!"

I laughed in tolerant disbelief but went over to look anyway. Sure enough, still visible on the glass bulb was the legend MAZDA 150 WATTS. (Little did I know that several years later in India I would learn what Mazda means to the Parsees!)

Gyrating with the Devil Dancers were numerous other Indian dancers wearing high feathered headdresses, who twirled as they played their reed flutes and beat primitive drums.

A ride in a balsa was a must for Hal at Lake Titicaca. The name of this unique craft of the high Andes is often misunderstood: it is taken to mean a vessel made of balsa wood. Actually balsa is merely the Indian name for a special reed that grows freely on the shores of the lake, and the hollow, dried reeds are bound tightly together to make the high-floating boats which we saw being used by the Indian fishermen. We boarded one of these frail craft and found it quite lakeworthy but with a rather shallow seating area for passengers. Fortunately the one we rode in was new and dry, a soothing circumstance for me because balsas become waterlogged after a season or two and then tend to sink! The skipper for our outing was a stolid-faced Indian wearing the traditional woolen cap of the Aymara. His face could easily have been mistaken for that of an Inca chieftain in an old Spanish painting.

Homecomings are periods of hectic activity for us as Hal sorts and edits his thousands of feet of color motion picture film and I resume my role as housewife. All three of us also continue our live appearances on television, now that the re-run season is over.

Meanwhile I enjoy reliving our experiences as I check photographs I have taken, scrutinize footage, and help my husband prepare each week's program. And so it was that although we were thousands of miles removed from South America and the Caribbean, our assembled film again took us on the flight from Bolivia to Chile; the visit to the skiing resort of Farellones; to Buenos Aires, with its two-inch thick steaks; and to Montevideo, where we met the colorful gauchos,

those booted cowboys of the pampas with their baggy panta-
loons.

The color films and still photos telescoped the remainder of
our trip including glamorous Rio with its swirling mosaic
sidewalks and the cable-car ride to Pão de Açúcar (Sugar Loaf
Mountain), towering more than a thousand feet above the
beautiful harbor. Nightclubs that open for business at 1
o'clock in the morning and our wonderful stay at a luxury
hotel at Copacabana Beach are other indelible memories of
Rio. And then Trinidad, with its limbo dancing and calypso,
its "oysters that grow on trees" (they collect on the roots of
the mangrove trees along the coast) and its amazing lake of
pure tar. Curaçao followed, a little bit of Amsterdam physically transplanted from Holland and set down in the tropics.
And finally Panama and the Panama Canal Zone. By the time
we finished the preliminary preparation for our programs at
the start of the new television season, we usually found ourselves almost as exhausted as if we had physically retraced our
journey. Nevertheless, within two months after our return
Hal usually had to begin making plans for the next summer's
filming. But this time Thanksgiving Day came and went without his so much as hinting at our travel itinerary for the
next trip.

It was not until late, one evening some time afterward,
long after our dinner guests had left, that I learned his plans.
I tracked him down in the workroom at the rear of our house.
He was seated tilted far back in his swivel chair, his hands
locked behind his head as he studied a relief map of the world
on the opposite wall. On his lap was a sheaf of correspondence.

"You're so quiet and serious, Hal-minn," I said. "Is anything wrong?"

He smiled. "Far from it." And then his expression grew
thoughtful as he gazed up at me. "Have you been wondering
why I haven't said anything yet about where we'd be going
next summer?"

I put my arms around his shoulders. "Well, now that you've mentioned it, David and I *were* wondering."

He pulled me onto his lap and thrust the correspondence into my hands. "A couple of weeks ago an amazing opportunity came up, elskan-min. In fact it was so amazing that I immediately told myself it was too different, and tried to forget it. But I couldn't concentrate on anything else."

I knew that the correspondence I held dealt with this "amazing" opportunity but I wanted him to tell me about it first. "Let me guess," I exclaimed, teasing him. "We're going to visit an ice floe in the Arctic and film polar bears!"

For a moment he stared at me, then chuckled. "You're not too far off. Come to think of it, maybe we'll do that, too, someday."

Now it was my turn to look startled. He hugged me. "We've been invited to go on a big-game safari in Africa!" He paused and searched my face.

"You mean—to film famous hunters and people like that?" I asked.

He shook his head. "I mean that I'm to do the hunting as well as the filming."

I thought of the elephants, hippos, lions and other wild life we had encountered during our visit five years before to what was then the Belgian Congo and to the spectacular Albert National Park Game Preserve. We had toured the flat African veldt country in the company of a park Ranger and had filmed in comparative security. Even so, our guide had insisted on our remaining close to our car with the engine idling, in case we had to make a fast getaway from a charging animal.

Fortunately for us, the protected wild life had been tolerant, and since cameras were our only weapons, we had done nothing to rouse their anger. But actual participation in a big-game-hunting safari—

"I have never hunted anything in my life," Hal continued, "but this is such a marvelous opportunity for exciting footage.

After all, David is quite grown up for a ten-year-old and—" He paused. "You're rather quiet, darling." Before I could say anything he plunged on, "I'll forget the whole thing, if you're opposed to it."

"Oh no!" I exclaimed. "It just sounds so thrilling and exciting, I'm speechless. Actually I've always wondered what a real hunting safari would be like." His face brightened. "Will it be in Kenya?"

He shook his head. "Even more interesting country, elskanmin. Mozambique, Portuguese East Africa."

"Do they have lions there?"

"Of course. And cape buffalo, leopards and sable antelope!" His eyes crinkled with laughter. "I'm rambling along as though I really knew what I'm talking about."

He eagerly told me of his plans for us to spend three weeks in a safari camp and use a car with four-wheel drive, a Land-Rover, during the daily hunting.

"But you said it would take only three weeks—the safari, I mean. What about the rest of the summer?"

"Oh, *that*." Hal's tone and expression were elaborately casual. "It'll probably be routine, perhaps commonplace. Let me show you—"

I stood and watched him indicate an imaginary route across the wall map. "Let's see now. We'll hop the Atlantic, spend several days in Paris again." He paused to wink at me. "Perhaps we'll let you do some shopping this time. Then we'll fly to South Africa. From there we'll go to Mozambique for the big-game safari. After that it'll be on to Dar es Salaam, Zanzibar, Nairobi and then to Bombay, where we'll film northern India and Kashmir." He paused again and watched me with twinkling eyes.

"After Kashmir," he resumed, "we'll continue eastward to the Kingdom of Nepal, Calcutta and Bangkok, then visit Cambodia and the Lost Cities of the Khmers before we touch down at Hongkong. From there we'll take a long shortcut home—by way of Australia."

"But—that means we'll have gone around the world!" I gasped.

He grinned. "For the second time, elskan-min, since we've been married! But the first time we traveled counterclockwise; this time we'll proceed clockwise!"

The first time I saw Paris I was seven months pregnant, young, gay—and we were broke! It had been our first filming adventure together after our marriage, and we had to count every penny we had. We had stopped off en route from England to Finland. Even so, despite my physical condition and the state of our exchequer, Paris had been vibrant, alive—a wonderful experience. I had even insisted on climbing the eleven stories to the top of Notre Dame Cathedral to see the view.

Now, eleven years later, the City of Light was an even more wonderful experience, especially since we reveled in good hotels and fine restaurants and could afford the conveniences that had been so far out of our reach the first time.

Our prime film target in the French capital on this trip was the Louvre with, among so many other masterpieces, the "Mona Lisa," "Venus de Milo" and "Winged Victory" or "Nike of Samothrace" as our specific objectives. However, obtaining permission to enter the hallowed museum proved to be another matter. Help came from the concierge of our hotel. These majordomos literally know everything and can do anything if they're on one's side. In this case our concierge came to our rescue by pinpointing the exact procedures necessary. We learned that not only special permission was required to bring cameras into the Louvre but that the permit must specify the exact masterpieces to be photographed. Furthermore, a permit could be granted only for days when the museum was closed to the general public.

So one Tuesday in early June, Hal, David and I found that we had the huge treasure of priceless art virtually all to ourselves. Incidentally, we also discovered that our names as television personalities had spread farther than we had realized.

I had hurried to our car, parked by the entrance, for extra film. Hal came out on the balcony just above and called out, "Halla, please bring the exposure meter along with the film."

A disconsolate-looking couple sat below the balcony near the closed doors during our shouted dialogue. They were visitors who had not known that the museum is closed on Tuesdays. However, when they heard Hal call my name, the man came up to me and said, "Say—aren't you the young lady who travels all over the world with your husband and son and appears on a TV program?"

Hal leaned over the balcony. "Yes she is. Do you watch us in Los Angeles or New York?"

The man smiled and shook his head. "No. We're from Salisbury in Southern Rhodesia. Our name is Jeffries. My wife and I watch you every now and then on our local television channel."

We had a pleasant impromptu visit with the Jeffries and learned, among other things, that many of the native domestic workers employed in Salisbury homes have recently seen "magic pictures" on television for the first time. There were only a thousand sets in all of Southern Rhodesia, we were told.

"They're simply fascinated by Wild West films," Mr. Jeffries said. "What mystifies them, however, is the strange habit Americans seem to have of brushing their teeth after they have killed a few Indians!"

Hal, David and I were startled.

Our South Rhodesian fan laughed. "It's the commercials, you see—we have them, too, and they're forever breaking into the continuity of the Westerns. For some reason or other, there always seems to be a white man or woman brushing his or her teeth after the most bloodthirsty encounters between redskins and cavalrymen. Has the natives confused no end!"

Our jet flight from Paris to Johannesburg in South Africa spanned nearly 7,000 miles with a single refueling stop at

Brazzaville, just across the turbulent Stanley Pool of the Congo River from Leopoldville.

When our plane circled over Leopoldville before landing, we stared down at the strife-torn capital of the new Republic of Congo. When we had first visited the Congo in 1956 while it was under Belgian control, we had covered more than 10,000 miles by river steamer, plane and automobile in a then-peaceful country whose prosperity and progress seemed to make it a shining example of how a colony should be governed. We had never encountered political unrest, and the white men and natives had seemed to get along well together.

We had visited military installations, private homes and communities maintained by the huge Belgian-owned Union Minière, a vast industrial complex with headquarters in Brussels. We had been the guests of tribal chieftains and had accompanied mission priests on their rounds of native villages. But nowhere had we found any hint of the bloodshed and destruction that were to follow the granting of independence to the Congolese.

After our extended exploration of the Congo when it was under Belgian rule, we had always regarded the area—many times larger than the state of Texas—as a progressive, hospitable land which within the foreseeable future would gain its own identity and rightfully join the community of new nations. But now, with unrest and bloodshed rife there even as we waited at the Brazzaville airport for our jet to slake its thirst, we could only stare with a numb sort of horror across the boiling Stanley Pool toward Leopoldville and shudder over the awful fate that had befallen so many of the people, white and dark, who had befriended us during our visit five years before. We were able to relax only after our plane had taken off and arrowed through the night for the South African metropolis.

Johannesburg, or Jo'burg as natives and travelers refer to it, is a sprawling, modern city that has gradually thrown off the raw frontier atmosphere that characterized its early days during the rich gold strike in 1886. With a population of one million souls, Jo'burg straddles the gold-bearing ridge called Witwatersrand (White Waters Ridge).

From our hotel we could see many multistoried office buildings and high-rise apartment structures, but looming in the background, almost everywhere we looked, were huge heaps of soil discarded during the process of extracting gold from mined ore. On our first morning we were assailed by a haze which we at first assumed was a smog similar to the blight that frequently hovers over Los Angeles. It later proved to be dust blown from innumerable slag heaps, however. Walking through it when it was stirred by a brisk wind, pointed up the seriousness of Jo'burg's problem. It made me wonder which of the two, smog or Jo'burg dust, is worse for human lungs. The irony is that both evils are man-made.

Coming as we had from the United States, where desegregation is such a burning issue, Jo'burg's apartheid was especially noticeable. The blacks of South Africa, who outnumber the whites some four to one, are kept in rigid, unyielding segregation. And the policy of apartheid applies not only to Negroes but also to Asiatics, particularly those of East Indian descent. This is somewhat ironic, since the multitudes of India are for the most part considered Aryan in origin. But the key word here in South Africa was "white" rather than "Aryan."

It was interesting to learn that the majority of the Negroes of South Africa actually came to this area long after the first whites. The early European settlers in the 1600's had found only Hottentots, a primitive race which has now almost died out. The present-day Negro tribes drifted down after the whites made their first settlements.

However, we were there to film for our program, not to become involved with the country's racial problems. The white South Africans were charming, friendly and zealous in their desire to make our stay as pleasant and comfortable as possible.

One manifestation of this hospitality was a visit, arranged for us by the South African Tourist Corporation, to the Doornfontein gold mine, one of South Africa's largest, located about an hour's drive from the center of Jo'burg.

It meant a very early start; we were due at the mine by 7 in the morning. During a hurried breakfast I reminded Hal of the other time we had encountered a mine during our travels together. That had been in Wales, on our first trip, when I was seven months pregnant. I had waited in the car, calmly knitting, while Hal took pictures. He was to be down an hour or so, I thought. When hours had passed and he'd not returned, I began to worry. But my Icelandic reserve would not permit me to get out of the car and start asking questions. Besides, a large group of prisoners in striped uniforms, working nearby under the supervision of an armed guard, were the only people I could have asked, and I was afraid of them. When Hal finally did rejoin me, almost at nightfall, I could only stare with amazement at his face covered with coal dust and his smudged clothing. He had been down the mine for five hours. Delayed by problems of filming, he had been unable to communicate with me from a mile below the surface.

Now, at the dressing rooms of the Doornfontein mine in South Africa, even while our hosts smilingly equipped the three of us with white coveralls, high rubber boots, lamp-bearing "hard hats" and raincoats to wear over the coveralls, I reminded Hal of my mystified and rather anxious wait eleven years before.

"Well, this time, you'll see for yourself how I get footage a mile beneath the surface of the earth." He laughed.

Our hosts were Neville Hayne and Collin Fenton, two of the mining engineers. When we set foot in the tiny elevator that held only six adults, the engineers told us, with clipped South African accents, that the mine employed some 800 Europeans and 7,674 natives, mostly of the Zulu nation.

"We'll be going down to Level Nine which is almost five thousand feet straight down, y'know," commented Fenton.

No, I *didn't* know, I thought. And then the elevator literally dropped out from under our feet. I struggled to catch my breath, and as we shot down the air got progressively warmer and more dense, with noticeable pressure on our eardrums.

Our "landing" was abrupt but smooth. "A point of reassurance, ma'am," Mr. Hayne, the other engineer, said. "Although we're almost five thousand feet below the surface, we're still some four hundred feet above sea level. After all, Jo'burg is almost six thousand feet above sea level, y'know."

We found ourselves in a huge cave with railroad tracks headed in every direction in different tunnels. The air was becoming oppressively hot and the raincoats we wore as a precaution against moisture dripping from the tunnel roofs were beginning to feel like steam-heated straitjackets. A smiling native, helmeted and with a metal arm brassard reading BOSS BOY, came along and said a few words in Fahnagalaw, the lingua franca of the Transvaal.

Fenton translated. "He says there's no dripping water today so we can shed our raincoats."

This was the best news we'd heard. We lost no time getting out of the coats which by now had become almost unendurable.

Although Hayne's comment that we were nearly a mile underground but still above sea level kept running through my mind, I was conscious of the closeness and denseness of the air. The odor was strange—a mixture of clay, rock dust, rubber hose and warm dampness. As we set forth I asked Hal if the Welsh mine had been like this.

"Worse," he answered. "The coal veins were only three feet high and I had to crawl the whole distance on my hands and knees."

Our guides lit the electric lamps attached to our helmets. The batteries that supplied the power were tied around our waists. They then led us through a passageway some fifteen feet in diameter which had been hewn and blasted through solid rock. The footing was precarious for me, even though I wore the rubber boots they had provided, because the flooring was slippery and covered by the narrow-gauge railway tracks and ties. Burdened as Hal was by equipment, he was as surefooted as the two engineers. And David, had he been allowed to have his own way, would have raced along like a subterranean mountain goat!

The lights from our helmets bobbing with our steps made shadows and highlights that interwove as though projected from some unearthly magic lantern in harsh black and white and occasional flashes of somber gray. It was as though the devil sat at a projector and amused himself by aimlessly changing slides without rhyme or reason.

Fenton paused and said, "Now here we must all be careful!"

We had arrived at the opening of a smaller tunnel. It was quite steep and covered with loose shale. When we started down, I found myself struggling to keep upright on the slippery footing. It was on the tip of my tongue to make a comment to Hal about the treacherous footing when a din of pneumatic drills suddenly exploded from around a bend. The sound hammered hard against our eardrums. For some unexplained reason, it seemed to make breathing more difficult.

Fenton shouted to us, "We're at the Mali Reef—the money reef!" He pointed to yellow chalk lines that marked off areas to be probed for gold. And then we rounded the turn and found ourselves confronted by native drillers and their white supervisors.

Mr. Hayne explained that the natives manning the pneumatic drills were preparing holes for dynamite charges. "After we blast, gold-bearing ore is pulled into the shaft," he said, almost shouting to make himself heard above the din. "The ore is taken to the tracks and placed aboard cars and later reaches the surface by elevator."

I stared at him. "Are you going to blast *now?*"

He shook his head. "Heavens, no! We clear out first and *then* set off the dynamite."

It was a reassuring thought. The native workers and their white supervisors had become aware of us. They paused momentarily and stared with friendly nonapartheid curiosity.

While the engineers explained the methods of commercial gold mining in South Africa, my husband set up his camera, tapped the mine's electrical supply for light, and proceeded to film the underground operation. After some two hours of this, we returned to the surface to capture the processing operation—"the rest of the drill," as one of the engineers put it.

When we emerged from the shaft, the noon sun was almost blinding at first. Then as we rapidly resumed our normal existence as surface creatures rather than helmeted cave dwellers, we noticed that the air was refreshingly cool and sweet, almost heady after the heated density below.

The surface operation proved fascinating. After the dynamited ore was crushed, it was mixed with water into a thick, muddy solution that was then poured over moving runways. This fairly simple procedure separated gold nuggets from the mud, since the globules, chunks and fragments of the precious metal adhered to the corduroy surface of the runways. The remaining mud was then mixed with cyanide and passed over revolving drums with inner suction devices that extracted additional gold and the cyanide, leaving only the mud. The next step consisted of separating this residue of gold from the cyanide. The raw gold was then melted down in carborundum containers. Even slag—the waste remaining from this final operation—was reprocessed to extract the last particle of gold.

As a climax, our hosts permitted us to watch and photograph the workers as they neatly stacked fifteen 65-pound bars of pure gold, each worth roughly $30,000. The bars, fairly wide on the bottom and tapering toward the top, looked like loaves of oddly shaped yellow bread. One of the supervisors volunteered the information that we were in the presence of about half a million dollars' worth of the metal.

"This lot you're looking at represents about ten days' work at this mine," he added. "Here, lad," he said, noticing the interested look on David's face and leading him to the gold, "if you can pick up one of these bars with *one hand,* mind you, with the narrow side up, you get to keep it!"

David gritted his teeth and tried his best. When he finally gave up, he turned to me and said in Icelandic, with just a hint of moisture in his eyes, "I tried, Mommy. I wish I could've done it. I'd have given it to you for a present."

I hugged him.

Hal looked at the supervisor. "Has anyone ever lifted a bar, single-handed, from above like that?"

"It's a standing joke." The man shrugged. "It's quite impossible. One can't get a grip on the bar. It slants too much."

Before leaving Doornfontein, we were invited to visit the company-owned housing area for the labor force of approximately 6,000 natives recruited from tribal reservations.

The workers put in six months a year at what is considered a substantial wage plus a minimum of 4,000 calories of nourishing food daily and, of course, housing. After the half-year work tour, the native laborers are allowed to return to their villages for six months. If they choose to return, they receive salary and privileges commensurate with the seniority they attained before going home. However, if they return after a year or more, their pay scale and privileges begin at the bottom again.

Mr. Fenton explained all of this and added that this procedure was similar to that used by oil companies that bring American technicians to wells and refineries in the Middle East.

"Another good thing about it is the boss-boy system," he went on. "When a native becomes a boss-boy, he has specialized in one trade or another in mine work, and this ability stands him in good stead when he returns to his tribe. For instance, boss-boys are taught advanced first aid. Frequently they become 'doctors' after they've gone home, and they do quite nicely."

When we started the tour of the mine, we'd noticed a sort of arena adjacent to the housing area.

"Oh that!" Fenton chuckled. "That's so the natives can let off steam on Sunday mornings!"

We discovered that "letting off steam" meant tribal dances in authentic costume, primarily for the entertainment of the other miners. In fact, miners from the various "diggings" in and around Jo'burg made their own costumes, devised their own choreography, and then carried on a friendly but spirited competition, tribe against tribe or mine against mine. We later returned for that Sabbath ritual and found it to be a stirring and spectacular experience. The entire assemblage was colorful, both spectators and participants, and the atmosphere was extremely festive.

A mine official named Micklejohn acted as a sort of master of ceremonies. He spoke Fahnagalaw and appeared quite popular with the natives. Evidently he understood their humor because his comments to them frequently provoked gales of good-natured laughter.

In English, he explained to us that we would see and hear the dancing and music of Pondo, Xosa, Batswa and Nguna tribesmen. The first dance, performed by the Pondos, who come from the coast halfway between Durban and East London on the Indian Ocean side, was vigorous and done to the accompaniment of their strange music, which we recorded. Their dance concluded with what we learned was a characteristic crouch and turning away from the audience.

The next performance was by the Xosa, who attached rattles called *toti* to their legs. The dance was actually an exercise in gymnastics called the Amakenkwi. The overall effect was more or less similar to our own dance, the twist.

In between each number, Micklejohn made announcements, first in Fahnagalaw for the benefit of the natives, and then in English with now and then a few rapid phrases in Afrikaans for the benefit of the Dutch-speaking members of the audience.

The dances of the Batswas, who come from Mambona in Portuguese East Africa, were of particular interest to us because we were scheduled to visit that part of the continent immediately after leaving South Africa. The music for the dance was provided on a xylophonelike instrument identified for us as a *timbila*. The youthful performers were magnificent physical specimens whose stamina and agility were amazing.

The final performance was staged by the Nguna, northern Zulus who live in the Lebombo Mountains near Swaziland. These warlike people, who fought against both British and Boers, re-enacted what must have been fierce chapters from their long history as fighters. In many ways they reminded us of the towering Watusi dancers we had photographed during our visit, half a decade before, in Ruanda-Urundi, near the Congo.

The Kruger National Game Reserve was named after Paul Kruger, the Boer President who was defeated by the British in the South African war at the turn of the century. It is probably the world's most famous game reserve.

It was to be our last stopping place in South Africa before flying to Mozambique to begin our hunting safari. The drive from Johannesburg traversed more than two hundred miles of beautiful countryside.

Our headquarters in Kruger was Camp 14 in Pretorius Kop. And our shelter consisted of a rondavel, a native-type hut provided for visitors by the South African Government.

A vast place (200 miles long and from 30 to 60 miles wide), Kruger has been known as a wonderland of scenic beauty and wild-animal life since the original Dutch explorer-settlers first set foot there during the 17th century. A sanctuary where no weapons of any sort are allowed, it has game of almost every conceivable variety living unmolested by human beings.

With approximately 1,400 miles of fair-to-excellent roads with adequate signs in both English and Afrikaans, it is possible to get about without a guide but certain regulations must be adhered to and park Rangers are constantly patrolling to make certain that visitors obey them, for their own safety.

Definite "musts" to be observed include such precautionary measures as staying inside one's car while on the roads and bedding down by dusk, and only in one of the regular camps. The authorities make no bones about the fact that it is the animals that are protected. Aside from the regulations already mentioned, humans are strictly on their own.

While the animals have grown accustomed to people in automoblies, they are disturbed when a person leaves a car and walks about. When that occurs, elephants, hippos and lions are as apt to charge as they are to trot away. And since some of the predatory beasts are nocturnal prowlers, the hazard of camping out in the open at night can well be imagined. Despite all this, there are seldom any mishaps to visitors, we were told. Possibly this is because of the awesome surroundings and the obvious danger which can hardly fail to impress even the most thoughtless and unheeding tourist.

We had had an extensive exposure to wild life in the Congo's vast Albert National Park, but that had been years before. Since then we had taken so many trips that our recollections of our Congo adventure had become somewhat hazy. (At the time of the visit to Kruger National Park the three of us had explored over 75 countries during our 11 years of married partnership.)

When we reached Camp 14, we were greeted by a white South African Ranger captain who volunteered to drive us cross-country for our filming instead of keeping to the established roads. We would use a British-made Land-Rover, a large, four-wheeled-drive vehicle rather like a king-sized jeep. This was a stroke of good luck. Wheeling away over hill and dale rather than being confined to main roads, we'd be able to bag more game—on film, of course.

We had been exhausted after our long trip from Jo'burg, but after a night in the comfortable rondavel hut, our early morning start found us ready to enjoy the bracing air, the sheer beauty about us and the excitement of the forthcoming adventure. No sooner had our Ranger driven beyond the confines of Camp 14 than we found tempting targets on all sides.

It was stop-and-go, stop-and-go as the animal kingdom put on an unending parade for us. Giraffes and warthogs were to be seen everywhere. Just over the hill from camp we encountered and filmed a pride of lions. When we drove toward a stream, we were intrigued by a large sign in Afrikaans: PAS OP VIR OLIPHANTS (Beware of elephants).

And even as our guide was translating the sign for us, David looked up and excitedly cried, "Look, Mommy—Daddy!"

Ahead of us, swaying on its massive legs and waving its trunk, stood one of the huge, intelligent animals. Nearby was a small herd, its family, we assumed. It watched us while Hal filmed. When we drove on, it kept staring at us, as though trying to determine what we had been up to.

At a nearby stream we ran into hippos. One of them was huge, with teeth that must have been at least half a yard long! It moved slowly, ponderously. I knew that its slow-motion was deceptive. When alarmed or enraged, a hippopotamus such as this big fellow that may have weighed more than three tons can move with devastating speed and hit an enemy with the destructive force of a charging tank.

Our Ranger parked by a thicket on the bank of a good-sized stream and led us to the water's edge. Here we found the African version of alligators—sinister-looking crocodiles with narrower, more pointed, heads than their American counterparts but possessing just as many long, needle-sharp teeth.

One of them blinked up at us hungrily and yawned, exposing its fearsome maw while Hal's camera whirred.

When we returned to the Land Rover, I stopped short and grabbed David. Squatting on the engine hood was a tremendous spider with long, armored legs. It resembled a spider crab. I thought of the tarantula I'd encountered in Mr. Wong's camp on the Amazon, but now I was not afraid. I picked up a stick and held it out. The creature slowly climbed onto it. I raised the stick while Hal began to film a close-up. But afraid or not, when my husband had taken sufficient footage I thankfully flipped the creature into the underbrush and hurriedly got into the car.

On our way back to camp we filmed many impala, members of the deer family. These graceful animals can cover as much as 35 feet and soar 10 feet high in a single leap.

But the impala's speed was nothing compared with that of the greater kudu, which can move so fast that experienced game hunters call it the Gray Ghost. We stumbled across one, and Hal barely managed to capture the deerlike animal on film as we drove along. It paused, stared, and then took off like a launched missile, leaving us behind as though we were standing still!

Along the road at dusk we saw a lone hyena sitting on its haunches, almost as though it were begging. It looked like a grotesque dog, and David wanted to feed it. Our Ranger captain was horrified.

"Keep your hands in the car, sonny," he said when we stopped to film. "That hyena is sick and he can't hunt. That's why he's begging in desperation. I've heard about him. Yesterday a car stopped and a woman reached out of the window of the car with her reflex camera. In a flash the hyena leaped and crunched the camera in its jaws, just missing the woman's hand. Those jaws can break a bone like a matchstick."

I kept my own reflex camera in my lap and allowed Hal to film the hyena—with the telephoto lens!

When we met a herd of zebra, David finally got the answer to a question that had evidently come up in school. He asked our Ranger whether a zebra is really a black horse with white stripes or a white one with black stripes. After scratching his head the Ranger guessed that the animal was a horse with black-and-white stripes!

8

Zebras Taste Better Than People

TONY FAJARDO, the "White Hunter" who would initiate us into the delights and perils of an actual shooting safari in Mozambique, came bounding up the steps of the entrance to the Embaixador Hotel in Beira, Portuguese East Africa.

A tall, lean, broad-shouldered man with sun-bronzed features and touches of gray at the temples, Fajardo looked more like a motion picture star enacting the role of an African hunter than the genuine article. He had actually served in the Portuguese Consular Service before deciding to become a White Hunter! He was "in uniform"—immaculate safari-type bush jacket, creased khaki trousers and the inevitable large-brimmed veldt hat.

"Mr. Linker? Mrs. Linker?" His smile revealed startlingly white teeth. Hal returned his handshake.

It was oppressively hot and humid in the seaport of Beira. Ever since we had driven to Laurenco Marques by car from Kruger National Park and flown to Beira, Hal had occasionally complained of a sinus headache and sore throat. Waiting for Fajardo in the hotel situated in the center of Beira, my husband had begun to feel worse.

I myself felt ready to wilt in the steamy, hot air, and even David moved with a languor alien to a healthy youngster.

It would have been preferable to postpone the start of the safari until Hal could rid himself of the disquieting symptoms which had actually begun during our descent into the bowels of the earth at the Doornfontein gold mine. But as Fajardo had pointed out over the telephone, there were others coming after us to hunt and the original schedule would have to be followed.

Fajardo took over immediately, drawing up wicker chairs to a table in the refreshment area of the lounge, summoning waiters, and then immediately getting down to business.

First we would require proper attire. This suited David fine. The notion of wearing a floppy hat, bush jacket and khaki trousers revived our son almost immediately.

While a waiter was bringing a tray of tall, cooling drinks, Tony produced maps and began to outline what we could expect the next day.

"It's quite a drive to the safari camp. First, however, we'll be traveling over to the Gorongosa Game Preserve which is chock-full of all sorts of animals—for filming only, that is!"

"We've already hunted with our cameras—in Kruger," muttered Hal.

"But Gorongosa is ever so much more spectacular and much better. It'll be excellent preparation for our actual hunt!" He beamed at us.

Miserable as Hal felt and uncomfortable as I was, we couldn't help but return his smile.

"Cheers!" he said, raising his glass. Then he checked his watch and added, "I'll return at six and we'll have dinner and get better acquainted. Right?"

Before we could answer he finished his drink, swept up the maps, and arose, all in one smooth, continuous motion.

"As the first order of the day, to save time, why don't I take you to a tailor where you can get outfitted?"

We found ourselves walking behind him in the blazing sun. Parked by the curb was a battered open-back truck of uncertain vintage. We had looked for something more modern, but Fajardo opened the creaking door of the cab of the truck.

"Here we are," he said. "Hop in!"

"It looks tired." Hal frowned.

"Not this lovely creature." Fajardo fondly whacked one of the bent and rusted fenders. "She's taken me everywhere one can imagine. And the engine's in tip-top shape."

"I suppose the car we'll use on the safari is—newer," I ventured.

Fajardo stared at me. "Why no, Mrs. Linker. This"—again the affectionate wallop on the fender—"is what we'll use."

Once we had squeezed ourselves inside (it reeked of stale tobacco smoke, ancient upholstery, superheated metal and raw gasoline), Fajardo pressed the starter and the engine snarled into life.

"Sounds powerful," Hal said in my ear. I glanced up. Rivulets of sweat were running down his face. He looked miserable. I made up my mind to take him to see a doctor, safari or no safari.

Fajardo put the truck into gear and we lurched down the main thoroughfare. The seaport of Beira, founded in the 16th century by the Portuguese, had not changed basically since that time. The architecture was a hodgepodge of colonial Portuguese intermingled with Arabian and East Indian structures. As we rattled and puffed along the main thoroughfare, we did see several modern buildings protruding above the muggy skyline, however.

Everyone moved slowly, almost sluggishly. Even the traffic policemen, all Portuguese, waved their white-gloved hands indolently. We had read that Mozambique's lowlands are plagued with malarial mosquitoes and the tsetse fly, carrier of the dreaded sleeping sickness. I quickly brushed the thought from my mind, however. We would be heading inland where our chances of avoiding malaria and encephalitis would be improved, I hoped.

The tailoring establishment was owned by a short, obsequious East Indian who tilted his head and shook it when he meant yes and nodded it when he meant no. Fajardo made sure that everything would go according to plan and then left us, promising to return in time for our evening engagement.

Since both Hal and I could still use the safari gear we had bought for our Congo adventure five years before, we were not in need of outfitting. David was another matter.

When the tailor had finished with his measuring, he looked apologetically at us and said, "I'm afraid that this will take rather long—at least three hours. We're shorthanded, you see."

It was then just before noon. Hal and I stared at him. "You mean you'll have everything done by three this afternoon?" I said.

The tailor seemed to cringe. "I regret the delay. But as I said—we're shorthanded."

"Oh—that'll be all right. We won't be needing it until six tonight," Hal said.

The tailor brightened. "Then that gives us very much time indeed."

I was skeptical of his ability to cut the material, sew and finish it in less than a full day, let alone a mere three hours. But when we returned at 4, following a visit to a doctor— which I had insisted on—to our astonishment the outfit was waiting, finished exactly according to measurements and all other details.

The Portuguese doctor had diagnosed Hal's ailment as a virus that had attacked his respiratory system. He prescribed antibiotics which we happily found could be obtained in Beira. But despite the medication the evening with Fajardo proved less than successful. We ate dinner in a tiny restaurant overlooking the Mozambique channel leading out to the Indian Ocean, and Hal felt worse and worse as time wore on.

We excused ourselves and retired rather early. The night was one of the worst that Hal had ever experienced: he alternately burned with a raging fever or shivered from chills. It was too much like malaria, I thought, as I alternately removed or piled on blankets.

None of us had much sleep that night. We were still tired out the next morning when Fajardo arrived bright and early at the hotel for the start of our safari. With his help and that of a retinue of hotel bellmen, we managed to accumulate all our gear and pile it into the ancient three-quarter-ton truck that Hal dubbed "Old Faithful." Tony's two helpers rode the back of the truck while we three squeezed into the cab with him.

And then finally we were off. Amazingly enough, once we were committed to our adventure, we all felt better—including my husband who even felt strong enough to take footage during the lurching, clattering ride through the outskirts of Beira.

Fajardo was a competent if daring driver. He navigated Old Faithful around curves and along the narrow road as though it were a low-slung sports car rather than the top-heavy, swaying monstrosity it was. The drive to our overnight quarters at the Chitengo Rest Camp in the Gorongosa Game Preserve would not take more than "three hours."

Alas. When we were halfway along the ninety-mile journey, the truck's engine quit. Later we'd discover (and not as a surprise) that this was chronic with Old Faithful. Hal then changed its name to "Old Faithless." The trouble lay in the ignition, Fajardo announced after tinkering under the up-lifted engine hood.

"Have to put a new one in, once we reach my place," he said, wiping his grease-stained hands. "Meanwhile, she'll do for the time being."

After entering the confines of Gorongosa Preserve, we had the interesting experience of being ferried across the Pungu River in a native barge. Motive power was provided by cheer-ful, lean-flanked natives wielding long poles. There had once been a pontoon bridge here but it had been washed away by an "unseasonal flood" (to quote Fajardo) and never replaced.

"Besides, it gives the natives a chance to earn a few escudos," he added, wrestling with the bucking steering wheel.

When we reached Chitengo Camp it was growing dark.

After another restless night for Hal, we awakened about dawn in our rondavel hut, almost a replica of the one we had used in Kruger Park at Camp 14.

We found our gear packed and stored in the bed of the truck. Fajardo introduced us to a "passenger" who was to accompany us. He was a native park Ranger, and his mission was to make sure that we hunted with cameras and not guns, since—as at all the other preserves—shooting, even in self-defense, was forbidden.

Tony's native assistants rode in the cab this time. Fajardo, Hal, David and I, together with the native Ranger who said little, merely grinned, rode in the back of the jouncing, swaying truck.

My role was to be that of "still-camera woman." Two Rolleiflexes were slung around my neck and David carried the light meters and his own Rolleicord. Hal had the movie camera and his heavy tripod.

Gorongosa's roads were not up to those of the Kruger preserve, but the animal life seemed more plentiful and we shot hundreds of feet of color film. And the journey was actually more exciting than the one to Kruger. Not because of the wildlife, but because of Fajardo's truck. The thing seemed on the verge of taking off and flying every time it came to a rise. All we could do was hang on while the driver and his grinning assistant sent us careening across the veldt.

And then Fajardo looked at us brightly and said, "Now I'll show you something you'll never see anywhere else!"

He waved toward what appeared to be a tiny settlement on the horizon with perhaps half a dozen small buildings. We squinted through clouds of dust kicked up by Old Faithless.

"Looks like some sort of European settlement," Hal observed.

"It *was* an encampment," Fajardo said.

"Was?"

Tony nodded. "It's been abandoned—at least by people. If I were you I'd have the cameras all set."

His advice was unnecessary. Our cameras were prepared for immediate use. We peered with curiosity at the looming structures. The buildings were rectangular, like small European railroad stations rather than those one would expect to find on an African game preserve. As we drew closer, we could see that the windows had no panes. And then the truck came to a groaning halt in front of the foremost building.

"There!" Fajardo said, waving toward it.

"There, what?" Hal asked, perplexed. And then he glanced toward the roof.

Lying on the very edge, returning his stare, was a lioness. For a long moment we stood frozen and then Hal began to take pictures. The lioness merely eyed him. I managed to overcome my initial shock and went to work with my two cameras; one was loaded with color film, the other with black-and-white. At first my hands trembled with excitement and my movements were clumsy.

Fajardo spoke quietly. "This used to be an advanced camp —for people who wanted to get as close as possible to the animals. Well—it was too close. The animals resented it, kicked the people out, and moved in!"

Hal moved out of the truck and prepared to film from another angle. The lioness watched him; it was hard to tell whether she was curious or merely bored.

I finished one complete roll of film and as I started to reload I measured the distance from the big cat to where we stood on the exposed back of the truck.

"Do you suppose she could leap on us from up there?" I asked.

Fajardo shook his head. "No. We're out of range, I think."

Hal looked up from his camera. "I wish she'd move so I could get some action."

Greenland—
At Holsteinsborg the
archway to the church
is made of whalebone.

Amazon—The chief of the Yagua tribe shows David how to shoot a blowgun.

Peru—The dancers of Cuzco, who had defied their "commissars" to dance for us, pose after their performance.

Bolivia—
A fierce-masked Devil
dancer at the
fiesta in Copacabana.

Bolivia—Army troops parade in German-style uniforms.

Bolivia—David's cut is treated in the first-aid station after we were stoned by the mob.

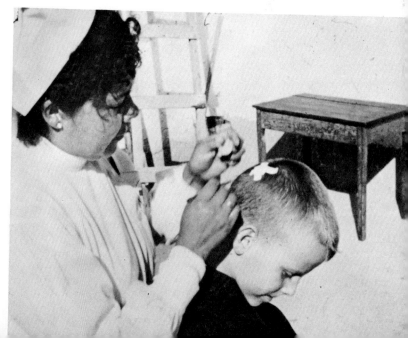

South Africa—Hal filming the Mine dancers as they start their tribal dances.

Mozambique—After shooting a Cape buffalo, Africa's most dangerous game.

India—Three lovely girls at the Taj Mahal.

Nepal—Admiring the statues in the holy city of Pathan.

Nepal—The "all-seeing" eyes of a Tibetan *stupa* stare across the walls.

Nepal—The Kathakali dancers in front of the temple in Bathgaon.

Ethiopia—With
Emperor Haile Selass
and his Court
Chamberlain *(left)*.

Ethiopia—At Aksum
priests of the Church
of St. Mary display
some of the famed
crowns of Ethiopia's
earlier rulers.

Ethiopia—David
with Tojo, Haile
Selassie's pet lion.
A moment after this
picture was taken
Tojo clamped David's
ankle in his jaws.

Left, Near Timbuktu—The Dogon dancers. Some of their masks tower twenty feet into the air. *Right,* Timbuktu—A veiled Touareg tribesman with amulets.

Timbuktu as seen from the mosque.

Our White Hunter chuckled. "Why don't you take a picture of what's sitting in the doorway of the next house?"

The three of us looked to where he was pointing. David gasped. There, not seventy-five feet away, sat a tremendous, fully grown male lion with an immense black mane. He gazed steadily at us and then his eyes seemed to lock with mine. I couldn't help shivering.

"*Behind you*," hissed Fajardo. "Quick!"

I turned slowly. Lying in the shade of a tree was still another male lion. And we were standing exposed in the open back of the truck!

Then Hal's urgent voice came to my rescue. "Quick, Halla, put a fresh reel into this camera while I use the spare!"

Keeping myself busy helped steady my nerves. I remember completing my task and looking up to hand the camera to Hal as I heard Fajardo suck in his breath.

The lioness, evidently growing bored with the entire procedure, rose, stretched, and then, without a backward glance, proceeded to walk down a circular outside staircase from the roof to the ground floor. She was the owner of the property and her action made this perfectly clear. She favored us with one last disdainful stare and then paced toward a nearby stream.

"Look over there, Mr. Linker. You'll be able to get something unusual." Fajardo pointed. "See—it's a whole pride of 'em. The entire family, including cubs. They're going to the stream for water."

While Hal filmed the scene I watched what appeared to be a family gathering of the beasts by the river. From where we stood they seemed as tame as pussy cats. The cubs rollicked about the lionesses and males. It was a peaceful scene, at least from a distance.

I began to wonder what I would have done if the lioness had leaped at us from the roof. I did not, for one moment, trust Fajardo's claim that we had been out of range.

Our guide turned to Hal, who had lowered his camera. "Think you got enough?"

Hal nodded. "For the time being, Tony."

"Good. We'll come across even more before we leave the preserve." He pounded on the top of the cab. The native driver started the engine. The racket made some of the lions raise their heads and stare in our direction.

I felt a great sense of relief when we pulled away from the former encampment that had been appropriated by the animal kingdom. And I sensed that my relief was shared by the Ranger, who had stood by, tight-lipped, while we had taken our pictures.

"For wild beasts, they seem quiet enough," Hal remarked.

Fajardo pointed toward the horizon. There, at a safe distance, was another family of lions sharing the carcass of some unfortunate animal.

"That's why they're quiet," Fajardo said. "That bunch out there, they're lunching on a zebra. The only time a lion will go after a human is when he or she is too old to catch fresh four-legged game." He grinned. "We're food for them only when there's nothing else available!"

Evidently lions don't particularly like the flavor of human flesh when delicious zebra or wildebeest are available—a kind of discrimination I don't at all resent.

The trail approached a grove of trees. Lying in the shade of a big tree was another immense male lion. As we got closer we could see that he was old.

"Now take this fellow," Fajardo said. "His mane is ragged. His eyesight's probably failing. He can't run fast enough to catch game, so he's been kicked out of his tribe, so to speak."

I swallowed. "You mean—he's the sort that might like people? Like us?"

Fajardo shrugged. "If he were hungry. But look at his belly. It's bulging. He's full. We're safe."

I thought we were going to drive on. Instead Fajardo

pounded on the cab to signal the driver to stop and the truck
came to a halt not more than a dozen yards from the lion.

The aging beast stared at us and then parted his formidable
jaws in a huge yawn. One of his teeth was missing but the
remaining ones looked formidable enough to me. I put my
arm around David's shoulder.

Hal aimed his camera and began to get a close-up.

"Wait!" exclaimed Fajardo. "I'll get him to move for you."

"Don't bother," Hal said. "This is good enough."

"No, really," said our guide. "It'll make a better shot for
you." He lightly jumped off the truck, stepped in front of the
engine, and shouted at the top of his voice. The old King of
the Beasts slowly turned his head from us and peered at
Fajardo—and yawned again.

Fajardo's face grew red. I found myself almost giggling.
When Tony waved his arms, jumped up and down and bel-
lowed, *"Heyaaaa!"* I found myself laughing. But it was not
funny to the lion. He sprang to his feet, let out an earthshak-
ing roar, and charged at Fajardo.

For an old animal, that lion moved like lightning. But
Fajardo was even faster. He literally sailed into the air, landed
almost on top of the cab, and began to yell in Portuguese and
pound for the driver to get going. Our native Ranger's face
turned gray. The engine-starter began to grind and grind.
Nothing happened. Fajardo's face, now pale, turned toward
us. I saw Hal deliberately pick up his tripod and hold it like
a weapon as he moved his body between us and the lion.

And then I forced myself to look over my husband's shoulder. The lion was merely sitting on his haunches, watching us
with—I could almost swear—a grin. Once he had succeeded in
making his tormentor run, he was satisfied.

The engine finally came to life. Fajardo's face was dripping
with perspiration as the driver put the truck into gear and
we began to move away.

"First time *that's* ever happened," Tony muttered.

I watched the old lion. He slowly got up, shook himself and

returned to the shade of the tree where he had been so comfortable before we came along to make nuisances of ourselves.

"You see," Fajardo added, "he was full. That's why he didn't really attack. He just wanted to frighten us."

"He succeeded," said Hal.

"Had he actually been hungry, he'd have kept right on coming," Fajardo continued.

Hal looked at him. "I'd bear that in mind the next time you meet one if I were you."

9
Safari in Mozambique

WITH our White Hunter at the wheel, we lurched and clattered across the African veldt. I sat in the cab next to Tony Fajardo. Hal, David, our native Ranger and Fajardo's two assistants stood in the open bed of the truck, immediately behind the cab. At the wheel was a Portuguese-Indian from Goa, also named Tony, whom we immediately took to calling Antonio, to differentiate him from Fajardo.

After the episode with the spry old lion, we made several other stops to film additional specimens including some of the largest crocodiles and hippos we had ever seen. Each time we came to a halt, Antonio turned off the ignition. When he tried to start the engine again, it was always several minutes before it would spring to life.

In fact, after the pause at the Pungu River, he had ground the starter over and over until the battery showed unmistakable signs of exhaustion. It was then that Hal prevailed on Fajardo to let the engine continue to idle during stops. Tony had agreed reluctantly and then taken the wheel himself.

Now we were finally heading back to the Chitengo Camp for our overnight stay. Government regulations require that people seek the protection of camp barriers before dark. The animals then have the complete run of the range.

"Out here at night," Tony explained, "people are considered eatable unless they are behind proper protective barriers. In fact, if a visitor is found outside after dark, he is
punished by the authorities."

I thought of the lions that had taken over the abandoned
camp where we had filmed earlier in the day. "What happens
if a lion leaps the barrier at Chitengo Camp and attacks a
human being?" I asked.

"Oh, in that case he would be shot," replied Fajardo.

"The person?" David spoke up, with bright-eyed curiosity.

"Heavens, no!" Fajardo blinked. "The lion."

That would have been small comfort to the person involved, I thought, but I decided to say nothing.

Despite the clatter-bang of our passage and my hanging
onto the windowsill to keep from getting entangled with
Fajardo and the controls, I felt myself growing drowsy. Then
suddenly Fajardo let out a yell that brought me bolt upright,
half expecting to find the old lion climbing into the cab.

"Elephants!" He shouted, pointing past my nose toward a
distant clump of thickly foliaged trees. "There's a big herd
there!"

He applied the brakes and leaped out for a consultation
with Hal.

I overheard Fajardo say; "We'll have to be careful. I'll
drive off the road and then back up toward them. In that way
we'll be able to leave fast—just in case!"

"Fine!" Hal replied happily. He leaned over toward my
window. "Elskan-min, never mind trying to take still-pic-
tures. I'll just get footage with the telephoto lens and then
we'll be on our way! They're half hidden in the tall grass,
about twenty of them."

"I can see them," I assured him. I swallowed hard. "Oh,
but I want to get some stills, Hal-minn."

"Well, we'll see."

Fajardo put the truck into low gear and started cross-country. We crept toward the animals that were browsing on the

leafy, lower branches of the trees. As we slowly wobbled over the uneven ground, I remembered having read somewhere that elephants were nearsighted. I wondered if they were also hard of hearing. The racket of our approach should have triggered them into enraged attack or precipitate flight; instead they seemed utterly indifferent.

We finally came to a stop about two hundred yards from the herd. Here Fajardo and the Ranger had a long conversation. It turned out that they were trying to decide how to approach the animals downwind and thus keep from alarming them with our scent.

"Can you film from here?" Fajardo called to Hal in a stage whisper.

My husband looked dubious. "It's a little far. All I can see through the view-finder are their backs."

Fajardo shrugged. "All right. We'll get closer. I'll back in so you can film from the rear of the truck." He got in, shifted gears and began to manipulate the truck this way and that until its open bed was pointed in the direction of the herd.

Fajardo steered backward by alternating glances into the rear-view mirror and twisting his head through the side window. Somehow we navigated around fallen logs, barely missing massive tree trunks. I leaned out and looked back. We seemed almost on top of the browsing beasts, although they were probably about a hundred yards away.

Fajardo stopped. "This is as close as we dare get," he said. It was welcome news for me.

He got out of the cab and looked up at Hal. "Can you film better from here?"

"Yes, but this truck is shaking too much," Hal answered. "I need a steady camera platform."

"No problem." Fajardo smiled brightly. "I'll fix."

Before I could utter a sound, he reached in and shut off the engine. I sat momentarily frozen while through my mind ran memories of the *grind-grind-grind* of the starter and the engine's reluctance to turn over. I thought of the lion that had halfheartedly charged and then stopped. Suppose an elephant finally decided we were intruders and came galloping our way —and the engine refused to come to life?

I took a deep breath and unlimbered one of the two Rolleis draped around my neck. Better to be busy than to brood, I told myself, and swung around to get some pictures. I saw Hal setting his telephoto lens into position on the camera. And then there came a sudden, bloodcurdling shriek from the Ranger followed by a deafening pounding on the roof of the cab, the emergency signal. In that instant Hal's expression changed from surprise to horror. Fajardo bounced into the seat next to me. I peered back and saw a tremendous elephant, trunk upraised, huge ears flapping, bearing down on us with the speed of a runaway locomotive. It was trumpeting strident bellows as it charged—almost shrieking in rage.

There was no time even for prayer. As though in a nightmare, Fajardo's hand seemed to float toward the ignition. His foot pressed the starter. The engine roared into immediate life! Fajardo jammed the truck into gear and we started full speed ahead.

If the ride had been unsettling before, it was spine-shattering now. I wrapped my arms around the corner post of the windshield and held on with all my strength. David was clinging to one of the wooden seats that lined the sides of the truck's bed. Hal had one arm over the horizontal side of the truck and held his camera, tripod and all, with the other. The lens was pointed to the rear. Later I was not surprised when he said he had kept his finger on the trigger during our frantic retreat. The footage, although jumpy and blurred, recaptured all the drama of that near miss when we finally televised it.

But at the time the question of whether or not he was getting footage did not matter to me. After what seemed an eternity of hellish, bouncing flight during which the trumpeting of the enraged elephant was louder than the roar of engine and the grinding of gears, we finally came to a halt. And just in time. I was on the verge of being thrown out of the cab.

Fajardo uttered a sigh of relief and shook his head. "Do you know, senhora—" he began.

Again that violent pounding on the roof of the cab, with Hal's voice, nearly frantic, the shrill treble of the Ranger and Fajardo's assistants forming a frightening chorus.

"What did you stop for? For God's sake keep going! He's still coming!"

Fajardo turned white. Fortunately the engine was still idling. He released the emergency brake and shoved the throttle to the floor. The truck careened. Several times I could have sworn that all four wheels left the ground simultaneously. I clenched my teeth, otherwise I might have bitten off the tip of my tongue.

After what seemed like a year, we reached the dirt road that led back to Chitengo Camp. Fajardo stopped the truck. All was quiet. The elephant was far behind us, out of sight.

We got out of the truck and stared at each other and our pent-up fear turned to uncontrollable, nearly hysterical, laughter. Somehow the incident seemed funny, like slapstick movie comedy. We bantered choked-up comments about how hilarious it had been when Fajardo had calmly stopped the truck while the elephant was still charging full speed ahead.

"To tell you the truth," Tony gasped, "an elephant doesn't usually keep charging when you run away like that. This one must have been a female with young, and you know how mothers are when they're protecting their children." The latter was said with a glance in my direction. "Either that, or it was a demented rogue elephant," he added. He looked up at the sky. "We'd better hurry back. As it is, we'll barely make it before dark."

We climbed back on board.

After I resumed my seat in the cab I turned to Fajardo. "Tell me, Tony," I said. "If the elephant had overtaken us back there, what should we have done—stayed with the truck?"

"Oh *no*, senhora," he said and he shuddered. "Never do that. The elephant would have aimed for the truck and tried to tear it apart. The only thing to do would be to run as fast as we could—we'd all have scattered and hidden behind trees!"

I made a mental note of that.

We reached Chitengo Camp just as the sun went down. Our first stop was at the Rangers' compound, where we deposited our Ranger. He was cheerful, it seemed, for the first time in hours. But as we waved farewell to him the engine coughed and expired. No matter how much Fajardo cranked the starter, it refused to budge. The motor was absolutely dead. Fajardo swore in Portuguese and gave up. Our Ranger, who had stood by watching, wore a big grin. He held up a finger, obviously bidding us to wait (as though we could do anything else), and ran into the headquarters building.

The next minute he emerged, followed by half a dozen more Rangers. The group, laughing and chattering among themselves, put their shoulders to the back of the truck. With a deep-throated chant, they all began to push. Slowly—oh so slowly—we started to roll. And finally, courtesy of Ranger-power, we were pushed to our rondavel.

After we had tucked in for the night, I asked Hal what he'd have done if the truck hadn't started in time during the elephant's charge.

"Probably grabbed you and David and ducked under the truck, hoping the elephant wouldn't see us."

When I told him what Fajardo had said he grimaced. "Well, I'll know for next time—if there is a next time." And he promptly went to sleep!

The drive from Chitengo in the Gorongosa Preserve to Fajardo's safari camp two hundred miles into Mozambique's interior took from dawn to twilight. Our host was less than exuberant. Before we started he had been the picture of bleary-eyed exhaustion. He had worked almost all night, trying to exorcise the devils that possessed the balky engine.

Before we took off from Chitengo, he reassured us that the truck would behave during the cross-country trek. And much to his and our amazement, it didn't break down once during the long trip!

When we reached his camp he brightened considerably. And so did we despite our own exhaustion and our having swallowed dust all day on unpaved roads that dwindled to trails and finally to mere paths.

Actually Fajardo's safari camp was intriguing. He had established it on the bank of a small lake. His permanent staff of ten or twelve trackers and game skinners had built a row of thatched huts for themselves. Between these barracks and the lake shore were four small tents and a much larger one that boasted a splintery wood floor. We were told that this big one would be our dining hall.

In the deepening twilight, with a refreshingly cool breeze and the twinkling lamps of the camp, it was almost romantic. I stood there gazing at what was to be our home for the duration of the safari while Fajardo and his staff unloaded the truck.

And then he came to us and smiled. "There—everything is ready. Each of you will have your own tent."

The thought of lying all alone under canvas out in the open, unprotected by even a thornbush or barricade, was not pleasant. All sorts of images formed in my mind—prowling hyenas and decrepit, hungry old lions creeping into the tent to make off with David, not to mention Hal or me. I grasped Hal's arm. I could cope with anything, as long as we were together.

But before I was able to open my mouth, Hal shook his head and said, "That's out of the question, Tony. I can't have Halla or David waking up in the middle of the night alone and frightened by strange sounds with me yards away. We'll have to be together in one tent."

Fajardo looked perplexed. "But, senhor, it's so late, It's

impossible for us to start putting up a big tent now. Tomorrow morning, perhaps—"

For a moment I was afraid Hal would give in. I should have known better.

He folded his arms. "Put three cots in one of these small tents. We'll squeeze in for tonight."

The expression on Fajardo's face was almost indescribable. He stared at each of us in turn and then sighed, let his arms drop, and called to his helpers in a resigned tone of voice. We all knew that this was the first time he had ever taken an entire family on a big-game hunt; I had a feeling that he was probably vowing that it would be the last.

When the cots had been squeezed into one of the small tents, not an inch divided them and the canvas walls bulged. While we were peering in through the front flap Fajardo returned.

His debonair manner was back and his voice and step were buoyant. "Now that this problem's been settled, how about dinner?"

The long journey had almost anesthetized us, but his mention of food suddenly reminded us that we were nearly famished. We freshened up by taking turns at a washbasin that rested on a stand in front of our tent. The water came from a pitcher that had been filled in the lake.

Several of Fajardo's native assistants gathered at a slight distance and watched me with wide grins. Normally I would not have paid the slightest attention to their curious stares, but I was wilted from the long ride and feminine enough to feel awkward performing simple ablutions before an audience.

Fajardo saw my gathering frown. He guessed the reason for it and said, "You must realize, senhora, that white women rarely come here. In fact no women. These men are not permitted to bring their wives to camp during the hunting season."

I managed a smile. "Oh, it doesn't bother me the least bit." Hal gave me a quizzical look. I shrugged in reply.

Following Fajardo to the big tent, I wondered what sort of meal we could expect. The memory of Mr. Wong's cuisine on the Amazon was strong. But when we stepped into the large dining tent we were pleasantly surprised. The table was covered with a clean tablecloth, dishes and service were properly arranged, and the camp chairs were comfortable.

Butane-gas lamps provided illumination for a lavish dinner prepared by Fajardo's native chef. The thick vegetable soup was delicious, and the entrée of eland steak garnished with spaghetti and served with Portuguese wine that had been chilled in a Butane-gas refrigerator would have done justice to a better-than-average restaurant. This totally unexpected refinement of living more than made up for the decrepit transportation and Fajardo's bad guesses about the reactions of wild life the day before in Gorongosa.

When we turned in, I had a happy feeling of excited anticipation for the adventures ahead. And even as I lay there, impatiently waiting for the night to pass, I fell asleep and dreamed that Hal, David and I were seated next to a family of popcorn-eating lions in an amphitheatre while before our eyes Tony Fajardo, assisted by an elephant, cracked a whip at a gaily painted truck pirouetting on its rear wheels.

When the sun came up the following day, I awoke to appreciate the sheer beauty of early morning in an African safari camp. I was so inspired by the invigorating air, impudent chattering of monkeys and excited jabber of innumerable birds, that I quickly arose, dressed and tugged on my boots without bothering to see if any "boarders" had moved in during the night.

Once outside the tent, I was impressed by the efficiency of Fajardo's organization. The staff had been astir for some time and delicious aromas of breakfast drifted from the pots on the fire. Squatting adjacent to the flame was a "laundryman" who was carefully pressing one of Fajardo's bush jackets and my freshly laundered clothing of the previous day with irons heated over the cook fire.

He looked up at me, smiled and nodded. *"Boa dia, senhora."* And as other natives passed each gave me the same salutation.

I turned back to our tent. A tent boy who had been assigned to look after us was in the act of replenishing the water supply in our wash pitcher. A distant pounding made me look to the far end of the camp. Fajardo stood there supervising a work crew. I watched as a large new tent with a wooden floor began to take shape. As I surmised, it proved to be our permanent home for the duration of the safari. It was nearly as large as the mess tent, therefore quite luxurious.

Two smaller tents had been put up nearby. These were our commode and shower room, a rather ingenious setup. The lavatory plumbing of the commode consisted of a hole in the ground covered by a portable seat. The shower tent featured an overhead bucket with a shower head attached. Bathing was a simple procedure and merely involved having our tent boy fill the bucket with lake water with which to wash off the grime of a day's hunting. A disinfectant called Detol was sprinkled into the water to help remove whatever ticks one picked up while plowing through the brush. Hal always stood guard while I used these facilities; there are no locks on tent flaps.

The lake that first morning was crystal clear; not a ripple disturbed its tranquillity. I started to stroll along the shore, in peaceful reverie, when Fajardo came to my side.

"Boa dia, Senhora Linker," he said rather hurriedly, "but please do not wander too far along the shore."

"Oh, I won't get lost," I replied blithely.

"It's not that—" He hesitated. "You see—there are crocodiles in this water."

When he saw me start, he quickly added, with a reassuring smile, "After we built the camp here, they moved to the other side of the lake in those rushes over there."

My gaze followed his pointing finger but I saw only water and some marshy growth.

"They avoid us here. But just the same, let's not tempt fate by straying where they are. No?"

"Yes." I nodded. "I mean, don't worry. I'll stay strictly away from their side."

As nonchalantly as I could, I returned to our little tent to find Hal and David standing at the open front flap. Both were gazing at the African morning with the same rapture I had felt. I mentioned crocodiles.

Hal grinned. "As soon as I get the hang of handling a hunting rifle, maybe I'll be able to snare you a pair of shoes with a matching handbag."

Breakfast turned out to be as pleasant as dinner had been. Corn flakes, eggs and warthog bacon, coffee and even powdered milk for David. Immediately after breakfast, Fajardo had his staff wheel out an empty oil drum and place it near a tent. Then he paced off a hundred feet to a tree and nailed up a target.

Our White Hunter then produced his own battered .375-caliber Winchester rifle with a telescopic sight. Handing it to Hal, he smiled and said, "How good a shot are you, Senhor Linker?"

My husband turned the weapon over in his hands and then lifted it. "Frankly I don't know. I've never fired a rifle in my life."

Fajardo's mouth flew open. "Surely you must be joking. I never heard— Didn't I understand you to say you were in the war?"

"I'm not joking." Hal grinned. "And I did serve in World War II—as a naval intelligence officer in the Pacific. I was issued a .45-caliber automatic and had occasion to use it several times, but never a rifle."

Fajardo looked as though he were about to say something in protest. Finally he shook his head and in a dull tone of voice said, "Then I'd better show you what to do."

He took the rifle from my husband's hands, dug into a pocket of his bush jacket and produced shining cartridges which he inserted one by one into the gleaming, well-oiled magazine of the weapon. As he did this he rattled off a monologue, in somewhat resigned tones, on the destructive potential of the rifle, the speed of the bullet, its shocking power and all sorts of grim details. Hal listened attentively.

Fajardo worked the curved bolt handle of the rifle. *Snicksnack.* "Now it is loaded and cocked," he said. He thumbed a small mechanism. "This is the safety," he explained. "Now I've set it so—"

"So it can't be fired," Hal interrupted. "I know about safeties. The .45-caliber automatic I carried had a safety."

Fajardo grunted and flicked off the safety. "To fire, you raise the rifle to your shoulder, just so—" He lifted the weapon and placed his right eye close to the telescopic sight. "Look through this eyepiece and make sure that the cross hairs in the scope sight are centered on target. Then place your trigger finger on the trigger and squeeze slowly."

There was a sudden deafening explosion that made my ears ache. I had never heard a gun fired so close at hand. It was rather frightening.

I stepped back as Fajardo lowered the rifle and squinted at the target on the tree. "Bull's eye," he said casually. His hand worked the bolt. The spent brass cartridge case glinted in the air and then, *snick-snack,* the weapon was reloaded and he handed it to my husband. "Now you try."

Hal slowly lifted the weapon to his shoulder and gazed through the scope sight. He said aloud to himself, "Squeeze the trigger—just as I used to do with the .45—and then—" Again the gun uttered that piercing, concussive report, and once more my ears ached as the explosion echoed across the lake.

The chatter of birds and monkeys stopped abruptly. There was a watery stir in the distant rushes where the crocodiles lurked. Hal stood still, holding the rifle with its muzzle pointed to the sky. Fajardo stared at him, looked at the target and then back. Hal's bullet had penetrated the target almost on top of the shot fired by Fajardo.

"And you *never* before fired a rifle, Senhor Linker?"

"Scout's honor," Hal said solemnly, holding up his free hand.

Fajardo's lips tightened. "Try one more."

"Sure!" Hal imitated Fajardo's movements of ejecting the spent shell and thrusting a fresh one into the breech. David scrambled to pick up the empty cartridge and put it in the shell holders of his bush jacket.

"You made a bull's-eye with this one, Pabbi," he announced proudly.

I moved back even farther and placed my hands over my ears just as my husband fired again. I could still feel and hear the ugly sound but it was not as uncomfortable as before.

Fajardo strode to the tree, closely scrutinized the target, and then returned, shaking his head. "Another bull's-eye!" he exclaimed. "Well, I don't have to worry about you with *this* rifle!"

He rattled a command to one of his natives who nodded, leaped up from a squatting position and darted into the tent. "Now, Senhor Linker, we'll see how you can handle the *heavy* gun!"

The rifle the native brought seemed twice the size of the Winchester. It was brutish, formidable.

Fajardo took the ugly weapon from the native and pulled back the massive bolt. "This is a .458-caliber express rifle," he explained. "Have you ever seen one before?"

Hal shrugged. "Only on the forward turret of a destroyer!"

Fajardo took him quite literally. "I did not know your Navy carried express rifles."

"Oh, they do." Hal's expression was solemn. "They have for years, Tony. They call them six-inch guns." He winked at me. "We used to bombard enemy islands with them. But seriously, why do we need this big rifle?"

"For large game like elephants and buffalo."

We were all startled by his announcement.

"I don't want to hunt any elephants on this trip," Hal said firmly.

"Perhaps not an elephant, but we'll be meeting lots of Cape buffalo and they're not only one of the most exciting animals to hunt but perhaps the most dangerous. I'm sure you'll want to bag one."

"Buffalo!" exclaimed our son. "Gosh—like the Indians and cowboys hunt?"

"Not quite." Fajardo grinned at David. "Cape buffalo are also called Black Buffalo. They are big and tough, with huge horns." He stretched both arms wide. "Their hides are almost as hard as armor and they can run nearly as fast as an automobile!"

And then he turned back to Hal and began to explain the mechanism of the express rifle. "Now this one does not have a telescope sight. It has what we call open sights because it is used for close-range work." He raised the weapon to his shoulder. It was obviously heavy. He also braced his legs farther apart. "You aim so that the front sight at the muzzle is exactly in the notch of the rear sight. When the target sits on top of the sights, you squeeze the trigger and—"

The roar was almost ear-shattering and Fajardo's body rocked back under the impact of the recoil. He looked at the target. A black hole, immense in comparison to those made by the Winchester, gaped back at us. It was a bull's-eye of course. Fajardo wore a satisfied smile as he ejected the spent cartridge, a long, fat cylinder, and slid a new one into the breech.

Hal raised the express rifle to his shoulder.

"Careful, Senhor Linker. She has a terrible kick!"

Hal quickly aimed and fired. Although my husband is of medium height, his build is stocky, muscular and quite powerful. But I could see that the weapon's recoil jarred him nearly as much as it had shaken Fajardo, whose frame was more slender.

Fajardo threw up his hands. "A bull's-eye for you, senhor!" he exclaimed. "You're a crack shot!" His expression was sincere. "I guess we won't have to worry about your handling guns."

Hal smiled and absently rubbed his right shoulder. "I'd hate to have to carry this Big Bertha all day."

Fajardo nodded. "It weighs over ten pounds but"—and he rubbed the thick barrel with affection—"it'll stop almost anything on four legs, this one!"

He looked at the three of us. "Out here there are no stores, so we have to hunt for our food; otherwise we do not eat meat."

The uneasiness brought on by the unaccustomed sounds of gunfire faded at the realization that for the first time we were going to live under primitive conditions which, except for gunpowder, would differ little from those faced by our ancestors thousands of years ago.

It was a startling and thrilling thought. My own husband would provide meat for us by means of his own skill and ability as a hunter. I thought of the gaudy and glittering supermarkets back home and of the women shopping safely there and I wouldn't have traded with any of them the excitement I felt at that moment.

10

The Leopard

OUR three weeks on safari were unforgettable. Although our daily routine required that we be up before dawn each morning and we collapsed from utter weariness at night, we were thoroughly happy. We were living as close to nature as was possible without going completely native.

There were discomforts that normally would have been nerve-wracking, but we didn't mind them. We were constantly bitten by swarms of tsetse flies that insisted on keeping us company in the veldt. Fortunately the tsetse in this section of Mozambique does not carry the dread sleeping sickness, but they are annoying campmates; their bite is sharp and fierce and can pierce right through one's clothing.

Our diet, despite the culinary skill of the native chef, was spartan by urban standards. And although we had our own private "bathroom" with a shower and used lake water prodigiously, we were never truly free of greasy, sweat-caked dirt. And still we were gloriously content and wished that time would stand still!

The reason of course was that the numerous grinding pressures of civilization simply do not exist in a safari camp in Africa. Life, for us, was reduced to basics. The only necessity was the constant hunt for food. Otherwise we were gloriously free for perhaps the first time in our wonderful life together. No newspapers with shuddery headlines or ominous predictions; no raucous voices shrilling over loudspeakers; no crowds; no smelly, roaring traffic; no worries about what to wear, since we wore the same kind of khaki safari clothes every day. Each evening the dusty clothing was washed and pressed for us! And what glorious freedom to be wearing safari boots so large and comfortable that I had room to wriggle my toes inside them anytime I wished.

We could do as we pleased—stalk dangerous big game with gun and camera or merely lie in the shade of a tree with full stomachs and gaze up at the glorious African sky until our eyes grew deliciously heavy and we dozed off with no slight twinge of guilt!

The routine of a typical day on safari will best explain what I mean. We awaken before dawn, about five. The nights and early mornings are brisk but we enjoy dashing out of the tent and splashing ourselves with water from the basin that has been thoughtfully filled at the lake by our tent boy.

Often the three of us pause and almost reverently gaze toward the eastern horizon where the oncoming sunrise splashes the dark canvas of the night sky with a riot of brightening color. There is always a momentary hush and then the teeming bird and animal life raise their voices in salute to the new day. The air is clean, sweet and almost intoxicating. And as the first gleam of real daylight floods the countryside, objects near and far are clearly etched and seem close enough to touch.

Breakfast is always enjoyable. The aroma of food sets our mouths to watering and we hurry to the mess tent where the native boy stands with a big grin and greetings of *"Boa dia, boa dia, Senhora Leenker, Senhor Leenker, Senhor Dah-veed!"* We have appetites as voracious as those of lumberjacks. The breakfasts are huge. Back home we could never begin to cope with them; here we wolf down huge portions of fried eggs, potatoes, broiled eland, impala, hartebeest or pork that Hal has hunted down the preceding day. And the aromatic bread, freshly baked in an oven scooped out of a towering anthill is unforgettable. We gorge and ask for more and still leave the table just a bit hungry! But not an ounce of surplus weight do we gain. On the contrary the three of us grow firm and tanned.

As we set out on the daily trek, we feel tremendous anticipation. Even Fajardo and his native helpers eagerly look forward to what each day may bring. David and I squeeze into the cab of the truck. Hal, Fajardo and the trackers perch on the wooden seats in the back. And off we go.

No journey is the same. We do not follow set paths. The truck sets forth across the flat land like a 17th-century galleon lumbering across an uncharted ocean. We are jounced and shaken but we do not care. And as we drive along we flush animals and coveys of birds that flee in all directions and disappear from sight.

There is much game for shooting but often we've more than enough meat in camp. Only about forty hunters per season are allowed to hunt in this area, and a license must be obtained for each species of animal shot. The hunting is regulated so that the animal population is merely kept in check and not faced with any threat of extermination. Fines are levied for violations of the strict regulations, and Hal reminded me of the annual need to thin out the small buffalo herds in the national parks of the United States, to keep their numbers down.

We film magnificent nyala, herds of sable antelope with imposing horns, huge warthogs that lower their massive heads and menacingly point their tusks our way, serving notice that they would just as soon fight as run. We also see hundreds and hundreds of impala.

On this typical morning we confine ourselves to hunting with motion picture and still cameras. Hal has already bagged his share of trophies and now is primarily concerned with capturing the movement of animals and birds on film. However, both the Winchester and express rifle are close at hand. It is my husband's ambition to shoot a great Cape buffalo. There are literally millions of them two hundred miles to the north of us, and the factories of Beira send hunting parties there to get meat for their workers, but we have not seen a single buffalo since our arrival.

The truck charges boldly into groves of trees. And now we marvel at the simple and ingenious navigating method invented by Fajardo and the driver. Tony holds a long wand cut from a tree branch. Since he is standing high up in the open truck body, he can see over the top of the brush and around trees. He leans above the front of the truck body and points over the windshield with the wand. A swing to the left side, and the driver obediently turns the wheel to the left, neatly avoiding an obstruction he would not otherwise have been able to see from his own position. Another swing of the wand, this time to the right side, and we resume our original course. Holding the wand straight ahead means "Maintain this heading." It is simple and effective.

Meanwhile the briskness of the early morning has given way to the heat of the midday sun. We take off our sweaters. Our helmsman steers for a grove of trees. It is time for lunch. In Africa, "only mad dogs and Englishmen go out in the noonday sun." African game itself, along with the natives and experienced hunters, eat and relax, waiting for the cool of the afternoon. Our luncheon has been prepared at camp that morning and we carry it with us in the back of the truck. The meal is fairly simple, but so keen are our appetites that we find it delicious. We can imagine that we are on a picnic in a forest grove. It is peaceful and idyllic except for one thing —there is always the possibility of a visit by a leopard, lion, rogue elephant or even a Cape buffalo. The presence of the loaded rifles is a reminder of the fact that there *could* be danger.

But such is our acceptance of safari life by now that we are accustomed to conditions on the veldt. Hal casually removes his sneakers, traditional footwear for a hunt because they enable one to stalk quietly. A crushed scorpion drops out. He forgot to turn them upside down that morning!

After eating, we do as the others do—stretch out in the shade and let ourselves drift off into slumber. And so adaptable are we to this marvelous ritual that it seems not only proper but as though we have always indulged in this kind of daily restoration of body and soul.

We do not sleep long—an hour at the most—but we awaken thoroughly refreshed. Tony's assistants pitch in to tidy the campsite and repack the box, and then we resume our hunt. This time perhaps some waterbuck, hartebeest or even an ostrich provide fair game for our cameras.

The afternoon trek invariably stops for a while at 4:30—time for tea. Fajardo is as set in his ways about this as are his English colleagues. And the custom is pleasant. We have tea over an open fire, drinking mugs of it along with camp bread smeared with jam or marmalade. It helps pass the time until dusk begins to close in and the animals emerge to hunt.

After that we may be lucky and shoot what we need with camera or gun. Or we may go "rolling, rolling home," as the popular chantey has it—home to our camp, a shower, a change of clothes and the relaxation of an evening meal with sound, restful sleep to follow.

Perhaps if we had lived this sort of life for more than our allotted three weeks, it might have become a habit. The three of us have often discussed it and we truly feel that, equipped with enough reading material, a year might have passed just as quickly for us as did that short period of time. Since that hunt, we have even adopted the noon siesta at home.

We sometimes covered a hundred miles or more in the course of a day. Only once or twice did we come across a tiny native village of four or five huts, although we often saw natives when we used the back roads. After an exchange of formal salutations and a visit with the headman of one village who was also the official hunter for his little community, we were able to glimpse what "going native" would really be like.

Compared with these people's existence, our simple life at camp was security and opulence. I watched the women prepare a meal out of wizened, shriveled potatoes. And we noticed an array of spears, bows and arrows, and hanging nearby the drying skins of a leopard and a civet cat.

Fajardo told us that the leopard was probably one of the greatest menaces these simple people had to face. Thus far the village hunter had been lucky. We gazed at the thin-shanked but proud-looking native with new respect. To be able to defend his people and get food solely by means of his primitive weapons, made him a mighty hunter indeed.

Hal gazed at one of the drying leopard skins and then turned to Fajardo. "That settles it, Tony."

"Settles what?"

"Let's try for a leopard. I'll be doing these people a favor and I'll also have the excitement of removing a menace to their lives."

Fajardo nodded. "Good idea! But you'll find it requires a different hunting technique and it can be tedious."

The technique he outlined sounded exciting. Since leopards are primarily nocturnal predators, one must bait a trap with freshly killed meat. But it does not necessarily follow that the leopard will "bite" the day the trap is baited.

In our own case, days passed before one of the cats expressed an interest in what we had to offer. We had killed a wildebeest, given the best cuts to our native boys, and then dragged the rest of the carcass behind the tailgate of the truck for miles, thereby creating a scent which we hoped would lure the cat to where we finally suspended the bait from a low-hanging limb of a tree. We placed bait in three different locations. At dusk we settled ourselves under cover near one of the traps and waited. And waited. *And* waited.

Fajardo explained the theory behind the system. "The idea is to lull the leopard into expecting to find his meat easily rather than having to prowl for it. In that way he'll grow lazy and careless!"

Hal looked dubious. "What is there to prevent him from merely robbing the traps and growing fat and sassy while we knock ourselves out killing bait and keeping him well fed?"

Fajardo grinned. "We hang up more than he can eat at one time. Once he has eaten from a bait, a leopard always returns to what's left until it's all gone."

"But first we have to get him interested in our lure. Is that it?"

Fajardo nodded. And his plan finally worked. On the second day when we returned to look at the baits, we found claw marks on the trunk of a tree from which we had suspended meat. The bait was partly eaten.

We planned to return at dusk, but the weather suddenly changed. A quick, tremendous cloudburst turned the veldt into a quagmire although we were well into the dry season. We scampered into an abandoned native hut only to find that its present occupants resented our intrusion. It was my second encounter with Africa's huge, ferocious red ants. The first time had been in the Congo when we visited the Pygmies of the Ituri Forest. The tiny natives had picked some of them off David's clothing during our sojourn. But this time we provided a safe oasis for ourselves by building a fire inside the hut. We stayed on one side of the fire and the ants kept their distance from the flames on the other. This truce between us and the red army lasted until the rain stopped and we were able to escape to the truck.

The rain had completely washed out the scent of our bait, and we had to start all over again, dragging the bait and waiting. We had almost given up hope when Mister Leopard's greed finally betrayed him. It was just before dark when it is neither day nor night. I remember that I was about to doze off when, almost like an apparition, the leopard materialized in front of the bait we were watching.

I was wide awake again instantly but unable to move or

even to open my mouth. For an endless moment the leopard seemed to stare directly at me. In the mournful twilight its eyes glowed like phosphorescent torches. And then it stood on its hind legs and reached up for the bloody bait.

And I stirred. But in that same instant there was a terrible explosion that momentarily turned everything crimson and practically deafened me. I was too stunned to move again. As though in a dream, I saw Hal rise to his feet. I could hear that ominous *snick-snack* of his rifle, and then a second shattering report jarred my ears.

The reek of powder was most unpleasant in the muggy atmosphere following the rain. David came to my side and put his arms around me as Hal and Fajardo cautiously approached the leopard crumpled at the foot of the tree.

"Careful," said Fajardo. Then, "That's one leopard less for the natives to worry about."

Today that spotted, golden hide adorns the den of our home and I share Hal's pride in it as a trophy.

Our departure was only a few days away when we found our opportunity to shoot a tremendous Cape buffalo. It took five shots from the express rifle for Hal to bring down the huge, dangerous animal. Afterward we counted the bullet holes. Each of Hal's shots had scored. Any one of them would have finished the largest lion or tiger. This beast must have weighed 2,000 pounds, since five men were unable even to turn it over.

We wanted to stay on safari with Fajardo longer, but it was impossible. In the first place, another hunting party had chartered his time and facilities and was due to arrive by car the day of our scheduled departure. Also, we had played truant from our other obligations long enough. There were thousands of miles to cover and thousands of feet of film to shoot and expose before we could call our summer's work finished and return home.

A tiny Beechcraft plane was to pick us up at a primitive landing strip and fly us to Beira in an hour, thus enabling us to avoid the long ride back. It was waiting for us, the engine idling. We shook hands with Fajardo and his men.

A strong feeling of sorrow at leaving our idyllic existence welled up in me as we boarded our transport back to the modern world. But once we had taken off for Beira, we found ourselves eager to reach our next filming site—legendary Dar es Salaam, on the fabled Indian Ocean.

Dar es Salaam means Haven of Peace in Arabic.

Circling over the small capital of Tanganyika before landing, I crossed my fingers and hoped it would live up to its name. After all, we had been stoned in the last City of Peace we had visited, La Paz in Bolivia. While we had been enjoying a peaceful existence at Tony Fajardo's camp in Mozambique, there had been bloody rioting between Africans and Arabs in Zanzibar, a few miles away from Dar es Salaam. European residents had been caught in the middle, and native Askaris, plus Malayan and Indian troops wearing the distinctive blue berets of the United Nations, had been called in to help maintain order.

All this had taken place two weeks before our arrival in Dar, as it is called. This city has had a turbulent history ever since Arab traders first started to explore the territory in the 8th century. First it had been the Arabs, then the Portuguese took over in the 16th century, only to lose out to the Sultan of Oman.

Finally, together with Ruanda-Urundi, the territory of Tanganyika with Dar as its capital, became one of Imperial Germany's colonies in the late 19th century and remained such until after World War I when it was administered by Great Britain under a League of Nations mandate later changed to a United Nations trusteeship.

When we landed and made our way through immigration and customs, we proceeded to a hotel, flamboyantly named the Palm Beach. We were thoroughly wilted by the torrid heat and the oppressive humidity. The hotel, despite its promising name, proved to be a tiny and decrepit two-story structure that had been built during Kaiser Wilhelm's reign, sometime before 1914.

Operated by a Greek proprietor, the Palm Beach did have excellent food, even if the standards of sanitation might not have passed an American health-department inspection.

When we set about exploring Dar es Salaam, we saw immediate signs of the trouble of the preceding weeks in Zanzibar in the presence of UN troops in the streets and the gray hull of an Indian naval vessel lying at anchor in the harbor. It reminded us that the temporary peace could be shattered at any moment.

We found this city of over 127,000 people an interesting mixture of various races. Two thirds of its population were Africans, 25,000 were Hindu and Moslem, along with some 5,000 Europeans and 1,500 Arabs. Traces of Portuguese and Arabian influence remain in its architecture. More unexpected is the solidly Teutonic aspect of some of the former government buildings. And while most of the baroque German colonial structures have a certain amount of hot, weatherbeaten charm, it was amusing to note that whereas similar buildings elsewhere in the tropics are ocher, pink or chartreuse, the German structures in Dar es Salaam are predominantly battleship gray, a shade evidently preferable to the old imperial German colonists.

Actually the length of German rule was not long as history goes. It lasted from 1891 until 1918, yet the traces of German occupation are still strong. Probably one of the strangest reminders is the big Lutheran Church near the harbor. Architecturally, it would have been more suited to Berlin, Hamburg or Stuttgart.

Tanganyika, now united with Zanzibar and known as the Republic of Tanzania, primarily depends on sisal crops used in the manufacture of twine, cordage, rope and sacks. At least two thirds of the working population are occupied with either the cultivation of the plant or the harvesting and processing of its fibrous by-products.

During a visit to one of the factories, we found Portuguese East African tribeswomen, some of whom still bore "ceremonial" facial scars or wore wooden plugs in their upper lips. They were like the duck-lipped women we had filmed in the Congo, and—like their northern counterparts—they, too, had had their front teeth knocked out to make room for their lip plugs. These were mere signs of beauty in modern times but were originally intended to make them so unattractive that they would not be stolen by Arab slave traders.

My husband pointed out that these women willingly put up with the discomfort of working a season in order to return to their native villages with a "fortune" in wages. It was, he explained, much like California's *bracero* program in which Mexicans cheerfully worked at "stoop labor" in Imperial Valley ranches under the searing sun, so they could return to Mexico with a nest egg.

One vivacious resident of Tanganyika, determined to develop tourist travel as a supporting industry, was a charming woman named Mary Seabrook who had forsaken her native England many years ago to settle here and open a travel agency. Filled with enthusiastic plans, she went out of her way to make sure that we filmed everything that could possibly induce a watcher of our TV show, *Wonders of the World,* to visit Tanganyika. She was wildly enthusiastic about the future of her country under the leadership of Julius Nyerere, the native premier whom she felt was the only strong and at the same time moderate leader in all of the new nations of Africa.

When the time came to make the twenty-minute flight from Dar to Zanzibar, we boarded the plane with some trepidation. Because Zanzibar is a small island about 50 miles long and 15 miles wide, we hoped that the surrounding Indian Ocean would make it cooler than Dar. But we were also fearful because of the unpleasant rumors of new rioting in the city.

During the height of the disorders there more than eighty people had been killed. We were told that a large force of the Askari native soldiers had been brought in to keep order but trouble could break out all over again at any moment.

For centuries, Zanzibar had been under the domination of the Arabs. Then, too, it not only had been a sea fortress for marauding Muslim freebooters but a distribution point for slaves captured by Arabian raiders from places in Africa as far away as the Congo and the Gold Coast! Of course the population had always been predominantly African. In recent years the Arabs, outnumbered ten to one, had still managed to maintain their rule.

With the resurgence of African nationalism and the plum of independence dangling before them, the African Negroes insisted on rule by racial majority, thereby overpowering the Arabian minority. During elections the friction had come to a boil with resulting death and destruction.

We were wrong both as to climate and the danger of trouble. Zanzibar was just as sweltering as Dar, but before our visit, passions between the opposing factions had cooled, thanks to the presence of the British-trained Askaris with their red fezzes and white uniforms.

While Dar es Salaam was primarily Germanic, Zanzibar had an Arabian Nights quality, with citadels that were mixtures of colonial Portuguese and Arabian architecture and narrow "casbah" streets filled with women clad in the veiled dress of the Moslem purdah. The atmosphere was stimulating and intriguing despite the intense heat.

The entire history of Zanzibar can be traced by the way its buildings have been erected, one on the site of another. The huge and ornate Palace of the Sultan, for example, was constructed (in 1700) over a Portuguese chapel.

And to demonstrate the impartiality that history often reveals, when we climbed to the ramparts of the palace to film the impressive Anglican Cathedral, we found it had been built on the site of an old Arab slave market.

Although British influence is predominant, the continuing
Arab attitude toward the feminine sex was brought clearly
home to me when I blithely stepped up to sign the registra-
tion book at the entrance to the Sultan's Palace. Above it was
a sign in English which bluntly stated: IT IS NOT CUSTOMARY
FOR LADIES TO SIGN HIS HIGHNESS' REGISTER. The inference was
painfully clear to me: *no women's signatures wanted!*

The government offices were in a citadel called Beit-Al-
Ajaib, which translates into English as The House of Wonders. The wonder lay in the fact that when it was built in the
1880's, the first elevator ever seen in Zanzibar was installed.
Another wonder to us was the time indicated on the building's tower clock; it never agreed with our watches or with
other clocks in the city. The mystery was solved when someone told us that the clock was set on Mecca time. Regardless
of the hour of the day in Zanzibar, the faithful followers of
the Prophet Mohammed always knew the correct time in
Mecca, the center of the Moslem faith.

As one who takes delight in cooking, I found myself thrilled
to be on the island that, with its neighbor Pemba, produces
80 percent of the world's cloves.

Soon after my arrival in America from Iceland, I had secretly learned how to make an apple pie, to surprise my husband, and I remember the chest-bursting pride I had felt
when he praised my effort as "the best pie I ever tasted."
Cloves had been an ingredient in that initial attempt to win
my husband's stomach as well as his heart.

I progressed in my cooking skill to the point where I ventured to prepare baked hams for our guests, and here again
cloves were a part of the recipe. Now, after our travels
throughout the world, I often felt the urge to concoct the
exotic dishes we had first tasted in such places as India and
Japan; and whenever Chicken Curry Calcutta or some such
dish was on my menu, I again often found myself using cloves.

I had inhaled their fragrant odor with every breeze since

our arrival, and now Hal announced that he was ready to film the clove industry.

First we traveled to the outskirts of Zanzibar City to the extensive clove plantations that ring the metropolis. I learned that the trees grow from 15 to 40 feet in height and that the tiny, spicy cloves I had been using in my cooking were actually the small red flowers of the trees, gathered before they open, and later dried. It was fascinating to learn that almost 50 percent of all these cloves are sent to Indonesia, where they are used to flavor tobacco.

Back in the city, we entered a "godown" of the Clove Growers Association. This Chinese word, meaning warehouse, has now replaced all other designations of storage places for goods throughout East Africa. Here the fragrant spice is stored for the Arab traders who arrive each year in their lateen-sail cargo vessels borne on the trade winds from Arabia.

"Bit of luck, eh?" said Alfred Abercrombie, the slender, bespectacled, middle-aged manager of the godown who was to show us around. "Two of the blighters are here today buying some of our goods. I'll just trot over and see if they'll let you film them." He waved his hand casually and strolled away. No one ever seems to hurry here.

Hal busied himself filming the loading and unloading of the 200-pound sacks filled to the brim with the aromatic spice.

A few minutes later Mr. Abercrombie sauntered back. There was almost a smile on his face. "Old friends of mine, they were. No trouble at all. Let's give it a try, shall we?"

In a flash Hal had his camera and tripod on his shoulder and we almost had to trot to keep up with him as he headed toward the two Arab merchants who were waiting for us on the other side of the godown.

"Ali ben Ahmed—Mohammed Faki—Mr. and Mrs. Linker from America, and their son David."

Smiles broke out on the faces of the two as we were introduced by Mr. Abercrombie, and widened still more when my husband greeted them with "*Salaam Aleichum*—May peace be with you."

They were from Saudi Arabia and were dressed according to the customs of that country. One wore a traditional turban and flowing robes; the other had covered his head with a white cloth that fell down his shoulders and back and was held in place by a double band of gold-and-black ropelike material tied around his forehead. They seemed to have no fear of having their pictures taken, a dread we had often encountered in Moslem nations and attributed not only to the Prophet Mohammed's prohibition of graven images but to fear of the "evil eye," which can steal one's soul along with his picture.

As Hal began to film the merchants he suddenly stopped and a thoughtful look came over his face.

"Say, Mr. Abercrombie," he remarked, "they've forgotten their curved knives. Don't all Arabs wear them? You know the ones I mean."

"Ah yes, their *jimbeeyas*," our host murmured with embarrassment. "Don't suppose you could have known it, but since the trouble last week all weapons including the *jimbeeyas* had to be turned over to the police. The blighters were hacking away at each other all over town with spears and *jimbeeyas*. It was a bloody mess, I tell you." He paused and looked thoughtful. "But I suppose they'll get them back some day."

"Doesn't look right this way," Hal insisted. "All the pictures I've ever seen of Arab merchants show them wearing their knives across their stomachs. This scene won't look real." He stared straight at Abercrombie. "Say, how about borrowing two of the *jimbeeyas* from the police for the filming?"

Our host looked horrified. "Really, old chap, the police here just don't *do* that sort of thing. I shouldn't care to approach them on the matter."

I saw that certain gleam come into my husband's eye. "Well now, Mr. Abercrombie," he said slowly and deliberately, "one really can't tell what someone else will do unless one asks and definitely finds out, don't you think? And I wouldn't like to go through life never knowing for sure what the police would have said had you asked them. Of course, if you'd rather that *I* tried—"

"That won't be necessary," Abercrombie retorted stiffly. "I'll make the necessary inquiries." And off he stalked.

"Won't he just make believe he tried?" I asked worriedly.

"I doubt it," Hal said, with a laugh. "That would be unsporting and I think I've challenged his sporting instinct. He'll tell me exactly what happens."

Hal returned to filming the new shipments of dried cloves arriving on carts, with ten sacks to a cart, each vehicle pulled by from four to six straining Negro workers. Only a week or so ago they had been rioting and killing any Arabs they could reach and the Arabs had been retaliating. Now the urgent necessity of making a living had brought the enemies together again, whether temporarily or permanently, no one could guess.

About ten minutes later Mr. Abercrombie reappeared, walking slowly around the godown. A look of wonder was on his face and across his outstretched arms were two magnificent silver-filigreed *jimbeeyas* and their ornately decorated belts.

Without a word, he walked over to the two open-mouthed Arab clove merchants and handed a knife to each. As they buckled the vicious-looking weapons across their middles, I noticed that the Negro workmen who had just arrived with the latest shipment of cloves kept edging uneasily farther and farther away!

11

Mazda Is a Parsi God!

WE were back in Mother India after an incredibly long nonstop flight in a British-made Comet Mark-IV jetliner from Nairobi to Bombay. It had been nine years since I had last set foot in this country, during the rainy monsoon season. Any hopes I might have had that the weather had changed meanwhile were shattered the moment we stepped from the air-conditioned comfort of the Comet's cabin into Bombay's oppressively sultry heat.

Our headquarters was the Taj Mahal Hotel, a Victorian structure that faced the beautiful harbor. Just across the wide thoroughfare from our hotel, facing the harbor and the Arabian Sea beyond, is the famous Gateway to India, a monument built by the old British Raj to celebrate the 1911 visit of King George V and Queen Mary.

During World War I and through World War II, thousands upon thousands of Indian and British troops (as well as Australian, New Zealand and American) had stood in the presence of this gateway.

India is only one third the size of the United States. Yet within its 2,000-mile length and 1,800-odd-mile width are crammed more than 450 million people, according to the most recent census figures available. In all likelihood there are even more. In spite of famine, natural disasters and the appalling toll of pestilence, the birthrate rises by leaps and bounds. It seems that Mother India truly takes her name seriously.

Bombay, called Mumbai in the days of the Moghuls, is an intriguing cross section of India's diverse races, religions, customs and variegated tongues. During our first visit, years before, we had spent considerable time in Calcutta, once the second largest city in the British Empire. At that time Calcutta had seemed a crowded, sweltering melting pot.

But Bombay was much more bewildering, although much more modern. Near the Crawford Market, a place of temptation and financial disaster for unwary shoppers, we wandered through narrow, winding lanes and rubbed shoulders with Parsis, Maharashtrians, Tamils, Malayalis, Sikhs, Bengali and squat, broad-faced, stocky Ghurkas who, though natives of the independent Kingdom of Nepal at the foot of the Himalayas, still comprise the elite fighting branch of India's Army.

Each retained his or her regional individuality of dress and language. Although the majority of the Bombayans use Marathi as a sort of native lingua franca, the basic language of overall communication, social intercourse and business is English. While we were there, attempts were already being made by the government at New Delhi to establish Hindi (or Hindustani) as the official language.

Even at that time, people in Bombay resented the thought of being compelled to abandon Marathi in favor of a language arbitrarily chosen by New Delhi. In the daily English-language newspaper, we read of demonstrations and rioting that had begun to break out in cities and towns throughout the country, especially in the Tamil-speaking south. After we left, many of these public protests turned into minor but bloody insurrections.

The religions of India vary depending on the section and its inhabitants. Bombay is crowded with Hindu and Jain temples, Moslem mosques and the places of worship of the Parsis, who are descendants of the 8th-century Persians. Although the number of Parsis in all of India is less than a quarter of a million, they are highly successful merchants and as such tend to dominate India's financial structure.

Parsis have a relatively high level of education. They are Zoroastrians (fire-worshipers) and their supreme deity is Mazda—a name familiar to most Americans only as an electric-light bulb.

We were able to visit a temple in Bombay in one of their walled-off residential areas—self-imposed ghettos *without* poverty. Their priesthood is hereditary, a tradition that goes back to before the days of Darius the Great, ruler of Persia in the era of Alexander of Macedonia. And their burial customs—somewhat gruesome to us—are equally ancient.

We learned about these by seeing the gaunt towers that rise in remote areas and are generally attended only by flocks of India's "sanitation experts"—the scavenging vultures. These structures, we discovered, are called Towers of Silence, and the uncovered Parsi dead are laid to rest on iron gratings at their tops. When the flesh has been devoured by the vultures, the skeletal bones drop between the bars of the iron gratings. The rationale behind this strange custom is to avoid contaminating earth, fire or water with a dead body, because these elements are objects of worship.

When we had visited Calcutta when David was less than a year old, we had found the streets—even main thoroughfares such as Chowringhee—blocked by wandering cattle sacred in the Hindu religion. Traffic, regardless of time or weather, frequently came to a complete halt while these bovine creatures of veneration slept, fought, relieved themselves or even mated.

This weird situation is also found in Bombay, although the authorities have tried to gradually ease the sacred cattle into the suburbs. The thought of either putting these animals to useful work behind the plow or fattening them for slaughter to relieve India's recurring famines is sacrilegious to most Hindus.

But there was still much that enchanted me in Bombay, despite the monsoon. The women were charming and graceful in the magnificently flattering garment known as the sari. I couldn't wait until we had an interlude of relaxation between filming sessions so I could go on a shopping spree for sari fabrics and learn how to wear one correctly.

Saris are made of sturdy material for everyday use or of diaphanous, lustrous silk for formal wear. Many of the bolts of material shown by the energetic merchants were brocaded and elaborately decorated.

The sari, whether as a house dress or evening attire, is worn with a short form-fitting blouse called a choli, that leaves the midriff uncovered, and a petticoat with a drawstring around the waist. This method of dressing is complicated at first but with a little practice it becomes a thing of ease.

After the choli and petticoat are put on, the upper edge of the sari is tucked into the waist of the petticoat so that the material drops its full width to just below the hem of that garment. Then seven or eight pleats are fashioned by the wearer, using thumb and forefinger to measure width. These pleats are held together, tucked flat into the front of the petticoat, and permitted to fall straight and smooth. The remainder of the sari is then draped over the left shoulder and allowed to descend casually from one shoulder to the back of the knee.

The method of wearing a sari is also dictated by race and area. Hindu women drape the garment over the left shoulder, while their Parsi sisters wear it over the right. I acquired several saris and often wear them at home and on formal occasions. The fact that I'm Icelandic and quite blond seems to cause special delight in the "visiting" Indians I am honoring by wearing their national dress.

New Delhi, capital of the republic, was planned as a model city by its founders, the English rulers of the British colony. The wide streets, tree-lined boulevards and graceful "cir-

cles" are airy and handsome. The huge government buildings, built by the British during the last decade of England's
rule, lie in an immense circle at the end of what used to be
known as King's Way but is now called Raj Path.

The architecture can only be described as a mixture of St.
Peter's in Rome and St. Paul's in London, with a touch of
the capitol in Washington, Windsor Palace, the Taj Mahal
and Frank Lloyd Wright!

The overall effect, however, is not only overwhelming but
rather beautiful in an awesome, massive fashion. Our own
American Embassy, designed by Edward D. Stone, has blended
contemporary design with Indian tradition. While the structure is massive and dominating, it has a deceptively ethereal
quality which, together with its pool and inner courtyard covered by a delicately filigreed roof, made us feel almost cool
despite the blistering midmorning monsoon heat of 100 degrees.

Adjoining New Delhi is Old Delhi—a crowded area dating
back to the time of the Moslem Moghuls who were the ruling
descendants of the conquering Mongols of the 15th century.
Our eventual destination was picturesque Kashmir, high up
in the blessed foothills of the Himalayas. But we were grimly
determined to make the journey by slow stages, despite the
monsoon, in order not only to visit New Delhi but also Agra
and the famed Taj Mahal. Hal had seen the Taj on his first
trip around the world, the year before we were married, and
he wanted me to enjoy its beauty as he had done.

Getting about Delhi, New or Old, can be accomplished in
many ways. One of the most popular is by bicycle. People by
the score, in all kinds of dress, could be seen pedaling briskly,
evidently oblivious to the awful heat and humidity. And
when frequent rain squalls descend, they keep right on about
their business. Another and increasingly popular method is
by motor scooter, noisy little Italian-made contraptions that
dart about like earthbound, gas-scented hummingbirds. The
gharries, two-wheeled, horse-drawn carts with their drivers

squatting on poles almost on top of the horses' rumps, are still another method of getting about.

There are also buses of varying types, ages and stages of repair, many private cars and taxis, the latter for the most part driven by huge, bearded, turbaned Sikhs.

We chose a cab with an interior and engine that strongly reminded us of Tony Fajardo's safari truck. Fortunately, after leaving the government circle, the cab steadily though unspectacularly managed to putter its way to the temple of Kutb Minar, which is almost fifteen centuries old. The eleven-mile drive through the suburbs was interesting. There were more monkeys on the loose than we had seen on safari or even at Wong's camp on the Amazon. Here, of course, they are sacred, like the cows. No matter how much of a nuisance they become or how much food and grain they pilfer from farms, hovels and food stalls, one is not permitted to molest them.

After filming some of these audacious creatures, we turned our backs on them and began to film the tower of the temple, which rises 238 feet. Actually this tower is a "new" addition: it was erected by Moslems in the year 1193 and called Kuwwat Ul Islam Mosque. The mosque itself, near the base of the tower, had been built on the site of a Hindu temple and was composed of fragments of twenty-seven Hindu and Jain temples which the Moslems had destroyed. Whoever the Islamic architects and builders were, they evidently did not worry that no two columns in the courtyard matched. The most absorbing feature of the temple was an iron pillar that had been fabricated in the fourth century. Just what its function was or what ingredients went into its construction so that it has survived centuries of exposure to rain and heat without showing the slightest trace of rust, is a historical and metallurgical mystery. No one has ever solved this ancient secret.

No mention of Delhi would be complete without touching on India's snake charmers. While hurrying through the streets between cloud bursts, we came upon one with his reed flute, squatting beside a covered wicker basket. Hal dickered with him. We had learned that Indians love to bargain, and this entrepreneur was no exception.

The snake charmer finally removed the top of the basket and began to pipe a series of sharp sounds that evidently charmed and beguiled cobras but that grated on my ears. While Hal began to film (with the usual crowd of passers-by gathered around), David crouched near the basket and stared into it in fascination. I stood back several feet. Wringing wet with perspiration and monsoon rain, I was tired and stood thinking about our air-conditioned suite at the Asoka Hotel when, to my horror, not one but *two* cobras emerged with extended hoods.

Although by this time I have grown accustomed to all sorts of creatures during our travels, the sight of reptiles always terrifies me. I grabbed my son's arm and pulled him back from those two swaying heads.

After my husband had finished filming, he assured me that "performing cobras" are perfectly safe: their poison sacs have been removed.

"That may be, Hal-minn," I replied, "but they still looked at me with a rather hungry expression."

Richard Halliburton, the travel-adventure idol of stay-at-homes during the 1930's, once wrote of having swum in the pool of the Taj Mahal under a full moon. At the time he wrote, the area was remote and inaccessible to the ordinary traveler. From America, an ocean voyage of almost a month, followed by dusty miles overland, was required.

Gazing at the beautiful but extremely shallow pool that stretches toward the imposing marble edifice, I remembered his words and realized how modern jet travel and methods of communication have combined to place formerly remote parts of the world within easy reach.

So much has been written about the exquisitely beautiful Taj Mahal that I perhaps cannot add anything significant.

But my first glimpse of it was a profound emotional and personal experience.

Almost everyone who has visited the Taj—whether under the light of a romantic moon or during the sticky heat of a monsoon day—seems to have experienced a similar reaction.

Reading or hearing about the Taj beforehand is one thing. It is said to be beautiful. It is called a "silvery castle in moonlight" or a "dazzling white citadel under a bright sun." It is all of these but it is also much more. And unlike so many first impressions, I find that the Taj's enchantment grows stronger as time passes, instead of fading.

Its sheer marble beauty was thrilling. And when I delved into the story behind the Taj, I felt a gentle sadness and sympathy for the unhappy monarch who had built this lasting monument in memory of a love that ended tragically.

The builder, Shah Jehan, fifth of the Moghul emperors who had conquered India and founder of Old Delhi, ordered the structure built in the year 1630 to honor his favorite wife Arjuman Banu Begum, also known as Mumtaz I Mahal. She had borne the Shah thirteen children and died giving birth to her fourteenth. The brokenhearted monarch ordered the building as a mausoleum for her. When it was completed after eleven years, the Taj became his wife's resting place and was called Taj Mahal, a shortened form of her name, which means Beloved of the Palace.

Ironically, shortly after this the Shah Jehan's two sons, Aurungzeb and Muarad, seized and imprisoned him for many years and he was liberated only by death. His repentant sons then decided to make such amends as they could by burying him in the Taj beside the tomb of his beloved.

When we first approached the area, we entered an immense walled garden through an imposing gateway. Before us stretched the long reflecting pools and fountains which Halliburton had described. The Taj itself rises from a marbled terrace and overlooks masses of dark cypresses. The dazzling white structure is dominated by a bulbous dome that rises more than two hundred feet. The exterior walls of Makrana marble are inlaid with semiprecious stones that have been worked into Arabic inscriptions and floral and geometrical arabesques.

Before we could enter the mausoleum, we were required to cover our shoes with cloth overshoes which, the guardian explained, both protected the marble walks and floors and also adhered to the Mohammedan custom that prohibits shod feet from entering a Moslem shrine.

The interior is lofty and the outside sunlight is filtered through carved marble screens. We spoke in whispers as we approached the two large marble sarcophagi. Even so, our whispers seemed to echo and re-echo in the strange, almost breathless, quiet of the tomb.

The beautifully decorated marble sarcophagus of Mumtaz I Mahal lies directly in the center under an eighty-foot-high inner dome. Around its border are inscribed the various endearing names the Shah had called his wife.

His resting place, marked by a larger block of marble, is to the left, where it was placed by his sons. Its position interferes with the symmetry of the interior in a way never intended by the Shah.

After we took pictures of these tombs, our guide told us that the sarcophagi are actually unoccupied. "The real burial places are below us," he said, tapping his foot to emphasize his words.

Was it possible to go below and film there?

Certainly. But for—*ahem*—a consideration, of course.

In Mexico they call the extended hand the *mordida*—the bite. In India it is called baksheesh.

Mordida or baksheesh, we pressed a rupee in his palm and followed him down a flight of stairs to a smaller, rather somber, chamber that contained two marble sarcophagi identical to those in the main rotunda.

As we entered the room another guide tossed some colored powder on our shoulders and smiled expectantly.

Our own guide coughed pointedly. "That's for good luck, sahib."

Hal understood. Another rupee changed hands, this time going to the "new" guide.

We went through the ritual of getting cameras and lights adjusted and filmed the second pair of tombs.

"*Ahem,* sahib," our guide murmured apologetically when we had finished. "Sahib—they are not buried here either!"

The three of us exchanged glances. It was uncomfortably warm down there.

"All right," said Hal. "Where *are* they buried?"

The guide shrugged. He pointed to the floor. "They are buried six feet under these tombs as is the Moslem custom. But," he continued, to Hal's obvious relief, "that cannot be filmed. It is sealed."

At the top of the stairs we were met by still another guide. Smiling broadly, he pinned little flowers on each of us. "For good luck, sahib!" he murmured. Word had apparently gotten around that the Americans had arrived! Another rupee changed hands.

Once outside in the blinding sunlight, we paused to carefully record on film the graceful minarets that adorn each corner of the Taj. We devoted considerable footage to the Arabic inscriptions and designs in the marble. And we made an interesting discovery for our television audiences. The letters and designs in the marble grow larger and thicker toward the top of the tomb. Thus, as you look at the inscriptions from below, they seem to be of the same size all the way up, since the larger inscriptions higher up counteract their longer distance from the eye.

This is actually similar to the method used by the classic Greek architects in the construction of the Parthenon in Athens, which we had seen and filmed on another of our trips. Called entasis, which means stretching, the technique causes the Parthenon columns to appear straight when seen from below by enlarging their size and the width of their grooves toward the top.

This subtle Greek optical illusion remained unnoticed in modern times until the 19th century when architects took the trouble to measure each of the Parthenon's columns painstakingly. So it is with the Taj's inscriptions and designs, many of which consist of semiprecious *pietra dura* stones. Whether standing close by and gazing upward or viewing it from a distance, the words and arabesques on the Taj appear uniform and in perfect alignment.

By now we should have become accustomed to the stifling dampness of the monsoon, but as an Icelander I found the heavy humidity and heat almost suffocating. The only thing that kept us going was the knowledge that within hours we would be on a plane bound for Delhi, where we would stay just long enough to board a connecting flight to Srinagar, at the foot of the Himalayas.

There we planned to visit the enchanting Vale of Kashmir where, aside from the spectacular scenery and a luxurious houseboat on Lake Dal at Srinagar, we would be at an altitude of more than a mile—and *cool*. But first we had to see Jaipur.

We had chartered a car of undetermined vintage, owned and driven by one of India's bearded and turbaned Sikh chauffeurs, and had arranged to be driven to Jaipur, the pink capital of the state of Rajasthan.

Unfortunately the vehicle was in worse shape than Tony Fajardo's truck. We broke down six times during the two-hundred-mile drive. The carburetor had to be cooled with wet rags soaked in nearby streams—it was overheating the gasoline!

But once at Jaipur our fascination with the pink-walled buildings erected around 1728 made us temporarily forget our transportation problems. We had an enjoyable luncheon in a pavilion cooled by breezes and slowly rotating ceiling fans on the grounds of the Rambagh Palace, formerly the home of a maharajah. We visited the abandoned old city of Amber, about five miles away, and as a pièce de résistance we even had an elephant ride. The undulating back of the pachyderm jostled and bounced us almost as severely as our Sikh's car did.

When we returned to the car for the drive to the airport, our bearded Sikh had a woebegone expression which we now realized meant more car trouble. This time it was worse than before: the engine itself had expired and gone where all faithful worn-out engines go. We had barely half an hour in which to get to the airfield.

Hal paid off the poor man and then led us, burdened with our equipment, trudging along the road to the airport. A few moments later a crowded bus overtook us. My husband planted himself in the center of the road and waved both arms. For a frightening moment I was afraid that the driver would run him down. With a squeal of brakes, the vehicle stopped and we inched our way—cameras, suitcases and all—into its closely packed interior.

When we came to the airport the driver kept going. Hal shouted and pounded. The Indian passengers sympathized with our predicament and added their voices to the uproar. The driver finally stopped, grudgingly. Willing hands helped us alight and there was a chorus of cheers in different dialects, including some singsong English, as the three of us, disregarding the risk of heat prostration, ran frantically toward the terminal and the transport whose propellers were already beginning to turn.

The airline station manager informed us that we were too late and that passengers simply *must* report at least twenty minutes before departure.

Hal pointed to the plane's door, which was still open. "That's our flight and we've got to be on it." There was a tone of finality in his voice.

The manager shook his head as if to say, "Ah, those Americans!" and waved us on.

We wearily marched past him and climbed the stairs to the cabin. As we strapped ourselves into our seats, the plane was already taxiing toward the takeoff. Although the cabin's temperature must have been almost 110 degrees and we perspired as though in a Finnish sauna, I closed my eyes and almost immediately felt cooler as I visualized the high, snowcapped, pine-covered Himalaya Mountains in Kashmir, our next destination.

12

Houseboat in the Himalayas

ALTHOUGH I have known many luxuries in the course of our adventures, our stay in a houseboat on Lake Dal in Kashmir is firmly stamped on my memory as one of the most delightful experiences of my life.

We fell in love with this place, with its altitude of about a mile, from the moment we stepped from our plane and breathed the cool, refreshing mountain air. A smiling Moslem named Haji Karima Ramzan Goroo made his appearance at the airport to greet us and escort us through the city of Srinigar to the lake.

When he introduced himself, Hal immediately said, "I see you've been to the holy city, Haji Goroo."

Goroo blinked with astonishment and then beamed. "This is so nice!" he exclaimed. "Very few Americans know that the pilgrimage to Mecca entitles one to be known as Haji."

Although my husband had not intended it, his comment about the honor conferred on Mr. Goroo by his religious pilgrimage gave us tremendous prestige with him. He was financially successful as the owner of several houseboats on Lake Dal, and during our stay in this paradise we could do no wrong.

Mr. Goroo drove us to the lake and ushered us into a long,

narrow, canoelike boat, a sort of water taxi known as a "shikara" with a canopy for protection from the sun. We paddled out on the lake on the way to our houseboat and I noted with a smile that our shikara's intriguing name was ABODE OF LOVE —DELUX—SPRING SEATS—FAST SPEED. The lake, a gemlike body of water tucked into the foothills of the Himalayas, was mirror-smooth, and the cool air instantly washed from our minds and bodies every trace of the monsoon that smothered most of southern and Southeast Asia.

Our floating hotel was a palatial houseboat that had been completed only weeks before our arrival. Built of cedar, the multidecked craft had a delightfully fragrant odor that was a blessed contrast to the mouldy smells encountered during the monsoon in the lowlands.

The boat was named the *Lone Star*. Moored not far away was another and older craft called the *California*. We felt a little unpatriotic choosing the *Lone Star,* since we live in Los Angeles, but it was the newer of the two. The lake, which is barely five miles long and a mere two and a half miles across at its widest point, is shallow and dotted with these floating hotels which are reserved months in advance by well-to-do Indians, Nepalese and knowledgeable foreigners as a refuge from the monsoon heat. The houseboat names were bizarre: *Cherryripe, Jazz, A-Jazz* and *Lucifer* were just a few.

While a staff of smiling servants, part of the *Lone Star's* crew, took charge of our baggage, Mr. Goroo showed us around. There was a living room with a porch out over the water, a dining room with an overhead fan, two bedrooms, each with private bath and hot and cold running water, and a kitchen.

Our life on the *Lone Star* will always stand out as almost the ultimate in sheer comfort. As a housewife and mother during the long winter months, I found the new life a paradise. Our rooms were huge, airy and spotless. We had a staff of servants—bearers as they are called—waiting on us from morning to night.

Our food was delicious and perfectly served. Our clothing was aired, brushed, cleaned and pressed without our having to give it a thought. Food shopping? That was taken care of by the houseboys. It was truly a heavenly reward for a hard-working homemaker. And because the atmosphere was so unlike that of a typical luxury hotel and more in keeping with the private home of people of affluence, we found ourselves not only thoroughly enjoying our temporary status as millionaires but growing quite accustomed to this delightfully easy life!

One of the charming "hazards" we encountered during our Kashmiri sojourn was the floating "doorbell-ringer." Almost before we had settled ourselves, watergoing merchants selling everything imaginable were paddling up to our front porch and offering bargains.

Indians love to bargain and the Kashmiri were no exception. There was no such thing as saying firmly, *"Nay mongta"* ("I don't want it"). They smilingly persisted. It takes a person with a heart of stone to keep saying *teek-nay* (no good). The word had gotten out that Americans (they pronounce it Amrikans) were back, and paddles stirred up waves on Lake Dal as the fleets converged on the *Lone Star*. The incidents of the past few years between India and Pakistan, both of whom claim this area, had seriously damaged their formerly thriving tourist industry.

There were tailors who brought bolts of all kinds of material, jewelers with silver and goldwork and gems, many undoubtedly spurious but a few exquisite and obviously valuable. Furriers showed their pelts. Woodcarvers, vendors of papier-mâché items, milliners, dollmakers, fruit-and-vegetable peddlers surrounded us at most times of the day and made a polite chorus while we tried to pretend they weren't there.

We did not escape entirely unscathed. Hal expressed a casual interest in some gabardine that was being waved by an excited tailor. That did it. The man thrust his boat toward us, shoving competitors aside, and climbed aboard with the agility of an old-time English pirate boarding a 16th-century gold-laden Spanish galleon.

Before this smiling but insistent onslaught Hal was helpless. He ordered a suit made to his measurements for the huge sum of $35 in rupees. An equal amount bought me a beautiful fur coat made of snow leopard. Actually both purchases were excellent investments. My husband's suit was turned out with a finish worthy of Brooks Brothers, and my snow leopard coat has remained a favorite of mine ever since.

During the first days of our visit to this Eden, everything seemed perfect. We greeted each experience, no matter how commonplace, with enthusiasm. I can only account for this odd state of euphoria by the fact that Kashmir was such a fantastic contrast to what we had experienced in the lowlands.

In our shikara, *Abode of Love,* we were paddled to the gardens of Shalimar near Srinagar.

The Shah Jahangir had built Shalimar for his wife; it was their son Shah Jehan who had constructed the Taj Mahal. To me, the realization that those two monarchs had placed their wives on such exalted planes was fascinating. The word Shalimar means Abode of Love.

The gardens, which are enclosed, have a delicate, almost fragile, quality. In their center is a large black-marble pavilion surrounded by beautiful terraces with playing fountains.

Like the Taj Mahal, the beauty of Jahangir's Shalimar defies description.

As we were preparing to film, unconsciously speaking reverently and in hushed tones, I was stunned to hear what sounded like gunfire.

Hal and I stared wonderingly at each other and I remembered the "firecrackers" during Fidel Castro's attack in Santiago. Through my mind ran snatches of what I had read and heard about the Kashmir dispute between India and Pakistan.

"Good heavens, what's that?" I asked as the shooting resumed at intervals, as though some sniper were efficiently picking off specific targets.

Our good friend Mr. Goroo seemed quite unconcerned. "Is there something wrong, perhaps?"

Hal peered around the gardens. "It sounds like someone shooting."

"Shooting?" For a moment I wondered if Goroo was hard of hearing. Then he grinned. "Oh, that noise!" He shrugged. "It's the caretakers. They are cracking whips to frighten birds away from the fruit trees."

We must have still looked doubtful because he nodded over his shoulder. "Come. I show you!"

We followed him to a grove of trees bordering the pavilion area and came face to face with our "sniper," who was casually strolling along, expertly snapping a tremendous bullwhip.

Mr. Goroo chatted with the youth, obviously explaining who we were. The latter grinned and proceeded to demonstrate his virtuosity with the whip. Where it had sounded like spaced shots before, it now crackled like volleys of rifle fire!

While Hal took the opportunity to film this performance, David came close to me and said, "Gosh, Mommie, even if I were an eagle, it'd scare *me!*"

Just then we heard the wail of strange instruments in the distance.

Mr. Goroo's eyes lit up. "Pairfect!" he exclaimed, snapping his fingers. "I arranged to have some musicians and a dance here so you could listen to our music and see our dancing." By "our" he obviously meant the Moslems of Kashmir.

We followed him back to the black-marble pavilion. There we found a rather heavyset young woman draped in a white costume—a tunic fell to her knees and revealed baggy white trousers. Her feet were bare, and wound about her dark hair was a veil which also looped down to her knees.

Seated before her on an Oriental rug were four musicians who paused when we made our appearance. Mr. Goroo introduced us. They nodded and smiled rather shyly. And when

Hal set up his camera, I could see them blush under their swarthy skins. Then they began to play. Their instruments were fascinating. One, called a sarengi, resembled a mandolin. Another was a harmonium—rather similar to an accordion. The third musician beat a cadence on the drumlike gara. The remaining performer strummed on a stringed instrument that Mr. Goroo identified as a rahab. The music sounded bizarre to our ears as the girl twirled and gyrated through a repertoire of dances that, our host assured us, reach back into antiquity—"Even before the time of the Moghuls!"

"Mistair Leenker, how would you like for to shoot a bear high up in the mountains?"

"What kind of a bear?" There was a glint of interest in my husband's eyes.

David excitedly leaned forward across the overladen dinner table aboard the *Lone Star*.

"They are Himalaya black bears. Big ones." Goroo nodded as though reaffirming the fact to himself. "Since firearms are not permitted except to foreigners because of the troubles, the bears have multiplied and they sometimes become dangerous to villagers. So"—he paused and beamed—"you get some excitement, pairhaps some good movies, and we do a favor for the people."

Hal warmed to the idea. "But what about a permit and a rifle?"

Mr. Goroo indolently waved his hand. Obviously such details were mere trifles. "A permit for you, a foreigner, is easy."

Hal turned to me.

I spoke up quickly. "Why not, Hal. Let's do it."

Hal hesitated. "Just because I've had a little experience with big game in Africa, that doesn't necessarily make me a Great White Hunter, Mr. Goroo."

"I assure you that there will be no—er—criticism if you happen to miss."

"Which *could* happen." Hal chuckled. "And probably will."

At the crack of dawn two days later, we left the *Lone Star,* and still half asleep, were ferried on the *Abode of Love* to the landing where Goroo waited with his car. It was misty and somewhat chilly as we started off on a winding, climbing road that headed straight for the dark mass of the Himalayas.

There was a brooding, eerie quality to the landscape. In some places the mist turned to almost impenetrable gray fog. Here and there we could see fragments of fields, a splash of color, an occasional human being or a grazing animal. The overall effect reminded me of Japanese or Chinese color prints. And then, as if emerging from a tunnel, we came into early morning sunlight and saw that we were skirting mountains flanked by gorges.

The road gradually turned as it climbed, and we looked back down and saw Lake Dal and Srinagar slowly come into view as the climbing sun continued to dissipate the lingering mist. It was a spectacular, breathtaking view—another in my collection of many splendid moments of sheer beauty.

Our first stop was at a trail that led off from the highway. Here we were supposed to leave the car and mount horses for the climb to a lodgelike cabin, at about a 10,000-foot level, that marked the "arena" for our bear hunt.

The time of our rendezvous with the horses and guides had been set for high noon. Normally our up-with-the-rooster start would have given us ample time to keep to our schedule. But an old Moghul fort on the way, the magnificent scenery and the interesting tribesmen along the roads had all been too tempting. After all, our prime objective was filming; the hunt had to take second place, so we had stopped innumerable times.

When we finally did arrive at the meeting place, it was nearly two in the afternoon. No one was there. We assumed that the horses that had been arranged for by special courier (dispatched in advance by Goroo) had not yet arrived.

"Nay." Goroo shook his head. "I know these mountaineers. They got here and when we did not appear they probably thought we had changed our minds and so they went back home." He shrugged.

Hal had been studying the trail, which wandered from the clearing higher into the mountains. "We've still a few hours of daylight left," he said. "Let's try to drive to the cabin."

Goroo shuddered visibly. "It's never been done. I mean, take a car up there."

"There's always a first time."

Our host looked unhappy and then sighed. "All right. Maybe it will work." But his expression plainly showed his skepticism tinged with apprehension, not so much because of the physical danger as the possibility of damage to the car.

The drive up the trail was an adventure in itself. We made frequent stops to seek ways of navigating around boulders, skirting jagged holes or crawling inch by inch on the edge of canyons without tumbling hundreds of feet to the bottom.

Meanwhile the sun was sinking lower on the horizon and the weather was becoming uncomfortably chilly for our blood, thinned by the monsoon heat of the lowlands. When we finally did reach the base cabin, it was with the same sense of relief that I imagine early sea rovers felt when they finally discovered land.

There was a small delegation of tribesmen there, headed by a lanky, broad-shouldered individual who turned out to be the headman of the nearby village and a famous bear-hunter. He had, we were told, personally slain scores of the 400-pound Himalaya black bears, several of them virtually with his own hands! He strongly recommended an immediate hunt.

Hal sighed and with an apologetic look of "How did we ever get ourselves into *this* fix?" shouldered his equipment while David and I picked up the smaller cameras we normally carried at such times.

"We're ready," Hal said.

"Atcha, sa'ab." Goroo reached into the car and produced a small leather sack roughly the size of an airline bag.

Hal looked questioningly as we proceeded along a narrow, soaring path that led from the forest into the high mountains above us. "Cameras, Mr. Goroo?"

"Oh no." Our host grinned at us, patting the bag. "The gun!"

"Gun?"

"Of course. How else can we shoot a bear?"

David stared in fascination at Goroo's leather bag. "Do you think he's carrying a submachine gun like those gangsters in the movies on television?"

Our footing was precarious. We followed a narrow trail over shale and small rocks which could easily turn an unwary ankle. And as we toiled upward, the increasing altitude brought back alarming memories of our experiences in the highlands of Peru and Bolivia. Finally we could only take three or four steps at a time without resting, our chests heaving for a few minutes before we could continue.

We struggled upward for two hours. I was sure that each step would be the last I could take, but I always managed another. David felt the climb least of all.

Our advance scout, the redoubtable headman, was a dim figure on the other side of a ridge when he froze and signaled to us with his hand.

"He's sighted a bear," whispered Goroo.

When we reached the ridge, Hal took a film sequence of the bear on a distant slope; our telephoto lens can make a distant object appear to be as near to one as his hand.

Then he turned to Goroo. "Now where's the gun?"

Goroo opened his bag. He produced several pieces of metal and wood which he proceeded to bolt together as though they were parts of a jigsaw puzzle. The finished product was obiously a rifle of sorts. Mr. Goroo handed the weapon to Hal.

Hal examined it dubiously. He glanced at me, shrugged,

and then said, "This seems rather puny for bears as large as the ones you claim roam around here."

"Oh, it's effective," said Goroo. "Here, let me load it." He took the weapon from my husband and slipped a small shell into the breach.

Hal whispered to me. "This thing has a caliber scarcely larger than that of our tiny pistol. I'm afraid a hit would only annoy a bear."

"And don't worry about anything," Goroo reassured us. "These bullets work. I filled them with powder myself!" He was quite proud.

Hal shook his head. "How'd we ever get ourselves into a fix like this?" He handed me the movie camera. "I think there's enough light left for you to get some action *if* I'm able to see the target."

I fingered the camera. David came close to my side. The two tribesmen who were along as extra beaters remained with us, and Hal and Goroo went forward to join the headman.

I was shivering as I placed my eye against the view-finder and watched my husband through the crystal-clear glass aperture. I saw the headman point and I could see the bear on a distant slope, and then the three men plunged into a ravine and disappeared from sight.

The sun abruptly dipped behind a distant notch in the mountains. For a few minutes we were enveloped in a dim half-light. I heard a distant flat *whaap* that sounded like a large stick being broken in two, but the hollow echoes that followed, repeating themselves from ravine to ravine, told me it had been a shot.

Another of those strange sound effects followed and then as darkness began to fall, the echoes fragmented and finally faded, leaving only the sound of our heavy breathing.

Although it seemed like hours, it could not have been more than twenty or thirty minutes before we heard Hal, Goroo and the headman approaching. The latter appeared first, as fresh as though all the hiking and scurrying about had been no more than a stroll down a shady lane. Hal and Goroo were both winded. In between gasps Hal told me what had happened.

They had stalked the animal and Hal had taken aim and had fired from extreme range as the bear was about to go over a distant ridge. The hand-loaded bullet had landed far short of the animal. Hal had loaded and fired again, this time purposely aiming more than a dozen feet over the animal's head as it climbed the distant slope. The thud of the bullet striking flesh plus the bear's grunt told him that he had scored a hit. The animal had managed to climb over the ridge and immediately plunged into the brush on the other side. From the amount of blood they found on the foliage, both Goroo and the headman were convinced that the bear had received a mortal wound, but neither of them felt we should risk pursuing a wounded animal with night at hand.

"We'll have to camp in the cabin and start out after him at daybreak," Hal said.

I thought of the luxurious *Lone Star* anchored back on the lake and sighed so deeply that Hal put his arm around me in sympathy.

And now the darkness enveloped us. The two tiny kerosene lamps carried by the tribesmen cast a fitful glow on the difficult, dangerous trail as we retraced our steps down the slippery, rocky path. In single file, slipping on loose, muddy shale, we toiled down and down until we reached the cabin. Here we would rest for what remained of the night.

Our "rest house" was primitive and had only one cot in a small separate room. The climb had almost completely exhausted us. We were not only cold but thirsty and famished. We had resigned ourselves to the prospects of an enforced fast, but to our happy surprise we found a fire waiting for us and an almost scalding sweet tea plus a thick soup that contained large pieces of lamb. It was truly simple fare but as far as we were concerned it was a gourmet's feast.

Goroo seemed merely to peck at his bowl. He wore a rather

glum expression. Hal finally asked if anything was wrong.
For a moment Goroo tried to be evasive and then he made a
full confession. His reputation as a knowledgeable guide,
bear-finder and whatnot was at stake. "Unless we shoot a
bear, Mr. Leenker."

"But I've shot a bear. And come daylight I hope we'll find
him."

Goroo shook his head. "We must make sure you get one,"
he said. "In the morning we'll really look—with beaters, everything."

I longingly thought of the *Lone Star* again and how nice
breakfast on that pleasant houseboat would be. Hal gave me
an apologetic glance and shrugged.

I smiled and put my hand over his. "Just think, Hal-minn.
A bearskin will round off our den at home."

I turned to our son. David's face was cradled in his folded
forearm which rested on the roughhewn table. He was sound
asleep.

Merely looking at him made us yawn with renewed exhaustion. We roused him and led him to the "bedroom." There
Hal told me he would share a straw-filled mattress with David.

"Nonsense!" I exclaimed. "There's room for David and me
on the cot."

"It'll be a tight squeeze," Hal mumbled.

"It's cold," I pointed out.

My husband grunted and stretched out on the mattress laid
out on the floor. David toppled onto the cot. By the time I
joined him, balancing my body on the opposite side, he and
Hal were both dead to the world. And before I knew it I also
dropped off to sleep as though I had been poleaxed.

A moment later, or so it seemed, my husband was shaking
me gently. "It's three o'clock, Halla. Time to get moving."

I ached all over. David stirred but I urged him to go back
to sleep, promising that we'd come back after we'd finished our
bear hunt. But David's recuperative power was as strong as

ever. He bounced up from the uncomfortable cot, ready, able and eager to push on with us.

Whatever grogginess I felt melted the instant we shuffled into the main room of the cabin to find hot tea and homemade biscuits awaiting us. This simple but effective *chota hazri* (the Hindustani equivalent of the continental breakfast) suddenly made me feel enthusiastic, almost gay, about our adventure.

Setting forth in the predawn darkness with only the flickering light of the headman's kerosene lantern to guide us, I was more conscious than ever before of being in a "forest primeval."

The sound of our passing roused unseen animals into premature wakefulness. We heard querulous, sleepy chirps and gruntings which Goroo whispered came from monkeys. For two hours we walked through the woods in the black of night, following an almost invisible trail.

It was 5 o'clock and dawn was near when we found ourselves atop one of the ridges which march like waves, higher and higher to the eternal Himalaya Mountains. Here our expedition halted. Goroo and the headman explained the strategy. David and I and one of the tribesmen were to remain here while he, Hal and the chief went on to waylay the bears. The tribesmen with us would shout and drive any bears that appeared up toward where the hunters were waiting.

Hal, David and I listened intently. The technique was as simple as it was ancient and universal.

And then Hal started worrying. "Which way did you say the bears would be driven?"

"That way," Goroo said, pointing.

"But what if they come this way instead of toward where we're waiting?" I asked.

"Oh, we'll be able to shoot them before they get this far," Goroo assured me.

My expression mirrored what I was thinking.

Hal came to my side. "The devil with it," he said. "We'll just get some pictures and call it quits."

But something stirred within me, perhaps an adventurous feeling that came from my Viking forebears. "No—we've gone this far and we might as well see the whole thing through."

My husband hesitated and then reached into his hip pocket and brought forth the tiny .25-caliber pistol he always carried when we were in out-of-the-way places.

He handed the weapon to me. I was quite familiar with its operation, since I had fired it once or twice on a range back home.

"Just in case, elskan-min," he said. "You and David hide in these rocks. If a bear should come your way, fire in his direction but make sure you don't hit him! The tiny slug would only enrage him, but the noise will scare him off."

I casually fingered the pistol and urged my husband on. "I'll use this only if I have to."

David and I and the native tribesman, who was ordered to stay near us, sat down near some rocks as the sun began to peek over the mountains. The time passed slowly. At first the morning daylight revealed a canvas of natural scenic beauty that thoroughly absorbed our attention. But the warm sun brought out something else. Mosquitoes. They swarmed from the brush. A few of their "scouts" sampled my Icelandic blood and went buzzing off. Their retreat did not fool me. I'd experienced this before. I knew that they were shouting in mosquito language, "Hey, fellers! Fresh blood! Come a-running!"

I told David to prepare himself. And as we both pulled our socks over our slacks, turned up our shirt collars and thrust our hands into our pockets, the main army attacked in force.

There was nothing to do but sit and wait while myriads of tiny engines whined and buzzed in our ears as one hungry mosquito after another circled, "peeled off" and zeroed in on us again. Then we heard a single reverberating shot quickly followed by two more. We forgot our insect tormentors and jumped to our feet. In the distance, atop a ridge, I saw the tiny figures of Goroo and the turbaned headman standing and waving to us. Our native guard, who had been dozing all this while (the mosquitoes ignored *him*), sat up just as David and I began to run toward Goroo, and followed us. We literally flew over rocky, uneven ground, crashing through the brush as surefooted as though we had spent a lifetime there.

Goroo grinned broadly when we reached his side. "Memsa'ab!"—he waved into a gorge—"your husband has got his bear!"

It was barely 6 o'clock in the morning. Even as I went over to congratulate Hal, I was mentally calculating time and space—a determined hike downhill to the car and then a fast drive and, with luck, we'd have a wonderful dinner and sleep in solid comfort aboard the *Lone Star.*

The black bear was large. It weighed at least 300 pounds. With much happy chattering, the tribesmen took over while Hal looked tired but pleased. David and I watched. They cut down saplings from a nearby tree, gathered several long vines, fashioned poles and tied the bear to the poles. Then, singing a chant, they formed a victorious cavalcade and set forth for the cabin, taking turns carrying the bear two at a time while the others kept clapping Hal on the back and shouting unintelligible remarks that were undoubtedly words of high praise.

Hal felt rather embarrassed by all this fuss, but the pleasure of the villagers over his kill was so genuine and vociferous that any qualms he might have had about shooting the creature quickly vanished.

Back at the cabin, Goroo, beaming expansively, prepared tea and a luncheon snack while more villagers—among them girls and women who wore magnificently decorated silver earrings and ornaments in their nostrils—gathered and watched the headman skin the animal.

Although Hal and David watched, I preferred to gaze at the scenery. The job was finally finished. The skin, complete with head, was placed in a sack and presented to the "sah'b and memsah'b and chota" (little sah'b) and we were at last free to begin our descent toward the comforts of civilization.

Just then a panting tribesman came running up from the other direction. It was the one who had been with us on our long climb the night before. He gasped out a torrent of words to Goroo, whose face broke into a broad smile.

"Ah, Sahib Linker, you are indeed lucky! They tracked the bear you shot last night and found it dead in the thicket. You have *two* bears!"

Only the obvious joy of the women and children of the village at this news of the removal of another potential danger took my mind off my typical housewife's problem: Where in the world will I put that second skin?

13
Devil Dancers of Nepal

TRAVELING from Kashmir to the tiny Kingdom of Nepal, mountainous homeland of the fierce Gurkhas, was like flitting in and out of a moist bake oven.

The "oven" was monsoon-stricken New Delhi, where we paused long enough to transfer from the DC-3 that had flown us from Srinagar to another plane that flew us to Katmandu, Nepal's capital. Both Srinagar and Katmandu are in the Himalaya Mountains, but there is no direct route connecting them, and New Delhi must be used as a transfer point.

Katmandu nestles trustingly at the feet of awesome, ice-helmeted sentinels—mighty Mount Everest, Makalu, Gauri Sankar, Annapurna and Kanchenjunga. Although during our inbound flight and for days afterward these peaks had worn mantles of thick monsoon clouds, we were very much aware of their brooding presence.

A tiny country with an area of less than 55,000 square miles, with northern and southern borders extending for several hundred miles along the boundaries of India and Tibet, Nepal turned out to be a colorful museum of antiquity interspersed here and there with evidence that the Nepalese are casually trying to catch up with the rest of the world.

191

Although the country is predominantly Hindu, Buddhism still retains a hold on a great number of Nepalese. I discovered that they are really two entirely different peoples: the classic short, stocky, bandy-legged Gurkha with the Mongolian characteristics often described by Kipling; and the slender, tall, lighter-complexioned Nepali. Despite the ethnic backgrounds of the two, they have one thing in common—energy and optimism for their country's future.

For centuries the Gurkhas had formed the elite battalions of Britain's Indian Army. Since India has gained its independence, there have been Gurkha regiments in its ranks. And we were surprised to find that an equal number of these fierce little warriors still fight under the banner of Great Britain as "Soldiers of the Queen." Although I never thought to inquire, I would not be at all surprised to learn that there are Gurkhas, or at least their first cousins, wearing the uniform of the Pakistan Army.

In the teeming, narrow streets of Katmandu we saw many of these compactly built fighters wearing their British-style military shirts and shorts with Australian "digger-type" campaign hats jauntily cocked on their heads.

Our Katmandu headquarters were in the Royal Hotel, a rambling baroque building which was once the residence of a prime minister. Our host was a somewhat mysterious White Russian in his middle fifties named Boris Lissanovitch, who had been in Nepal for a number of years. The story we heard was that he had rendered a number of services to the government, and among his rewards had been this property, which he immediately transformed into a hotel.

Like all such smallish cities in out-of-the-way places, Katmandu's knowledgeable circles—which include both the Nepal upper class and the foreign colony—hinted that Mr. Lissanovitch's background was full of international foreign intrigue. From information dropped in casual conversation, Hal and I inferred that, as a person privy to the king, Lissanovitch exerted considerable influence on Nepal's affairs and that the hotel bit was merely camouflage.

In appearance and deportment he was polite, rather reserved and always impeccably dressed, as befitted a successful hotel owner. Or spy? We rather felt that the latter role was the more authentic.

His wife, an attractive woman perhaps half his age, went out of her way to make our stay most agreeable. They had three sons: Mischa, four; Alexander, eight; and Nicholas, ten. They of course made our visit to Katmandu perfect for David; the boys got along famously.

The hotel itself was fun, even if accommodations were somewhat primitive since the structure had not originally been built as a hotel. There were rows of rooms and corridors running in every direction. We frequently got lost on the way from our rooms to the dining room and found ourselves wandering through ornate ballrooms and other chambers that must have seen many a state function during the days when the building was occupied by a personage holding high office.

Nicholas told us, quite seriously, that every now and then the family made new discoveries, not only of passageways and chambers but of interesting relics of the past, many of which turned out to be of historic value.

The windows of our rooms were screened. However, the transom openings over the doors had no protection against mosquitoes and flies. When we pointed out this omission to the native desk clerk, he nodded and promised to screen the transoms immediately. Meanwhile we used sprays of insect repellent. When the screens were finally installed, three days later, we had grown accustomed to the DDT routine and continued, as a matter of routine, the nightly ritual of spraying before retiring.

The city itself was like no other we had seen in the world. Possibly its strangeness was due to the heavy wooden timbers, ornately carved, used in construction. Balconies of carved wood extended over the streets and produced a flavor reminiscent of many medieval towns we had visited in Europe.

Here and there we saw fairly modern structures, mostly built with technical and financial aid from Great Britain and the United States. The pedestrian traffic was heavy, cheerfully noisy and extremely colorful. Intermingled with the cocky uniformed Gurkhas, all of whom carried their formidable kukri knives, were the taller Nepalese males, who wore long tunics and tight-fitting jodhpur-type trousers. The women wore either long, brilliantly colored skirts or saris. Here and there were fierce-looking Tibetan tribesmen with long, tangled black hair and bracelet-adorned, muscular arms. These formidable individuals were refugees from the Chinese invasions of their homeland. From their appearance one would suppose that they could more than hold their own with the Gurkhas. It was astonishing to realize that the shorter, more agreeable and by far cleaner, little Gurkhas were actually their superiors, man for man, in warfare!

Actually the most interesting aspects of Katmandu were the many Hindu and Buddhist temples and the Royal Palace grounds. Shopping opportunities for tourists are limited to souvenirs such as the kukri, which is a heavy-bladed, curved weapon akin to the machete of Latin America. Kukri blades have a reverse curve. By that I mean that the sharp point swoops forward—just the opposite of, for example, an Arabian or Turkish saber or scimitar, whose curve arcs toward the rear. The blade is fairly narrow at the hilt and widens toward the top as it curves forward. They are razor-sharp, rather dangerous, and all are encased in leather scabbards. Affixed to the scabbards are two small receptacles, one containing a small, sharp knife to be used for eating, the other a file for sharpening the kukri. According to legend, Gurkhas are supposed to draw the kukri blade from the scabbard only to draw blood. If there is no battle to be fought, a Gurkha

will prick his own skin and draw token blood before returning the weapon to its sheath. Kukris, theoretically at least, are
never used for such utilitarian purposes as hacking through
jungle. In Latin America, machetes—almost as formidable as
weapons—also serve as tools and hatchets.

Hal bought an ornate, beautifully decorated kukri to add
to our growing collection at home. Later, after we had returned, a visitor who had seen the Gurkhas in action during
World War II told us that the doughty little brown warriors
had cheerfully used their kukris on Japanese soldiers!

The temples at Pathan, the holy city a few miles from Katmandu, are fantastic. We entered Durbar Square and gazed
in amazement at a statue erected to Hanuman, the Hindu
monkey god, that stands in front of the Royal Palace. During
past centuries the Nepalese Hindus fed this deity sweets with
the result that the effigy's face has been completely reduced
to a sort of sticky glob!

This monkey god, Hanuman, according to the Hindu religion, is the central figure of the Ramayana saga. He helped
Rama, a reincarnation of Vishnu, recover his wife Sita from
the clutches of a demon.

The Narayan Hity Durbar Palace turned out to be a cam-
eraman's dream. We were able to get all sorts of angles for
both our motion picture and still cameras of the many statues
of Vishnu and of an elephant god shown riding on the back
of a mouse! I had read that imagination plays a major role in
Hinduism; this intriguing statue was positive proof to us.

The palace itself, guarded by a sentry clad in jodhpurs and
armed with an ancient symbolic musket, proved to be a mixture of Chinese and Indian architecture. Each structure bore
carvings depicting Hindu religious mythology, not excluding
Siva and his wife Parvati in a variety of intimate aspects more
typical of mere mortal life.

The streets of the "old town" also provided the usual sprin-
kling of Hindu holy men with unkempt, matted hair and
almost nude bodies who evidently feel that cleanliness must

be the devil's own weapon. Many carry tridents, the symbol of trinity in their religion. Photographing them is interesting—and tricky; their reactions before a camera are unpredictable.

Probably the most interesting Nepalese, aside from the Gurkhas, are the famed Sherpa mountain people. It is from this group that Sir Edmund Hillary recruited Sherpa Tenzing, who helped make the Englishman's conquest of Mount Everest possible.

Our exploration of Nepal grew more interesting after we were introduced to Shumshere Arjun, a former member of the ruling nobility which had been ousted from power. Arjun had been given a responsible post with Nepal's government tourist office. Although he had lost his noble rank, his style of living had not been at all affected. He still resided in a comfortable palace with his wife and his two charming daughters, sixteen and eighteen.

During a rather sumptuous luncheon at Arjun's home, Hal asked the girls to don their formal Nepali costumes and pose for his camera. The first costumes were beautifully brocaded garments that bore some resemblance to the Indian sari. The girls then changed into the wedding regalia worn by their parents. The younger daughter emerged in the garment worn by her father, while the eighteen-year-old appeared in a regal scarlet robe, jeweled headdress and ornate earrings with huge, semiprecious blue stones.

This costume, we were told, would be worn by her at her own wedding. And when we asked when that happy event would take place, she reacted as most young women do, with blushes, and giggles, and retired in happy confusion.

In all our travels we have always tried to capture the real atmosphere of nations and peoples through their unique costumes, music and dances. Nepal was no exception. Arjun and our mysterious Boris Lissanovitch arranged a performance at the hotel for the benefit of our cameras. While the music and movements were quite similar to those we had seen in India, their mountaineer energy gave each gyration an impetus that their lowland cousins could never have achieved.

This tiny kingdom is crammed with places to film. Arjun provided us with an authoritative guide, an almost ethereal-looking professor, J. P. Sharma, who taught at the university. In spite of his Nepalese features, he was the typically detached, mild-mannered, forgetful savant—forgetful when it came to his personal belongings and such practical things as food, but a fountain of information when he spoke of his nation.

While wandering through some of the city's temples (one of which showed in gruesome detail a blood-red Hanuman eating the vital organs of sinners), we came across a group of street musicians performing a weird cacophony of sounds while a tiny boy who couldn't have been more than seven or eight and wore nothing but a long shirt stood in front of them and shrieked at the top of his voice. It was quite deafening. At first we thought that he was berating the musicians for their performance.

Professor Sharma mildly corrected us. "He is what you would call, a troubador. He is singing about the national hero Sherpa Tenzing and how he conquered Mount Everest. These people are all Sherpas."

Hal looked at him. "Has he mentioned Sir Hillary?"

Professor Sharma smiled. "Not yet. Somehow I don't think he will!"

The town itself was fairly busy. Artisans were at work in open shops, fabricating decorative tiles with inlaid stones. Tailors and dressmakers could be seen haggling while sewing or fitting garments on customers. The food stalls were many and crowded with both people and flies.

Passing one stall, I happened to notice some women who sat on the ground engaged in making what appeared to be mudcakes. When I asked what these were, the professor seemed embarrassed by my question. I persisted, assuming that they were probably a sort of peat that is sold for heating purposes.

"It's fuel, Mrs. Leenker," he said.

"Fuel?"

He nodded, then continued academically, "It is actually cow dung which, when dried, is used for fuel for cooking."

Most of the villages and towns adjacent to Katmandu have remained almost unchanged through the ages and Bathgaon, the other holy city, is exactly as it must have been hundreds of years ago.

It has its own Durbar Square (as do most of the settlements in Nepal) and that means not only an ancient royal residence but ornate, rather overwhelming Hindu and Buddhist temples.

Our prime objective here was to film the Kathakali dances. While Hal, David and Professor Sharma were busy with arrangements for a special performance, I wandered over to a nearby four-storied temple. At first glance the carvings seemed typical of what I had seen in Katmandu and elsewhere, but a closer inspection made me gasp. The numerous figures that covered the walls under the eaves of the roof were gods and goddesses indulging in sexual acts of every conceivable type.

Several Sherpas, noticing my transfixed expression, paused and chattered in their own tongue, obviously amused by my reaction to the "art." My face flushed. Then I was saved by the sound of Hal's voice as he approached with David and the professor, all involved in earnest conversation.

I whirled around and ran to meet them. "Let's see what's down this side street," I urged, grabbing David's arm.

Hal, caught in midsentence, looked up in amazement. "But that isn't the way to the dancers," he explained patiently, giving me a perplexed look.

"I know, but I'm curious about this side street," I insisted.

The professor, glancing over my shoulder, understood immediately. With a solemn expression, he agreed with me. "By all means. There is something very interesting that I would like to show you in that street." He grasped the arms of Hal and David, gave me a knowing glance, and led my husband and son away.

Later on when I had a chance to tell Hal what had happened, he whistled and nodded in agreement. "Boy, oh boy!" he exclaimed. "A nine-year-old's questions are difficult enough to answer. Just imagine the ones David would have asked, if he'd seen those carvings! But that explains why the professor took us down that long street just to show us an ordinary wooden balcony on an ordinary house!"

The Hindu temple that formed the background for the dances was more (shall we say?) sedate. At least the carved figures were involved in matters spiritual rather than erotic. In an open area before the temple, guarded by four huge figures —each fifteen feet high and representing the elements of earth, air, fire and water—the Bathgaon dancers, waving swords and wearing demoniacal masks with huge, staring eyes, put on a rather bloodcurdling performance for us.

Directly behind them, guarding a stairway that led to the temple entrance, were two grotesque carved giants bearing massive clubs. The weird, wailing, screeching music and the weaving bodies of dancers in costumes representing animals and goddesses produced shivers along my spine. We filmed and recorded the wild music as the dancers leaped, gyrated and whirled, flailing about with their swords.

Professor Sharma explained that the dances had to do with the black goddess Maha Kali, consort of Siva. Kali is the goddess of death and destruction. The movements, music and costumes all told of her legendary experiences.

After an early start one morning, we found ourselves on the bank of Nepal's sacred river, the Bagmati. As in every other part of the country, the area was dotted with temples. Professor Sharma had us stop at one of these places of worship where clouds of thick, greasy smoke were rising to the overcast sky.

He told us that a Hindu cremation was in progress. Nepal also has its burning ghats, as does India. Hal filmed the procedure as a temple attendant casually added logs to the fire and poked at the still unburned flesh in the flame, to assure complete cremation of the body.

Our goal was a Tibetan lamasery dominated by a temple called a stupa in Nepal. The professor told us that these stupas originally were the graves of religious leaders. It was only "recently"—within the last several thousand years—that the stupa evolved from a grave covered by a large mound of earth into a place of Buddhist worship.

The lamasery we were to visit is called Boud-Nath Stupa and is 2,500 years old. Professor Sharma was not optimistic about our being able to move about too freely within the sacred confines. "It depends entirely upon how the spiritual leader, the Chinya Lama, happens to feel," he explained.

It was some time before the Chinya Lama made his appearance. As we waited, we smelled the odor of burning incense and watched the monks silently march by, each spinning the silver prayer wheels imbedded in the walls of the temple as he passed, muttering the words of the famous Buddhist prayer: "Om mani padme hum" ("Hail to the jewel in the lotus"). This commemorates the birth of Gautama Buddha who, according to tradition, was born in a lotus.

The atmosphere was rather awesome as we waited below the dome of the stupa's great, staring eyes.

Then the lamasery doors opened and out marched a short, bespectacled, genial-looking man who resembled Harry S. Truman, wearing the robes of a high Lama! Although his English was not easily understood, his gestures, wide smile and obvious eagerness were unmistakable. Like his far-off American double, the Chinya Lama was a gregarious, genial politician! Did we wish pictures of monks? Of course! A snap of his fingers, a few sharp commands, and we had an entire company ready to do our bidding.

A souvenir? Prayer wheels? Authentic Buddhist prayer wheels. Wonderful workmanship. Artistic. Most reasonable. And, he told us seriously, with Professor Sharma interpreting, they would make excellent investments; back in our country they'd be worth twice what we'd be paying for them!

David noticed a fantastic dance mask adorned with yak-tail hair. The Chinya Lama clapped his hands. Two monks immediately appeared with several masks for our inspection. Rubbing his palms, the Lama again turned to us with a beaming smile and an expression that plainly said, "And what else may I do for you?"

My attention had been drawn to a small Tibetan trumpet made of bone. When I called Hal's attention to it, our cheerful, businesslike Chinya Lama again snapped his fingers and, lo! we were the owners of a genuine Tibetan lamasery ritualistic trumpet used to summon the faithful.

Professor Sharma was surprised and perplexed. "Things have changed here," he muttered. "Perhaps they need money. Take this horn, for instance. It is made from the thigh bone of a dead monk!"

I almost dropped the thing. Hal stared at him incredulously. The Chinya Lama gazed from us to Sharma and then began to ask questions. The professor interpreted. When the Chinya learned the cause of our distress, he laughed and patted our shoulders reassuringly. Then he launched into a dissertation which, when translated, told us that Tibetan monks will their bodies to the lamasery. Knowing that their bones will be put to use, they evidently feel better about going forth to sit for eternity at the feet of Buddha. Since the money we paid for the bone went to the lamasery, the Lama felt that he was sticking to the spirit of the dead monk's wishes.

Our problem now was how to disengage ourselves from the lavish hospitality of the Chinya Lama. Professor Sharma brought matters to a head for us by insisting that since our time was growing short, we should film the dancing, chanting monks at once and return to Katmandu where—with an apologetic cough—"The Amrikans have to catch an airplane."

The Chinya Lama clucked with disappointment. But Sharma's little white lie worked. Our amazing host proved his ability as a theatrical entrepreneur and directed his dancing, chanting, bell-ringing monks through their intricate routine.

Following profuse farewells and the payment of additional baksheesh in Nepalese rupees, we finally escaped.

But once in the car Sharma paused. "And now let's visit the other lamasery."

"You mean there are two Tibetan lamaseries here?" Hal asked.

Sharma nodded. "And they are great rivals. Had the Chinya Lama known we were going to the other—a newly established one, by the way—he'd have been far less genial. Actually the lamasery we are about to visit was put up by survivors of an ancient Tibetan holy place overrun by the invading Red Chinese a few years ago. The monks set up their own temple after arriving here. The Chinya Lama did not like the—the—" He floundered for the proper expression.

"Competition?" Hal suggested wryly.

"That's it. Competition. There has been rivalry between the two from the beginning."

I was about to comment on the absurdity of two temples of the same faith not being able to get along when I remembered the interdenominational church rivalries at home and in other Christian countries. I decided to say nothing.

Although the new lamasery was rather tiny by comparison with the Chinya Lama's establishment, it seemed to have a more authentic atmosphere. Sharma explained that the monks carried out their daily rituals and living habits exactly as in the remote corners of Tibet. There was no commercial aspect here whatsoever. We were invited to enter the lamasery and immediately found ourselves in the past. The building was plunged in a gloom relieved only by small flames that burned yak butter in tiny dishes. Seated in two long rows, facing the pathway along which we tiptoed, sat chanting monks wearing maroon robes. The odor was overwhelming; bathing certainly was not part of their discipline.

They paid no attention to us, not even when we set up our portable lights and began to film them. It was as though we were invisible. It was a weird, moving experience and when we had finished and made our rather one-sided farewells, I felt much as a traveler suddenly transported into the past might feel upon returning to his own era.

Professor Sharma remarked, with a twinkle, "I assume you noticed the difference between this lamasery and the other one?"

I thought of the Chinya Lama's comparative luxury and nodded.

On our way back to the Royal Hotel, I remembered that the next day, July 27th, would be David's tenth birthday. I discussed this in whispers with Hal during our drive back to Katmandu. He grinned and assured me that "special plans" had been made. Professor Sharma nodded and I wondered what part the droll old savant would play in those plans.

Hal provided a birthday cake, and the Lissanovitch family, including their three sons, joined in the celebration. Then Professor Sharma's surprise arrived—a huge elephant from the household of the King of Nepal, fully turned out and with the royal decorations that had been painted on its head still visible, and guided by a royal mahout!

The latter, wearing a graven expression, had the ponderous beast kneel so David could climb aboard with all the ceremony accorded a maharajah, as though riding royal elephants was an everyday occurrence in his young life. After a solemn tour of the hotel grounds, David debarked and received the third surprise of the day—a miniature kukri knife presented by the younger Lissanovitch son on behalf of the entire family. The legend on the kukri was carefully preserved: the youngster gravely pricked his thumb with the needle-sharp point, to "draw ritualistic blood," and only then handed it to David.

As for me, I mentally vowed to have a serious talk with my son and tell him to forget this bloodletting nonsense when he showed off his present to his schoolmates back home.

14

The Lost Cities of Cambodia

THE arena was almost full when the car that had picked us up at the Rama Hotel deposited us at the entrance to Bangkok's boxing stadium. It was still a quarter of an hour before 5:30 in the evening, the official starting time of a typical professional Siamese prize fight program.

I hadn't really wanted to go. The sight of men flailing away at one another is not for me, but Hal had assured me that nowhere else in the world would I see anything even remotely resembling the Thai form of boxing.

We had been told that pugilism as practiced in this corner of Southeast Asia would be full of surprises. It turned out to be downright astonishing, to put it mildly. When we entered the stadium, our ears were assailed by a din of babbling voices competing with wailing, shrieking music produced by an energetic, perspiring orchestra that occupied two rows of seats among the spectators.

We settled ourselves and gazed at the ring. The gladiators scheduled to meet in the first bout were engaged in a strange ritualistic dance to the beat of the "music." They postured, gyrated, grimaced and glided from one corner of the ring to the other where they knelt and adopted a momentary attitude of prayer before leaping to their feet and resuming the entire routine.

One wore red boxing trunks, the other blue. Bound around their biceps were sacred cords, for good luck, we learned. Another cord, called the mongkon, was bound around their heads. But we quickly learned that this was removed before the fight began.

The dance was an act of homage to their teachers, the gods and of course to the paying audience. After ten minutes of this novel exhibition, the fighters were formally introduced to the audience which by now completely filled every nook and cranny of the stadium. The tourist office representative who accompanied us explained that although both fighters wore modern boxing gloves, they could use elbows, knees and feet as well as fists!

This particularly astonished David, who by then was learning the manly art of self-defense at his school's gymnasium. "You mean they kick each other?" He had to shout to be heard.

"Oh yes!" Our companion grinned. "However, they cannot use judo holds, butt with their heads, bite or spit. Also their toenails must be cut before the fight!"

The introductions were finished, the ring was cleared, and now there arose a mighty roar from the crowd. Then it grew quiet except for the music while the two opponents, both small, wiry young men, cautiously circled one another, each searching for an opening.

As they warmed to their task the music increased in tempo and volume. It reminded me of the old-time silent movies that Hal and I occasionally see in a Hollywood neighborhood theater showing Charlie Chaplin and Harold Lloyd comedies and the old D. W. Griffith epics. There a pianist established the mood for the silent scenes interspersed with subtitles. It was very much like that in Bangkok's stadium.

However humorous it may have looked to us, the fighters were taking a good deal of punishment despite the ballet atmosphere. Both men moved with lightning speed, particularly when they abandoned the use of their fists and "boxed" with their feet. Our tourist office companion explained that the French type of boxing known as *savate,* which also permits the use of the feet, originated in Siam.

When one of the opponents sagged against the ropes and the crowd's roar drowned out the orchestra, our host noticed me wince and avert my head.

"These are modern days, Madame Leenker. Now they use gloves. In the old days they wrapped hemp rope around their fists and sprinkled ground glass in the hemp. *Then* the boxing was *rough!*"

Three matches provided all the film we needed. We picked our way out of the stiflingly hot stadium and came outside into a refreshing sprinkle of rain that made the street lights of this fantastic Thailand capital sparkle like jewels.

We had been in this fabulous land of "Anna and the King" several days after arriving from Katmandu and Calcutta. Although we were in a land a mere ten feet above sea level and the monsoon was on, it was a comparatively mild kind of monsoon compared to those we had endured in India.

From the moment our plane had circled Bangkok (the name in Siamese is Krung Thep), I had fallen in love with this city of almost two million people. When I first met Hal, he told me of having visited Bangkok during his first around-the-world trip the year before he came to Iceland. Many times, first in Iceland before we were married and afterward at home in Hollywood, I had gazed at his films of Bangkok, its many temples—or wats, as they are called—and the graceful dancers whose hideously carved, gargoyle-like masks and towering spiked headdresses contrast with their deliberate, feathery dancing steps.

During our first trip around the world, before David was born, we had flown east to west from Hong Kong directly to Calcutta and East Pakistan, bypassing Thailand and Southeast Asia.

Now I was here in fabled Siam.

Bisected by the Chao Phya River and crisscrossed by canals called klongs, Bangkok is the Venice of the Far East. Although there are numerous cars and trucks as well as scooters, motorcycles and bikes, the populace's most important route of transportation consists of these waterways on which supplies of rice, poultry, fruit, vegetables and pork are floated back and forth.

I suppose that the first lasting impression I received after landing was the cheerful disposition of the Thailanders. They were all smiles, even the customs and immigration officials. I was not a bit surprised to learn that the name by which Thailand comes to be known to most visitors is the Land of Smiles. And it is significant that *mai ben rail*, which means "never mind," sums up their attitude to the exigencies of their daily existence.

Beneath their happy-go-lucky exterior, however, there lies a spirit of prideful independence. Rich or poor, the Thai walk erect, secure in the knowledge that they have always been an independent nation and have never been under foreign rule.

At the time of our visit Thailand was a welcome oasis of peace and stability in Southeast Asia, the rest of which was erupting in violence. Even then the United States's involvement in Viet Nam was starting to escalate from financial aid to military participation in the form of Army, Marine Corps and Navy technical advisers.

But in this charming capital of ornate temples, parks and floating bazaars, the ugliness of conflict seemed far away. After an early morning visit to the klong markets, we filmed the jammed traffic and noted the signs and towers of HST-TV, Thai television, which somehow do not seem out of place against the background of the magnificent marble Wat Benjama Bopit Temple and the 299 other Buddhist temples or wats to be found in and around Bangkok, or that of the tremendous, walled Grand Palace, with its glittering gold-and-porcelain spires.

Inside the Wat Benjama Wopit we found an aspect of Buddhist ritual that gave us much cause for thought. Filing past us came a group of monks wearing bright orange robes draped around their torsos like Roman togas. We were astonished to learn that they were actually Buddhist laymen, many of them professionals or businessmen who voluntarily give up a year of their lives to serve their religion by living the austere life of monks. They get their food by begging from door to door. The purpose of this practice is to instill in them a sense of humility, a cardinal virtue in the Buddhist religion. Hal and I have often wondered what would happen if some of our Western World's tycoons and statesmen embraced this remarkable religion and underwent such self-imposed hardship!

The grounds of the Royal Palace were like an illustration for a fantasy about life on another planet. In the spacious grounds were numerous memorial wats and temples adorned with gold. The Chakri Palace itself, actually the locale of *Anna and the King of Siam,* is guarded by enormous twenty-five-foot demons called yaksa, whose huge stone swords and ferocious masks are intended to frighten away evil spirits. Although they are only statues, I must admit that they were disconcerting to David and me. Their great, staring eyes and menacing grimaces seemed to follow us wherever we went. Later when we filmed Siamese dancers, we noted that their masks were replicas of the yaksa.

As though these demoniacal frighteners of evil spirits were not eerie enough, we next came upon the garuda, the winged demons that uphold the corners of a temple.

Nearby were other hideous-looking guardians consisting of leaning kinnari, bird figures with grotesque human heads! It was and still is, difficult for me to reconcile the gentle, good-natured Thai and the teachings of Buddhism, essentially a peaceful, philosophic faith, with all this rather startling belief in demonology.

But then again, in many ways the Thai are not too unlike the rest of us. After all, there is the boxing, which in one form or another is popular in most parts of the world. And even school children practice classical Siamese fencing with make-believe rather than real swords as part of the physical education of Thai students, and physical training is part of our own schools' curricula. When we attended an exhibition at a dancing school, we were entertained by a performance of the khon (masked drama) which dramatizes a battle recorded in the Hindu Ramayama wherein the deity Virunjumbung is shown helping his demon cousin Thsakarn in a battle against Rama or Vishnu on the ocean floor. And certainly drama and ballet are also popular in the United States.

The masked dancers act out each episode of this Hindu saga to the accompaniment of music that dates back for centuries. Each deliberate movement of arms, shoulders, fingers and even eyes tells a story. The dance ends with Virunjumbung's death at the hands of Hanuman, the monkey god whom Rama has pitted against him.

The performance is quite effective and after a while one gets the impression that the dancers are rather demoniacal themselves and not at all human. Only afterward when masks and headdresses were removed and I found myself confronted by flushed, excitedly smiling young faces, did I appreciate their professional artistic ability.

The battle epic was followed by a group of twenty costumed girls who performed a medieval Siamese classical routine depicting a group of angels celebrating a heavenly holiday. The performance ended with a blessing in the form of flower petals which the girls threw to the audience.

That night I found it hard to fall asleep, even in the air-conditioned comfort of our hotel. My head was too full of all that we had seen and filmed in Thailand. One thought led to another and before long I found myself staring up at the ceiling and seeing in my imagination fragments of South Africa, Tony Fajardo's camp, Dar es Salaam and the unruly, dangerous *dinamiteros* of Bolivia. It was like looking at a montage of motion pictures. And then as Chinya Lama's beaming, bespectacled features appeared and he began to speak in the dry Missouri accent of President Harry S. Truman, I finally drifted off right in the middle of a campaign speech!

The transport dipped low over the jungle and set us down at the outskirts of Siem Reap, in the center of Cambodia.

We had decided to explore Angkor Wat and Angkor Thom, the mysterious temple city and capital of the Khmers who built a mighty, flourishing civilization in the Cambodian jungle more than a thousand years ago and then disappeared without a trace, almost overnight.

The Mekong River had overflowed, as is usual during the monsoon rains, and the Great Lake, or Tonle Sap, close to Siem Reap, was swollen to seven times its normal size.

Hal had visited Angkor during his initial global filming jaunt in 1949 and had always wanted me to see the place. As we came out of the overheated plane into the humidity of Siem Reap, he gazed about the airport, which was little more than a muddy, unpaved landing strip, and remarked that the place had not changed much in twelve years.

But there *had* been a change. Our accommodations were in the new, air-conditioned part of the Grand Hotel; when he had first stayed there, mosquito bars on beds and ceiling fans had been the only conveniences.

Hal's first attempt to film the abandoned city had been partly frustrated by cloudy, rainy weather. "Probably in your honor, elskan-min, the weather is now excellent for photography," Hal remarked immediately upon our arrival.

We wasted no time getting to Angkor Wat and to the adjacent Angkor Thom. It would be well to point out here that Angkor Wat is primarily a city of wats or temples. Angkor

Thom was the actual residence of the lost populace and its rulers. The history of this mysterious lost civilization is intriguing. The Chinese rulers of the Middle Ages knew the Khmers and even maintained diplomatic relations and trade contacts with them. The catastrophe or other cause of the Khmers' disappearance must have occurred some six centuries ago. No one knows why or how this came abut. It is as though some gigantic force ended the existence of every Khmer of importance, leaving behind nothing but abandoned buildings. A strangely coincidental sort of mystery involves the fate of the ancient Mayans of Mexico and Guatemala. They, too, seem to have abandoned whole cities to the jungle, without any known reason, and to simply have vanished. It is interesting to note that two such mysterious events took place almost simultaneously in the 1300's on opposite sides of the world.

While it appears that the people who built these ancient monuments vanished without a trace, many of the Cambodians we met were living replicas of the Khmers depicted in the ornate temple carvings. They are undoubtedly direct descendants of those ancient people, just as the Mayas of today in Mexico's Yucatan and adjoining Guatemala can trace their antecedents back to that golden age of architecture, mathematics and science at Chichen Itza, Uxmal and Koban. But a mystifying thing about both races is the weird amnesia (I simply must so describe it) which seems to have overtaken the descendants of both gifted races. These progeny of masters of the sciences and arts are so far removed in learning from that of their ancestors that they can only gaze in awe at the marvels wrought by them and murmur, "The Gods must have built this. Only deities could work such wonders!"

I found an unusual geographical coincidence which may or may not link the Khmers with the Mayas. Aside from the fact that both civilizations seem to have disappeared almost simultaneously, there is the strange and thought-provoking fact that the main centers of the Mayas and those of the Khmers have certain similarities of geographical location. Both are about 15 degrees north of the equator and the Khmer centers are approximately 100 degrees *east* longitude, while those of the Mayas are about 100 degrees *west* longitude!

The encroaching jungle surrounding the vast, walled, dead Cambodian cities is a silent place, almost menacing, with but a few chattering monkeys and scarcely any bird life. When we approached the open portals of what our guide and driver called the Gate of Death to enter Angkor Thom, we had a feeling of profound awe. But when I looked through the portal and saw the two rows of hideous Khmer god demons holding the Naga serpent that stood guard at the entrance, I understood at once where the gate got its ominous name. It was easy to imagine how war captives of the Khmers must have felt as they were dragged in chains through the gate to slavery or death. Just gazing at the frightening statues was eerie.

This is only one of five gateways to the center of Angkor Thom. And all of them lead to roads guarded by demons and gods which serve as a warning to those who cross the surrounding moat on their way to the center of the ancient city —a city which, according to some archaeologists, was founded in 900 A.D.

Angkor Thom is laid out as a square. Each side is approximately a mile and a half long. The heart of the city contains the incredible Bayon Temple, an immense structure with 49 towers, 25 feet high, each with four hauntingly beautiful faces of Siva—altogether making up a total of 196 sculptured faces, each a little different from the others!

In our library at home we have a book called *The Four Faces of Siva,* written by Robert Casey almost forty years ago, detailing his visit to this awesome edifice. I had read it avidly —and now I was there myself.

We tiptoed through this ancient capital of a kingdom at one time populated by 30 million souls and finally reached the Gate of Honor. Here the massive elephants of visiting plenipotentiaries had once stopped to deposit their passengers, who were then invited to mount the steps and enter the inner sanctum of Angkor Thom.

We emulated those dignitaries of long ago and wandered into the inner courtyard. The main temple, close at hand, was breathtaking. Its front is a quarter of a mile long. As we stood there recording this majestic monument on film, a line of Buddhist priests—or bonzes as they are called—in orange robes passed us without even a side glance. We ventured into the courtyard and paused by one of its five towers. Stone stairs lead to their tops. The steps up to the shrine of Vishnu atop the main tower are extremely steep. The walls are covered with carvings of the famous asparas, the heavenly dancing girls, enchanting with their smiles and unique movements, captured in stone throughout the ages.

We puffed our way up to the top to film close-ups of them, and once at the summit, we took spectacular views of Angkor Thom spread out below us with the sacred city of Angkor Wat just to the south of where we stood.

Angkor Wat itself came into existence two centuries after the founding of Angkor Thom. Its outstanding attraction is the central temple with a sanctuary of Siva, the ultimate in Khmer architecture and design. It is an architectural symphony, with five soaring towers still remaining from the nine that once rose over the sweeping walls which are half a mile long. The buildings are adorned with intricate carvings, most of which seem to depict facets of Khmer religious life and which mirror the preoccupation of the builders with an afterlife. Our guide gravely informed us that the more lavish decoration seen in Angkor Wat was an indication of the wealth and power of the Khmer rulers during the 12th and 13th centuries. Evidently they wished to impress their neighbors in China and Siam!

Here, as at Angkor Thom, we filmed more of the startlingly lifelike carvings of dancing girls, this time wearing headdresses of a three-pointed design the central point higher than the others—symbolic duplication of the design of the temples at Angkor Wat itself.

We spent the entire day filming the seven-headed naga serpents, the carved lions of Angkor, the terrace of the garuda, the so-called Leper King statue and other thrilling sights this fabled place has to offer.

It was growing late and the jungle was no place to be after dark. We packed up our gear and as we hurried to the entrance we met two youthful Cambodians carrying a long pole over their shoulders. From a distance the pole seemed to have a coil of thick rope wrapped about its center. When I drew closer I stopped short. It was a huge boa constrictor—and it was alive!

I froze in my tracks while the youths grinned, chattering away. Our guide told us that the boa was perfectly harmless now. "It's been muzzled, madame!" He pointed out that it was thoroughly secured to the pole, therefore harmless.

Hal's eyes lit up as he raised his camera.

David started forward. "I'll pet it, Pabbi," he said.

I grasped his shoulder. "You stay here," I said. "It looks so cold and slimy!"

"It isn't," Hal answered. "I used to collect snakes as a boy and actually they're dry and warm to the touch. They're cleaner than cats or dogs, in fact!"

I took a deep breath and timidly put my hand on the boa's skin. Hal was right. I began to stroke the huge reptile. Its beady eyes looked at me and then closed. I could swear that it was enjoying being petted. It was an interesting experience but I was glad to see the Cambodian youths trot off with their specimen.

During our sojourn in the ancient Khmer strongholds we had let the outer world go by. But after the short flight from Siem Reap to Pnom Penh, we boarded an intercontinental plane for Saigon and home.

Before we landed at Saigon, one of our cabin crew members told us that the airport had been bombed by saboteurs a few days before.

"But it's all right now," said the stewardess, a pretty, smiling Vietnamese. "The army is guarding it!"

It was something to think about. When we touched down and came to a stop in front of the terminal building, the place was jammed with helmeted Vietnamese soldiers, all grim-faced, holding American-made automatic weapons. Swarming behind them were crowds of excited, frightened people who were obviously trying to leave the country. I felt apprehensive every moment we were there.

Ordinarily Hal was calm and cheerful in times of stress or danger, but here in Saigon he was a different, rather grim, person. When I asked him why, he confided, "Halla-min, what you are seeing for the first time is the tragic fringe of war. I went through years of combat in the South Pacific. This atmosphere is bringing back memories that I had hoped were buried forever."

Fortunately there was no violence at the airport or in the city during our very short stay. But later when we were basking on the sands of Waikiki on Hawaii's Island of Oahu, we read how Viet Cong terrorists had blown up the airport restaurant at Saigon and killed a number of innocent travelers. During our flight homeward Hal's cheerfulness had returned. Now, reading the story and remembering that the three of us had dined in that same restaurant only a short while before, his face again took on the grim expression it had worn in Saigon.

15
Ethiopian Adventure

IN Amharic, the language of Ethiopia, Addis Ababa means New Flower. While it isn't as beautiful as a flower, a great deal of it is new. A teeming metropolis of almost three quarters of a million people, it is the crossroads for air traffic from Nairobi, Salisbury and Johannesburg in the south to Khartoum and Cairo in the north, en route to Athens and the rest of Europe.

As cities are judged, it is a youngster. Menelik II, who handed the Italians their disastrous defeat at Aduwa in 1896, began to build Addis in the late 1880's. This sprawling city, distinguished by thousands of Australian eucalyptus trees planted during recent years, has a multitude of small, rambling business structures and a few large buildings that range from ornate wooden Victorian types to modern functional structures such as the gleaming, colorful Africa Hall and the Emperor's new Jubilee Palace, a gift from his people on the twenty-fifth anniversary of his accession to the throne.

Vehicular and pedestrian traffic is fairly heavy, with tiny, two-wheeled, horse-drawn carts, the tinkling of their warning bells competing with the loud *putt-putt* of Italian-made motor scooters.

Everywhere we were reminded of Italy's five-year occupation of the country by signs in Italian rather than in English. LAVAGGIO A SECO told us that the dry cleaners were often Italians who had remained behind when Mussolini's forces surrendered in World War II. Feelings against Italy ran high when the war ended, and most of Haile Selassie's advisers suggested that all Italians be exiled immediately. But the wise monarch realized that he would need their European skills and decreed that all those who had some special ability could remain. They have since formed a capable core of loyal technicians for His Imperial Majesty.

The traditional costume of both men and women includes a white, shawl-like cloth called a shama, worn over the shoulders. While the women wore long white dresses underneath their shamas, many of the men sported jodhpurlike trousers, tight-fitting from the knee down, and topped their costumes with a jaunty white or light-colored fedora hat. A dramatic sign of the changing times, however, was the fact that almost half of the men and women walking the streets of the capital wore European clothes. The largest motion picture house featured a tremendous poster of a scantily clad girl with her hands on her hips, advertising the American motion picture we know as *Damn Yankees*. For obvious reasons, the title had been changed to *What Lola Wants*.

The Russians did not seem to be doing so well here in Addis. The Cold War goes on politely here as elsewhere, and the United States Information Service building and that of the Russian Information Service face each other across one of the main streets. Our establishment is in a beautiful modern four-story building with a library and even a small projection room available for Ethiopian use. The Russian building is a one-story affair, quite old and decrepit.

A short distance away from our Information Service towers the one skyscraper of Addis, about eight stories high, a modern edifice that I was surprised to learn had been taken over by the Highways Department of the government. It had been built with United States funds. Somehow it seemed to me that

Ethiopian Adventure �> **219**

the Education Department or the Health Department would have been able to put it to better use. Ethiopia had only about twenty-five native doctors in the entire country at this time.

Our itinerary called for an interview with Emperor Haile Selassie, but when we arrived the government tourist officials suggested that since His Imperial Majesty's agenda was quite full, we should first explore the nation's interior and later return to Addis Ababa for the interview.

A Coptic Christian nation for 2,000 years and the country of the biblical Queen of Sheba, Ethiopia is a land worthy of years of study. Our problem was to select several subjects that would enable us to take back a comprehensive cross section of the country.

We chose Lake Tana, the source of the Blue Nile, Axum, home of the Queen of Sheba, and the remote religious city of Lalibela. The Lake Tana adventure almost proved to be the end of the Linker family!

We flew in a battered old DC-3 to the tiny community of Bahar Dar where we were to take a launch for the trip to an island in Lake Tana. There we hoped to film an ancient Coptic Christian monastery and the mummified remains of Ethiopia's former monarchs.

After a night in the bleak-looking rest house, the nearest thing to a hotel, we hurried to film the Blue Falls of the Nile, fifty miles away, and then returned quickly. Wobeshet Mekuria, our Ethiopian guide assigned by the Ethiopian Airlines, told us that it was dangerous to cross Lake Tana after dark.

We finally made it back to Bahar Dar just before noon, and in a cloud of dust our Land Rover brought us to the dock where our launch waited. The craft was about thirty feet long and had no cabin—only a canopied area in the center where the diesel engine was installed. Rolled-up side curtains gave it a kind of quaint "surrey" effect. Its general appearance was not reassuring to Hal, but Wobu (as he preferred to be called), insisted that it was absolutely seaworthy.

The skipper, a youthful, straight-limbed Ethiopian in his late twenties, appeared with an assistant about the same age and the assistant's young wife and infant child. A venerable Coptic priest who would act as guide and arrange for our safe conduct during our visit to the sacred island was also aboard.

None of the Ethiopians except Wobu spoke anything but Amharic. The only words of the language I had learned were *Tanastarlay*, which means "How do you do?" and *Embassaellie?*, meaning "Are there any lions around here?" I was always pleased when I got a negative answer to that question!

Our island destination was Dagga Stefano (Saint Stephen). The sky was clear as we started out and the lake had no waves to speak of, but the assistant's young wife began to show all the signs of mal de mer. She was along only for the ride, her husband proudly showing off his new job.

"*Tanasterlay*," said I.

"*Tanasterlay*," she replied.

And then we merely sat and vacantly smiled at each other. I felt that I would probably shock her if I asked "*Embassaellie?*" in the middle of the lake.

After three hours we reached our destination and I blithely prepared to accompany my husband and son and the other men to the dock, which was constructed of old, roughly hewn rocks. Our Coptic priest gave a moan of protest. Wobu ran up, and they jabbered back and forth at some length as the priest pointed at me. Wobu glanced my way apologetically and then waved his arms, obviously trying to placate the old man.

Wobu finally said dejectedly, "The island is taboo to women. If you set foot on the land, you would contaminate Dagga Stefano."

Somewhat annoyed, I asked what would happen if I went right ahead, taboo or no taboo.

"A terrible curse would be placed on you," Wobu solemnly assured me. "The priest says that one woman who disobeyed mysteriously bled to death from unknown causes later on."

Somehow the strength of my desire to break that taboo weakened considerably.

And there I was—or, rather there we were, the assistant's wife and I, two taboo females. Hal looked exasperated.

I knew that time was essential and quickly said, "Don't worry about me, Hal-minn. You can tell me all about the mummies later. Besides, I'll see it all in the film after we get home."

I watched the men folk disappear into the mysterious interior of the island, and then settled down to wait.

Hal later described their visit to the thatch-roofed, circular Coptic monastery lined with Christian religious paintings in the style of the Middle Ages.

They entered a narrow passageway which branched off to one side and was lined with numerous ancient books, many of them dating back nine centuries to the founding of this monastery.

The tombs of the kings turned out to be a tiny, mud-walled chamber some ten feet square with a ceiling only eight feet high. Close to the ceiling was a wooden shelf.

"But where are the mummies?" Hal insisted.

"In the coffins on that shelf," Wobu replied proudly.

"Behind that cloth covering? I can't film a cloth-covered box and tell everyone that there were mummies inside. Tell him the cloth must be removed and the box opened."

There was a shocked silence when this request was passed on to the young head priest. An animated argument followed, but finally the cloth was removed. Two rough wooden coffins could be seen. It was clear that this was as far as the head priest would go.

But Wobu produced his ace in the hole. It was a letter from His Imperial Majesty to all his subjects, with instructions to cooperate with us in every way. Our guide waved this in front of the priest, offering it to him to read.

Then, crestfallen, he turned to Hal. "He says he can read

only Geez. That's the ancient language of the priests. This letter is in Amharic. He can speak it but can't read it."

"Why don't you read it to him? You have an honest face," Hal urged, and Wobu's smile broke out.

He read the directive carefully, pointing out each word with his finger as he did so. The young priest's eyes wandered from the unfamiliar words to Wobeshet's face as he tried to decide whether he was being fooled. When Wobu finished there was a long silence. Hal held his breath. Then the priest, with an anguished sigh, nodded and agreed to let Hal film the actual mummies.

A rickety ladder made of tree limbs was placed against the shelf and the covers were lifted from the coffins. Hal and the priest mounted the ladder to the shelf. Hal scarcely had room to squeeze under the dirt roof and set up his tripod and camera.

For occasions when electricity is not available, we carry a very small but heavy battery that provides about twenty minutes of good light for color film. It must then be recharged. Hal pressed the switch, in an effort to get the light needed. Nothing happened! He tried again. The click of the switch brought nothing. It wasn't working.

Perspiration began to drip down my husband's face onto the camera over which he was crouched. The head priest began murmuring prayers and fingering his ornate Coptic Cross. Hal knew the priest was afraid that the spirits were incensed because the mummies had been uncovered, and at any moment he might decide to call off the filming to placate their anger. Hal asked David for a screwdriver from his camera case, and with fumbling fingers managed to uncouple the light and cross two wires to bypass the switch. A flood of light was the reward. He scrambled back onto the shelf and filmed the withered and shrunken remains at close range as the priest hovered fearfully nearby.

All of this had taken valuable time, and we had been

warned that we should try to be across Lake Tana before
darkness set in.

Hal was worried about this danger when he shouldered his
equipment and hurried back to the boat. I had been calmly
waiting for his return, but one thing had disturbed me. Our
boat had no toilet, and as time passed I grew rather uncomfortable. I gazed longingly at the island, especially the thick
brush nearby. And then I quietly stood up, left the boat and
stole into a thickly wooded spot. The Ethiopian woman and
her baby were asleep.

Fortunately my presence on the land forbidden to women
was undetected, but the guardian spirit of the island must
have witnessed my cardinal sin, because from that moment
things began to grow ominous.

When Hal and Wobu returned to the boat, I whispered to
my husband what I had done and we laughed about it.

By now it was late afternoon and our skipper was giving
every indication of concern. He kept glancing at the sky and
seemed to be scolding Wobu.

The latter turned to us and said, "We've taken too long
with the filming. He's afraid that we may not be able to reach
Gorgora, at the far end of the lake before dark. This is the
season of sudden storms, and they can be quite dangerous at
night!"

"Let's get going, then!" Hal exclaimed.

When we saw Dagga Stefano fall astern, I drew a relaxed
breath. We were all unusually excited about the filming. As
far as Wobu knew, such a visit to this ancient monastery had
never before been recorded on film. The afternoon was clear,
the weather balmy and Tana's broad expanse seemed mirror
smooth.

And then the curse of Dagga Stefano overtook us. It all
began with a low cloud on the horizon. Our skipper kept
glancing at it and shaking his head. At first the cloud seemed
to be no threat, but it approached with the speed of an express
train. The light turned greenish and then the sun seemed to

be strangled by patches of racing cloud. A wind set in and the surface of Lake Tana was no longer smooth.

As though someone had drawn a curtain, the sun was suddenly obscured and the scene quickly became one of alarming gloom. The waves grew progressively larger and more turbulent. Our cockleshell launch began to pitch and toss, and my worries grew. We had only three life belts on the launch and there were seven of us aboard including the baby.

Flashes of dazzling lightning lit up the eerie scene, each one momentarily revealing the storm-churned surface of Lake Tana. A shattering clap of thunder followed almost immediately, warning us that the lightning had struck nearby.

The bow of our thin-skinned launch rose high in the rain-drenched night and then, with a sickening lurch, slid down the side of an enormous wave.

For a moment our craft wallowed motionlessly. My heart skipped a beat. Were we destined to plunge to the bottom of the immense lake? I was frightened and found myself sobbing.

The battered launch somehow remained afloat but how much longer could the fragile craft withstand such a pounding? It had now been two hours since the fury of the storm had first struck us.

Wind drove the torrential downpour into my face. Was this going to be the end? Had I come all the way from my native Iceland only to drown in this vast, remote lake—and all because of some mummies of ancient kings of Ethiopia entombed on a mysterious, sacred island?

Hal left the native pilot's side and staggered to where I huddled in the center of the swaying boat. For the past few agonizing moments I had caught occasional glimpses of him during lightning flashes as he braced himself near the helm and consulted with the pilot.

Even before the sudden storm had hit the notoriously treacherous lake, we had suspected that the pilot was unsure of his navigation. Now it was obvious that we were hopelessly lost.

Hal carefully avoided stepping on the prostrate wife of the launch mechanic. The poor woman lay on the deck, and between spasms of retching, tried to protect her two-year-old child. My husband gave her a reassuring pat on the shoulder and then reached my side. Another of the almost incessant streaks of lightning brought our faces into stark relief.

Hal stared at me. Without uttering a word, he turned and grasped the arm of our ten-year-old son, who was crouched over our camera equipment in a rather futile effort to keep it dry. A look passed between them.

I saw David rise and then my son and husband flanked me. David soothingly stroked my arm; Hal held me tightly. His lips brushed my ear as he began to speak, raising his voice just enough to make himself heard above the bellowing thunder and the pounding of the rain.

"Easy does it, Halla-min." His calm voice and the use of our favorite Icelandic term of endearment almost immediately drove away my panic. "We'll be okay. You'll see. We've got life belts and all of us are good swimmers. The shore is only a mile or so away."

"But Hal-minn, I can't see how this boat can stay afloat another minute!" Despite my efforts to keep calm, my voice broke again.

He squeezed my shoulders. "It's stronger than you think."

"But those waves—we're hitting them so hard the bow will break off. Why don't we turn sideways instead of meeting them head on?"

"It's the only way we can stay afloat. If we turn sideways, we'll capsize." His lips brushed my cheek. "We've been through much worse before, Halla-min. We'll make it!"

There was another shattering clap of thunder, still closer this time. The lightning flash was almost simultaneous. Both Hal and David held me even more closely. And then the storm seemed to abate. It was as though that last thunderclap had been a final burst of artillery.

The rain began to let up. Although the waves still battered

us, the peak of their fury was obviously past. Hal checked the radium dial of his wristwatch. It was almost midnight. Now that the lightning had stopped, it was pitch dark.

"This is our chance to put into shore, Halla-min," Hal said. "I'm going forward to give them a hand."

The pilot ordered the engineer to take up a position in the bow with a flashlight.

"He thinks we're near Gorgora," Hal called to me. "Maybe we *can* make it to shore!"

My hopes rose as I saw the flashlight go on. The engineer was precariously crouched on the bow. The light itself seemed pitifully weak, but I could see Hal and the pilot silhouetted in its glow as they gazed intently ahead.

Then the light began to dim. Before my horrified gaze, it faded and total darkness closed in once more. The batteries were dead. The pilot throttled back the engine.

"It's no use, Mister Linker," Wobu said, in a tone of despair. "We'll have to stay out here all night. We wouldn't dare try to navigate in the dark."

"But don't you have another light?" Hal asked.

"This is the only one." Wobu's voice betrayed his exasperation as he added, "I told you that we had to get across the lake before dark—but you would film those mummies!"

The prospect of remaining afloat in cold, sodden clothing was unpleasant but not as frightening as the storm had been. I was used to physical hardships. Now that the waters had quieted, I felt more hopeful.

Still, the thought of staying on this boat all night in the still-heaving backlash of the passing storm was appalling. But I have come to rely on Hal to get us out of the unavoidable difficulties we sometimes meet, and this time was no exception. Quickly he went to our photographic equipment, and I could hear him mutter, "I'll get it to work somehow, if it hasn't been ruined by water. I hope I haven't used up all the power with those blasted mummies."

In a few moments he had hooked our portable photo battery to the floodlight we use for filming and carried it to the bow of the boat. There, clinging to a railing surrounding the pilot's compartment, he held the photo unit in the air and as I held my breath he pressed the switch. It worked! A flood of powerful light shone across the water and a matching flood of relief swept over me. I knew that our battery was good for only twenty minutes of light—and Hal had used much of this for the mummies—but I noticed that he flashed it on for only a few seconds and then off again, to conserve its meager power.

"Very good, sir, very good," chortled Wobu. "Now we can find our way."

And find our way we did, carefully inching into Gorgora through the rocky channel from the lake and arriving at 1 in the morning at the destination we should have reached at 6 o'clock the previous evening.

A battered old truck was commandeered to take us to Gondar, where we were to be picked up and flown to Lalibela, our next destination.

When we awoke the next morning in the tiny Italian-built hotel in Gondar, we learned that, as usual, the morning flight that was expected to pick us up at 9 o'clock would be late— perhaps as much as three or four hours. This was the plane that was to detour from its regular run and drop us off near Lalibela. It was to come directly from Addis with our food supplies and camping equipment, since there were no facilities whatsoever for caring for visitors at Lalibela.

We took advantage of the delay to explore Gondar, and Hal was delighted at the interesting sights we found to film. Unexpectedly, there was a series of Portuguese-style castles built over 400 years ago. Here it was that we learned of Gondar's connection with the famous European legend of Prester John in the Middle Ages.

For centuries, Europeans had heard of a distant land, some said in Africa and others in Asia, where a Christian monarch, Prester John, had held sway for many years. Such a tale had at first seemed fanciful to people in northern Europe, who themselves had but recently become Christians. (Much of Scandinavia did not adopt Christianity until about the year 1000.) It was inconceivable to them that in the wilds of Africa, let us say, a Christian nation had existed for ages. Yet the tale persisted.

In the early 1500's, the Portuguese, who were then exploring the coasts of Africa and settling there, followed a tip and sent an expedition to Abyssinia, as Ethiopia was then known. To their amazement, they not only found a long-established Christian nation as rumored but also learned that they had come just in the nick of time. The country was being hard pressed by its surrounding Moslem neighbors and was in danger of being overrun and absorbed. Portugal sent troops to help the Coptic Christians of the country and also taught them how to build massive fortresses to repel the invaders. Since Gondar was the capital at that time, the finest castles had been built there and the remains of these edifices provided fine scenes for our cameras while we waited for our plane.

I had no premonition of danger as our Lalibela adventure began, despite the fact that our sky chariot was an old Douglas DC-3, a twin-engined transport which must have been built about twenty-five years before. The ship, a dwarf by modern jet standards, laboriously climbed more than 13,000 feet in order to top the towering peaks of Ethiopia.

Our crew was all Ethiopian—tall, ebony-skinned, handsome men and women. The charming stewardess did all she could to make us comfortable. However, the ship, once it reached the churning air surrounding those jagged peaks and promontories, began to shudder and lurch as up-and-down drafts (called thermals) toyed with it as though it were a plaything. And when the Ethiopian captain made his way from the cockpit along the pitching aisle toward our seats, I looked up in the hope that he would announce the quick end of our ordeal.

He pleasantly asked us to fasten our seat belts and apologetically explained that it was getting "a bit rough." That was the understatement of our entire trip.

He flashed us a reassuring smile and then, leaning toward my husband, who was in a seat across the aisle from me, whispered something. Both roared with laughter, and when the pilot, staggering and weaving like a sailor on a storm-lashed destroyer, finally made his way back to the cockpit. I leaned toward Hal.

"What was that, Hal-minn? I could use a laugh."

For a moment Hal hesitated. Then he chuckled. "Well, he said that a flight through these mountains is always rough. The pilots call this route Vomit Alley, and the plane is known as the Vomit Comet!"

For a moment I was aghast and then the humor, grim as it was, overcame the increasing turbulence and I laughed, too, although a bit wryly. I fastened our belts more tightly around David and me and watched the shifting, rugged terrain below through the square window.

The pressure of a sharp turn pinned us against our seats and the blood seemed to drain from my face and arms—anything but a pleasant sensation. This, combined with the continuous rising and falling, began to play hob with my insides. I glanced at David, but such is the resilience of a ten-year-old veteran world traveler that he leaned against the window, eyes wide and nose flattened against the glass, as he stared with fascination at the scene below.

The trim stewardess put her lips to my ear. "We're circling to attract their attention." She almost had to shout to be heard.

"Whose attention?"

"The people in Lalibela!" She pointed to what looked like some twenty or thirty thatched huts nestled among the jagged peaks. What people? I wondered. I could see nothing below that moved. "We're now down to nine thousand feet. The landing place itself is lower, about a mile above sea level," the girl added.

I immediately glanced at Hal. With his tremendous chest and lung capacity, he quickly suffers at high altitudes when oxygen becomes rare, as we had learned in Bolivia.

Fortunately the altitude had not yet seriously affected him this time. He caught my glance and smiled as though he had intuitively read my mind and understood my concern.

The roar of the engines subsided abruptly and the ship leveled out. Boulders, brush and hummocks flashed past the windows at frightening speed. The wheels touched, bounded into the air, and then touched again—this time to stay. The tail lowered and began to roll over a rough clearing, a mere pasture crisscrossed by animal trails, and the plane came to a halt. We had made a "routine landing" for the Lalibela "flag stop."

The crew, natty in their uniforms, came out of the cockpit laughing uproariously with Wobu who, once again back in his own element as an Ethiopian Airlines employee, showed no traces of our Lake Tana experience of the previous day. Ever since we had taken off, Wobeshet had enjoyed himself up in the cockpit, exchanging airline gossip with the crew.

Now he said jauntily, "All right, Hal Linker and family—this is where we get off!" And as I loosened the seat belts and began to collect our belongings, he added, "I'll help you with your cameras, Mrs. Linker."

It took fifteen minutes for Hal, Wobeshet and the crew, all working together, to unload our baggage, which consisted for the most part of a large tent, canned food and bottled soft drinks. I hated to think what the excess charge would have been had we not been guests of the government.

When our gear had been piled some distance away and the ship, after a bumpy interminable run, had achieved an almost heart-stopping takeoff and faded into the distance, Hal turned to our guide. "Okay, Wobu—what are the plans now?"

"The plane will be back to pick us up in three days," he answered with a grin. "That is, if they can find this place again." And then as Hal's jaw dropped, Wobu calmly added, "Meanwhile we will wait until the villagers come down the trail with some donkeys for us. They should be here soon."

"You hope," Hal said.

"They'll be here," he insisted. "They know we're here. That's why we circled before we landed. It is procedure."

"How often does Ethiopian Airlines land here?" I asked.

He pursed his lips. "Oh, once a year—maybe!"

David tugged at my arm. "Look, Mommie!" he exclaimed, pointing.

We turned and watched a picturesque cavalcade of ragged but stately natives slowly approach on foot, leading four little donkeys. From a distance the men seemed armed; a few with rifles, others with large knives.

I swallowed and glanced at Wobu. "Friends?" I asked.

He nodded smilingly.

When we first saw them they seemed quite close. However, the clear mountain air was deceptive and it was quite a long while before they finally arrived. By now it was nearing 2 o'clock in the afternoon and Wobeshet wore an anxious expression.

"We'd better walk and use the donkeys for our equipment. It's too dangerous to climb the trail to Lalibela after dark."

My husband seemed dubious but agreed.

The tiny animals looked reproachful when we began to pile mountains of gear on their backs. The four of them could barely carry our food, shelter and equipment. We and the animals began to plod single file up a long, winding pathway that was infested by the African scourge of foot-travelers— thornbushes with cruel, two-inch spikes that eagerly rip and tear clothing and skin and cause lacerations that may become infected.

I carefully kept steering David away from the thorns that seemed to reach eagerly toward us from both sides. The path steepened, and breathing quickly became difficult in the rarefied air.

A rather elderly "donkey-skinner" walked with us, his rifle

slung over one shoulder. He urged his animals on with a switch. Preoccupied by his task, his Hamitic face had a somber, almost sullen, expression that was painfully in keeping with his weapon. But when he caught my eye he smiled and nodded, and the weapon suddenly seemed incongruous.

Our procession came to an abrupt halt. Hal and Wobeshet, at the head, engaged in an animated conversation. I hurried up in time to hear my husband exclaim, "You must be kidding, Wobu! That's an absolute impossibility!"

When I came to his side Hal turned to me. "Wobu says that it is still a four-hour hike, almost straight up, to Lalibela, unless we find more donkeys or burros. I told him that's out of the question. I simply won't have you and David making a hike like that without transportation."

"But we can't just stay down here," I said.

"He claims that the rest of the donkeys have not come down from the village yet, since it takes them more than two hours to even come downhill to the field. I've a mind to pitch camp right here and wait rather than hike in darkness. This trail will be downright dangerous then."

Wobeshet waved and pointed excitedly. "Look—donkey coming!"

We stared. Sure enough, trotting and panting down the narrow trail toward us were a turbaned old man and a young boy leading what looked like a veritable Samson of a donkey, even though it barely came to our waists.

Our mentor halted them and engaged in an arm-waving, spirited debate. Then he faced us with a wide smile. "I've rented this donkey!" he exclaimed. "Now someone will be able to ride."

There immediately ensued a Gaston and Alphonse debate between Hal and me. It would have been comical had it not been rather serious. I insisted that Hal ride, since he was carrying his favorite camera and heavy tripod and was filming along the way. And besides, he was so much more susceptible to high altitudes. He obstinately insisted that I ride, since I bore the awesome responsibility of being the "nurse" of the expedition.

I objected and then countered. "Let's have David ride. After all, he's only a child."

"What do you mean, child?" our son cut in frowningly. "I'm ten years old! You ride, Mommie."

For a moment I hesitated and looked at Hal. He shrugged. I tried to mount the donkey with ladylike grace despite my smudges of dirt and perspiration and a few rips in my bush jacket and khaki trousers.

As David helped me, the donkey turned its head and gave me a frosty glance. It stirred restively for a moment, but I managed to balance myself on its hurricane deck. Wobeshet and the natives, stifling their obvious amusement at this domestic byplay, again headed our entourage up into the deepening shadows of the late afternoon.

It could not have been more than forty minutes later, although it seemed like hours, when I again glanced back to see how David was faring. The child was walking at a slowing pace and steadily dropping behind. I called a halt and dismounted.

"David," I said when he caught up, rubbing myself meaningfully. "Would you do me a big favor?"

"Certainly, Mommie." His eyes brightened.

"I'm quite sore from riding this animal and I'm beginning to hurt. I'd appreciate it very much if you'd ride for a while and let me stretch my muscles."

He pursed his lips. "Okay." His tone was nonchalant. "If it'll do you any good and make you feel better, I'll ride."

He approached the animal and I prepared to assist him.

"I can get on by myself," he said, with an almost injured air.

"Oh of course," I murmured, stepping to one side. Hal's eyes crinkled with amusement as he set up his camera to film the scene. David readjusted his long-billed, bright-blue golfing cap and clambered aboard.

The donkey looked back at him and brayed. And then, to

my dismay, the animal began to buck like a bronco and started to slip toward a precipice whose bottom was lost in deep purple shadow below.

We stood there for a second, our mouths gaping. Then just as Hal and I simultaneously started toward the animal, the old, rifle-bearing native jumped ahead of us. He reached with one hand for the frayed rope that was a combination bridle and halter and placed his other palm over the frightened animal's eyes. The creature immediately stood still.

Slowly, carefully, the native led the donkey and our son away from the edge of the precipice and back to the security of the trail. We all felt weak-kneed. Wobu fired some questions at the man, who shrugged, grinned, and then reached up and removed David's blue cap.

As he handed it to Hal, Wobu shook his head. "It was the cap, the blue color. The animal has never seen such a brilliant color before!"

Hal and I exchanged glances and my husband folded the cap and thrust it deep into a pocket where it remained for the rest of our climb to Lalibela.

Our stay there didn't work out the way we had planned it. Living in a native hut was definitely *not* on our schedule. The numerous bundles and packages the airline had provided for our three-day stay were supposed to contain not only food and beverages to sustain us but also a big tent and "fine Army cots." But when we arrived at our destination just at dusk and hurried to get our tent up, Hal was horrified to find that the large Arab-style shelter had tent cords about as strong as the white wrapping twine our neighborhood drugstore uses back home. Each errant gust of wind resulted in a loud snap and a broken tent support. The headman of the village, who had been sympathetically clucking at our misfortune, now offered to let us use his hut for the night while he and his wife moved in with relatives. The growing chilliness of the night air made a decision easy. Hal accepted and we moved our equipment into the compound of the chief.

"Okay, cook! How about a meal?" Hal called out with a grin as soon as our moving chores were over.

As my "customers" hovered over me, I carefully opened the box marked FOOD. A loaf of bread was near the top. That was good. Then came can after can of expensive gourmet food! Tiny cocktail frankfurters, Belgian asparagus tips, imported Italian ravioli, boxes of Swiss chocolates. Then bottle after bottle of soft drinks—but not a sign of drinking water. Whoever had packed our food had apparently felt that Americans ate only exotic foods.

"We'll obviously eat well," I said, "but first, David, you'll have to wash your hands."

"Where, Mommie?" he asked.

"Where, Hal?" I repeated.

"Where, Wobu?" Hal echoed.

Wobu looked embarrassed. "Oh dear, I forgot to tell you. There is no water in Lalibela. Everyone brings what he needs in a gourd from about a mile away."

"Say, I've got an idea," Hal said musingly, holding an opened soft-drink bottle in his hand. "We'll use this." And he proceeded to wash his hands with Coca-Cola. In case the manufacturers are interested, Coke doesn't make a very good lather when used with soap, but it was better than no washing at all. Drying? Well, there was toilet paper in the supplies.

We were famished but as we gobbled the food that Wobu had heated on a fire in the center of the compound, I noticed that several young men had gathered near the door of our hut and were leaning on their spears and gazing at us with what I was sure were hungry looks.

"Here, Wobu," I called out, "give those fellows something to eat. They look hungry."

Wobu offered them bread and frankfurters. They drew back in horror. Wobu insisted. A torrent of words poured from them. Wobu took a bite of the bread and offered it to them again. They turned and fled.

"What was that all about?" Hal asked.

THREE TICKETS TO TIMBUKTU 236

"Well," said Wobu resignedly, "they said they didn't want any, and I ate some to show it was good, but then they said they were good Christians and couldn't eat unholy food. They consider this food sinful because it hasn't been blessed by a priest."

I realized that these people had been converted to Christianity when it was so close to its Judaic origins that they still maintained many Jewish religious customs including eating only kosher food blessed by a religious leader.

But having already gorged ourselves on the unblessed, sinful food, we then said good night to Wobu, who went off to find shelter for himself, and we lay down on our cots in the cramped hut, to try to get some sleep.

It was then that we experienced a night made miserable by thumping drums, chanting, fleas and a rooster that crowed all night.

When the first rays of sunlight streamed in through the cracks in the mud walls of the hut, I jumped up and preceded Hal and David out of the hut. It was a glorious morning with brilliant sunshine and I quickly began to forget all the discomforts of the night. That is, until I noticed a group of people gathered around a small bundle on the ground a few huts away.

"Good morning, Mrs. Linker," said a jovial voice almost in my ear, and I turned to find Wobu smiling, somewhat disheveled and unshaven but obviously feeling well. "I hope you slept well."

I managed to stifle a groan. "Oh, I've slept better. But tell me, Wobu, what's going on there?" I pointed at the assemblage around the bundle.

Wobu took a quick look. "Oh, madam, that's nothing important. Some child died during the night and they're getting ready to bury it."

A chill ran through me. Our Icelandic superstition about someone dying if a rooster crows all night might be true after all!

Hal and David came out of the hut and I blurted out the news.

Hal looked grave. "Just a coincidence, Halla-min. I'm sure that a rooster often crows all night without someone dying." I saw him glance over my shoulder. He took David and me firmly by the arms and led us back toward our hut.

"Is anything wrong, Hal?" I asked.

"Just a leper woman coming down the path. I didn't want her to be too close to you."

I turned and saw a woman of indeterminate age hobbling past us, using a tree branch as a crutch. Most of her features were missing, ravaged by the disease. One leg was just a stump and all the toes of the other foot were missing. The skin around the stump and other foot was the blue-gray color of steel, the distinguishing mark of this dread ancient disease. I turned my head away until she passed. Little did I know that I was to see more of leprosy than I wanted to in our travels in Africa.

Lalibela's attraction for us was its eleven stone churches carved out of living rock about a thousand years ago. This was hundreds of years after the country had been converted to Christianity by a Roman named Frumentius in the year 330 A.D. Under the guidance of St. Lalibela, the ruler of this area in the 800's, work had begun on the churches. The massive rock foundations were modeled inch by inch, to sculpture the outside; then the interiors were chiseled out, complete with windows, columns, arches and chapels.

The first one we saw was Beta Mariam or Saint Mary's Church. Like most of the other buildings, it resembled an underground fortification. Inside we found many medieval wall paintings, some of which included the Star of David. Only a little light filtered into its dark recesses through the tiny, carved windows, each one different from the others. None of the Coptic churches had pews for the worshipers, since the custom is to remain standing during the entire services lasting several hours. High staffs with crutchlike tops were available for the people and they could lean on these if they needed them. A small pool in the courtyard held water from the River Jordan, we were told, and was effective in inducing fertility in barren women.

The Church of St. George differs from the others in that it is shaped like a cross and is hewn deep into the center of a single huge rock formation. Standing at the top, we looked directly down on the ornate roof of the church and could see that the rock formation formed a wall four stories high around the structure itself. Entrance to the church requires a long detour around the hill on which the original rock rested and a dark walk through a tunnel slanting downward to emerge finally at the base of the church itself.

As we wandered through the narrow grounds of the church, I came upon a human skull and some thigh bones. I walked a few steps farther and then stopped short. The rock all around the church was pitted with caves and holes, and in these the devout were buried, as close to the church as possible. It was an open-air charnel house filled with grisly relics. Some of the bodies were mummified rather than decayed. I was not at all unhappy when Hal told me he was finished with his work here.

We filmed many of the churches including the Church of the World Saviour in which the paintings featured St. George and the Dragon. Our most terrifying visit was that to the Church of St. Gabriel. I thought this church was most appropriately named, since it could only be reached by crawling over a rickety log stretched over a chasm a hundred feet deep. As we crossed and recrossed this shaky "bridge," I was sure I could hear Gabriel's horn every time it quivered beneath me!

It was 4 o'clock in the morning of the third day of our Lalibela visit when we packed up, thanked our hosts, and said good-bye. We mounted donkeys and began our descent to the landing strip. The darkness was stygian. All we could do was hang on and assume that the donkeys knew their way, perhaps with built-in radar. Swaying on the uncomfortable razor back of my donkey, I found myself mightily yearning for daylight so I could see where we were going.

But the moment the rising sun brought light, I wished it was still night so that I could *not* see! When we had climbed up this same twisting trail, we had paid little attention to the terrain behind us. Now, descending, we could see how steep the precipices were and how awesomely deep the gorges below. It was a frightening experience, and our ancient, rotting saddles did not seem too secure to me either.

When we finally reached bottom I sighed with relief. And just then the strap holding Hal's saddle on his mount parted with a snap. Saddle and all, he tumbled to the ground. I frantically jumped off my own mount to help him, and as I came running up he was lying on one side with a bemused expression on his face. His camera was safe in his arms and he smiled up at me, but he didn't get up.

"Nothing broken here, Halla-min," he called out cheerfully. "I'm okay." Then he said, "But what luck! This is the only place we have passed all morning where I could have fallen without dropping over a cliff. Feels so good down here, I think I'll stay awhile."

I helped him to his feet and walked with him the short distance to where the airplane was supposed to pick us up. I held him tightly around the waist although the going wasn't rough at all down here.

It was now 9 o'clock, the appointed time for the pickup, but no plane was in sight. Another hour passed and Hal began to get restless. Then there was a speck in the sky and a distant humming. The DC-3 circled over our heads twice as the pilot evaluated the landing area, and finally it came in for a bumpy landing.

As we climbed aboard by a short ladder hurriedly hung from the door, I called up to the stewardess. "Say, am *I* glad to see you people! For awhile we were afraid you had forgotten about us."

"As a matter of fact," she admitted casually as she helped me aboard, "we couldn't find you. Our pilot and copilot have never landed here before and we've been searching near the wrong mountains. At the last minute the pilot decided to try this area—and there you were!" She smiled brightly. "Fasten your seat belt for takeoff, please."

The Ghion Hotel in Addis Ababa was like heaven after our experiences on Lake Tana and in Lalibela. I felt as though I had suddenly stepped from the Middle Ages into the modern world.

After we dumped our soiled clothing on the floor and bathed and dressed, we enjoyed a leisurely, civilized meal in the restaurant.

In the dining room we met a charming, educated young Ethiopian girl whom we had first met at the university. She said that she had noticed our absence, and when we told her that we had visited Lalibela, she was intrigued. While she had never been there herself, she knew all about St. Lalibela, who had ordered churches sculptured there.

"Oh yes," she exclaimed. "Our great Saint Lalibela was a personal friend of Jesus Christ!"

"Er—I believe you've made a mistake," Hal interrupted. "You see, Lalibela is known to have lived in the eight hundreds. That's quite some time after the time of Christ, so I doubt that they could have been personally acquainted."

"Oh no! He *was* a close friend of Christ," the girl insisted. "And besides, we Ethiopians have been Christians for three thousand years, long before Christ!"

Hal discreetly let the subject drop, and the rest of the meal was enjoyed in an atmosphere of harmony.

When we went back to our suite and opened the door, we gasped, strangled and retreated. The rooms were clouded with an insecticide mist.

Our indignant demand for an explanation brought an answer from the apologetic hotel manager. "Our room boys learned that you had been to Lalibela. They know what it is like up there and felt that your clothing and quarters needed fumigation."

Hal took it philosophically. "It's just as well, Halla-min," he said. "We're scheduled for an audience with Emperor Haile Selassie in the morning and it would be embarrassing to be scratching ourselves all during it."

"Oh, I don't know." I laughed." I won't be ashamed if I have to scratch myself. I'll just explain to His Imperial Majesty that it's because of the holy fleas from the holy city of Lalibela."

16

The Lion of Judah

WITHOUT any warning the fully grown lion clamped his powerful jaws around David's ankle. It was horrible, terrifying. And there was nothing I could do about it!

A few moments earlier the huge beast, royal mascot of His Most Imperial Majesty, Haile Selassie, Emperor of Ethiopia and Conquering Lion of the Tribe of Judah, had been quietly lying in the shade of a sycamore on the lawn of the Menelik Palace overlooking Addis Ababa.

We had just come from an audience with the Emperor in the ornate Victorian wooden structure built by his predecessor, Menelik II, before the turn of the century. The gentle monarch had not only granted us an interview but had graciously consented to pose before Hal's motion picture camera.

As we strolled toward our waiting car in the distant driveway, our escort, Hapte Selassie Taffessa, an official of the Ethiopian Tourist Office, was congratulating us on the success of our visit.

Emperor Selassie rarely granted interviews to people other than ministers and dignitaries of other states. Before we had been ushered into the Royal Presence, we had wondered if His Majesty would spare more than a few moments of his time to speak with us, much less consent to pose before a camera.

In the anteroom to the reception chamber we had been informed by the frock-coated Court Chamberlain that His Majesty spoke no English! The Court Chamberlain said that we should direct our questions to him. He in turn would translate them into native Amharic, for the benefit of the Emperor.

Furthermore, when we entered the reception chamber I was to curtsy and Hal and David were to bow. Halfway in our progress from the door toward the Royal Presence we were to halt and repeat these salutations. And when we finally confronted His Imperial Majesty, we were to pay homage for the third time.

As we strolled across the lawn, I smilingly recalled my nervousness when we had entered the reception chamber, furnished in a style reminiscent of the 1890's, its light subdued by drawn curtains.

During our wonderful years of traveling throughout the world, Hal, David and I had met with presidents, kings, tribal chieftains and dictators. An Emperor, however, was something else again. Haile Selassie and Emperor Hirohito of Japan are the only remaining emperors in the world. But when I finally found myself standing before the Lion of Judah, my nervousness vanished.

What immediately set me at ease was that his features were so familiar from countless photographs. A slender, slightly built man, his kindly smile and dark, compassionate eyes were at variance with his khaki uniform, which bore numerous ribbons and decorations. On his left arm was a black band of mourning for his beloved wife of many years who had died just five months before.

His voice was soft. When he spoke to the High Chamberlain in answer to our questions, I noticed that his gaze constantly returned to our son. After a while I realized with a start of surprise that David was actually conversing with His Majesty. And then it all came out: the Emperor understood

English quite well but preferred to pretend that he spoke only Amharic when meeting English-speaking visitors for the first time. By listening carefully to his guests for a while, he could decide whether or not he would be able to cope with their answers.

The Chamberlain explained. "There are so many different kinds of English—and many Americans seem to have languages of their own," he said.

I could sympathize with the Emperor. It reminded me of my own confusion when I had first come to the United States from my native Iceland to marry Hal. The English I had studied in Menntaskolinn, Iceland's college, was at first quite remote from such accents as those of New York taxi drivers and waitresses in the Deep South. It had taken quite a while before my ear became tuned to Americanese.

When Hal asked whether the Emperor would mind posing before the camera, giving as his reason the fact that our audiences would be most anxious to see His Majesty in our films, the monarch pursed his lips and then nodded smilingly.

As my husband began to ready his equipment, he delicately suggested that it would be much better if we could only prevail on His Majesty to step outdoors where the light would be so much more suitable.

The Emperor hesitated, and then David spoke up. "Your Imperial Majesty, sir." His little face was quite earnest. "Those ribbons on your uniform are very beautiful and they would look much nicer in the sunlight because my father is filming in color, Your Imperial Majesty, sir."

The Emperor smiled. "Of course," he murmured and led the way to a wide veranda.

I was proud of our son.

While His Majesty posed for Hal, the Chamberlain explained what had undoubtedly moved the Emperor to spend so much time with us.

"Right at this moment," he said, frowning at his watch, "he

has kept a Greek Archbishop waiting ten minutes. But it's because of your son—and the camera."

"Camera?"

The Chamberlain nodded. "His favorite son, who was killed in an automobile accident, was an avid camera fan. He used to take pictures of his father with a camera exactly like the one your husband is using."

I looked at His Majesty with a new awareness. And as I noticed the lines of care and suffering engraved on his sensitive features, I felt a lump of sympathy and understanding in my throat.

After our audience with His Majesty and as we walked across the lawn, Hapte called our attention to the languid lion. "Perhaps, Mister Linker, you'd like to get a picture of Tojo. Since the Emperor is known as The Lion of Judah, a film of his mascot might be appropriate."

My husband looked at him quizzically. "But why the name Tojo? Why on earth would His Majesty name the lion after the Japanese warlord of World War II?"

Hapte shook his head. "Tojo is an ancient Ethiopian name. There's nothing Japanese about it."

We gazed at the lion, which seemed oblivious of our presence. When we had first arrived at the palace, it had been in a roaring rage, leaping and trying to free itself from a heavy chain that secured it to a big sycamore tree. It had been a little frightening. Hapte had asked the keeper why the lion was acting so ferociously, and the man explained that the exhaust fumes of our car had enraged the beast. Lions, like people, get furious at smog!

When I reminded Hapte of Tojo's earlier behavior, he spoke to the keeper, who replied with a laugh. Hapte smilingly translated. "He says it's perfectly safe, now. There is no car around."

It was then that I noticed with a start that Tojo was no

longer chained to the tree. He was roaming freely, his chain dragging behind!

I was about to mention this when David spoke up brightly. "May I pet him?"

Hal hesitated.

Hapte said, "Why not? Everyone here does. Besides, as you can see, he's calm now."

My husband nodded dubiously.

David marched up to Tojo's side. The lion blinked up at him. When our son reached down to pet the huge, black mane, the animal disdainfully turned its head away.

"I believe this shot will make quite a sequence!" Hal unlimbered his camera and placed it on the tripod.

David straightened up and frowned at his hands. "Look," he exclaimed, showing his palms to us. "Tojo's mane is all gooey and oily."

Hapte chuckled. "It's the natural oil of a lion's skin. We've never found anyone here who'd volunteer to bathe a fully grown lion, so—"

David laughed and started to pet Tojo again while my husband started the camera.

I began to relax—and then it happened.

Tojo let out a sudden body-shaking roar. His massive jaws closed over David's ankle. I felt myself turning to ice inside. During all our travels, our son had never been in such frightful peril. And never had I been so utterly helpless!

I could feel the blood draining from my face. At any moment I expected that awful jaw to crush David's foot and make a cripple of him—if not worse. Hapte's face was ashen. From the corner of my eye I saw Tojo's keeper take a step toward the animal and then stop.

David stood stock-still, gazing down into Tojo's glowing eyes.

For what seemed an eternity we all stood like statues, hardly daring to breathe. And then Tojo wrinkled his nose, widened his jaw in a huge yawn, and released David's ankle. He favored all of us with something like proud contempt and turned away.

David slowly, carefully returned to our side. He raised his trouser cuff and we examined his ankle. There was not a mark. The keeper, scolding Tojo in rapid-fire Amharic, grasped the animal's chain and led him away.

Our escort mopped his brow with a hand that shook visibly. "Incredible. Who'd have thought—" He grasped David's shoulder. "And you, young man, to stand there so calmly—"

"He was like my dog Loki," David said seriously. "Loki does the same thing. He'll grab my hand or my foot, and I know I'll hurt myself if I pull away. So I just stand still and don't move until he gives up and lets go. I thought Tojo would do the same thing—if I stood still." He paused and searched our faces. "I wasn't worried."

I couldn't trust myself to speak. I put my arm around him and led him away from the sycamore tree. Hal shouldered his tripod and followed quietly.

Months afterward when we had returned to our home in Hollywood and processed all the motion picture footage taken during our Ethiopian visit, we were amazed to find the entire incident with Tojo recorded on film.

"There's only one explanation," Hal said, staring at the chilling scene. "When the lion closed its jaw around David's ankle, I froze because I realized that any sudden move could make things even worse. My finger must have been on the trigger at the time, and the camera continued to operate. But I didn't realize it. All I could think of then was, Don't move—be absolutely still!"

When we finally entered our car for the return to our hotel in Addis Ababa, I sank back in the seat and closed my eyes, still tightly holding onto David. It had been a frightening experience, and now that it was over I felt limp.

But not for long. Even as our chauffeur started the engine and the car left the palace grounds, my spirits began to soar once more. Our next stop was to be the capital of the Queen of Sheba!

Our flight to Asmara in a big DC-6 seemed like traveling in luxury after our previous experiences. The hotel there, colorfully named the CIAO (which sounds like the well-known Italian expression for "So long"), was operated by Italians and seemed opulent.

But the trip the next day required us to travel about five hours south into the interior, and the dusty ride was about four hours too long for my taste.

Breaking the monotony of travel through the barren, almost desertlike, hills, were the camel caravans we passed, each loaded with what our Ethiopian driver explained was "chat," better known in the Orient as hashish. It is an important article of commerce here. On the way we also passed the star-topped monument at the spot near Aduwa where a large Italian Army was thoroughly defeated by the warriors of Menelik II in 1896. This rankling defeat was the prime reason Mussolini invaded the country once again in 1935.

It was almost dusk when we arrived at Aksum and found accommodations at a sprawling rest house operated by a buxom Italian woman and her teen-aged daughter. All three of us slept as though we had been drugged.

Centuries ago, legend has it, when the Queen of Sheba came over from the Arabian peninsula and made this her capital, she decided to visit King Solomon. The state visit resulted in a very personal relationship, and from that meeting, without benefit of clergy, the present line of Imperial rulers of Ethiopia is said to have sprung. Haile Selassie himself claims direct descent from that union, and his claim seems to be borne out by his noble Semitic features which might have been those of Solomon himself.

But while Aksum may have indeed been the capital of an ancient nation, little remains to indicate it today—little, that is, except for the remarkable obelisks of Aksum. Some of these huge, granite columns are as high as seventy feet, and even taller ones are scattered here and there, leveled by earthquakes and storms. They are sculptured in the shape of buildings, with a "door" at the base and "windows" all the way up. Some authorities believe they may have preceded the establishment of Christianity in Ethiopia and may have had some connection with worship of the sun. It is thought-provoking to realize that these obelisks are completely different from those in Egypt, in spite of the proximity of the two countries.

High on our schedule of things to do here was the filming of the crowns of Ethiopia. We had been told that a vast number of the many crowns used by earlier kings and emperors of the country were preserved in a sacred area. But when we drove up to the Church of St. Mary with our equipment and started to unload, a black-robed priest with a dark, flat hat reminiscent of those worn by Greek Orthodox priests came up to our driver and an animated conversation ensued.

"I'm sorry, signor," our guide explained, "this is the head priest and he says that the grounds of St. Mary's Church are forbidden to women. Your wife may not enter."

"Oh no. Not again," I moaned. "And I suppose that if I disobey I will bleed to death from unknown causes."

"Yes, signora," the young man whispered, wide-eyed. "How did you know?"

"Never mind." I sighed. "Well, Hal, I'm in no mood to tempt the fates again. I guess I'll just have to pass up the crowns."

But Hal had been looking around thoughtfully. I know that look and can almost see the wheels turning.

"All right. Tell the priest we'll obey the taboo," he instructed, "but I'll need plenty of sunlight for filming the crowns. So show him the official letter from His Majesty and tell him he'll have to take fifteen or twenty of the crowns out into the sunlight for me."

A heated discussion ensued but finally the head priest threw up his hands and nodded agreement.

As Hal gathered his equipment together, he whispered to me, "Go back down the road about a hundred yards, where they can't see you, and then cut around that little hill. I'll get them to take the crowns out on the patio behind the church. I see that there's an iron picket fence there. You'll be able to see the crowns from there without actually stepping onto the grounds of the church. Just watch through the pickets."

Then, with a jaunty wave of his hand, he and David were off for the grounds of the church.

I followed his instructions carefully and as I quietly approached the fence, found I could easily see through the pickets, which were about three inches apart. And so it was that from about thirty feet away I got a fine look at the amazing crowns of Ethiopia as Hal filmed them, without contaminating the sacred soil of the Church of St. Mary. Apparently no Ethiopian stops to think that it is somewhat ironic that women should be forbidden to enter a church dedicated to that symbol of motherhood, the Virgin Mary!

As we loaded the equipment into our car preparatory to leaving, crowds of natives swarmed around us, some of them begging for alms. Normally we realize that poverty is so widespread in the world that what we could give one or two beggars would be like adding a drop of water to the ocean.

But this time, although Hal was quite busy, I tugged at his arm. "Have you a coin, Hal? There's a man there who looks like a wounded veteran. Maybe he lost his fingers fighting the Italians."

"Sure, sure," Hal muttered absentmindedly, reaching into his pocket. "Which one is it?" I pointed to the object of my sympathy. Hal reached over with the coin, and the man, who was wearing a tattered khaki coat, eagerly made a grab for it. His wounded hand, with the fingers missing, made contact with Hal's.

The driver gave a dismayed exclamation, then shouted wildly and chased the poor man away.

I was shocked. "Why did you do that?" I exclaimed. "The poor fellow is probably a veteran who sacrificed his fingers for his country. Why did you chase him away like that?"

"Oh, signora, please forgive me," our driver wailed. "I

should have watched more carefully. That man is not a veteran. He has leprosy!"

My heart seemed to stop beating. Hal, who had overheard, stiffened perceptibly. He had handed the coin to the leper with his left hand. He now looked at it as though it didn't belong to him.

"But please, signor, I think it was an arrested case. The skin did not have much of the typical steel color," chattered our now frantic chauffeur.

Hal continued to look at his outstretched left hand. Then he sighed. "Okay, let's see if we can find some alcohol or something. I'll scrub it well with soap. One is supposed to contract leprosy only after long contact with the disease. Let's hope that's right."

17

Moslems of Mali

WE were actually on our way to Timbuktu!

Even now, peering down at the seared hills of Mali from a window seat of an Air Afrique DC-6B, it was hard to believe that soon I would set foot in that mysterious city on the southern fringe of the Sahara Desert that represents the end of the earth in the minds of so many people.

During all our years of globe-trotting, I had trod upon every continent except Antarctica. I'd even had the unique experience of finding myself the only woman at the spartan mess of a remote DEW Line early warning radar station high on the Greenland ice cap, 250 miles inland.

After a series of fortunate contacts and negotiations with the United States Air Force, Hal had received permission to make a film there and the three of us landed at "DEW 2" in a military transport equipped with runners for landing on ice or snow. The technicians at the remote base were dumbfounded to see a woman in their isolated, barren domain. But their amazement had quickly changed to something like excited pride; I was a novelty, a conversation piece—the first woman ever to visit them. Their attention was enough to turn any feminine head. A group of them gathered around me in the mess hall.

Hal sat by, grinning with amusement. He knew how they felt, having experienced a similar sort of existence while serving with the Navy in the Pacific in World War II. In fact, he pointedly kept humming the refrain of "There Is Nothing Like a Dame" from *South Pacific*.

More amusing, however, was a telephone call from the even more isolated Radar Dome itself, which came while we were having coffee with the men.

A young life-of-the-party type named Kenny had seated himself next to me and was creating roars of laughter by his exaggerated attentions to me.

"Sugar? No? How about some cream? May I stir it for you? How about a doughnut? No? An apple, then?"

The phone on the wall rang and Kenny picked up the receiver. "Yes, this is Kenny . . . What's that, Georgie? You want to know what? . . . Oh, I can't be bothered with that right now. I'll have to call you back."

There was a pause while Kenny listened.

Then he broke in. "Now listen, Georgie, I can't be bothered with that. I'm busy talking to a beautiful girl who's sitting right to me. I'll have to hang up now."

A torrent of loud remarks which fortunately I couldn't make out distinctly poured from the receiver.

Kenny waited patiently until there was a momentary lull, then he said, "Now listen, Georgie, I'm *not* rock-happy. I'm really talking to a beautiful girl. Here, I'll put her on so you'll believe me." And he handed the telephone to me.

The faraway voice was still sputtering. "You and your wise-guy jokes! If you think—"

"Hello," I cooed into the mouthpiece, "I'm Halla Linker and I'm having a marvelous time here. How are things up where you are?"

For a long moment there was a shocked silence and as my grinning hosts listened I continued, "Hello! Can you hear me?"

The voice at the other end weakly gasped, *"Holy K-e-e-rist!"* Then there was dead silence.

Kenny took the phone from me and said, with a great show of patient forbearance, "You see, Georgie, I really *am* too busy to talk to you," and gently hung up.

Now as our plane circled prior to landing at Bamako, capital of the new Republic of Mali in West Africa, I couldn't help wishing for a moment that we were back on that Greenland ice cap with all that snow, for it was our fourth trip to Africa and I knew what the heat was apt to be like when we landed.

Somehow I hadn't expected to return to Africa so soon after our visit to Ethiopia. During the previous spring Hal had been rather vague about where our overseas filming trip would take us, once David's school vacation began. I fully expected to hear that we might go to Ceylon or Easter Island or perhaps even Little America in the Antarctic.

So I was surprised when he put his arms around me and, pointing to our world map, said, "Well, I've got it figured out. This year we can make it to Timbuktu!"

For a moment I stared and then his words registered. "You mean we're actually *going* there? There really is such a place?" I was tremendously excited.

He nodded and then explained that from New York we would fly to Dakar, the coastal capital of Senegal on the westernmost tip of Africa, and from there fly on, first to Bamako.

"We'll travel to Timbuktu by degrees," he said. "After we film in Bamako, we'll go up the Niger River to Mopti for more program material. And then we'll proceed to Timbuktu."

I couldn't sit still. I broke my rule never to interrupt David's homework and rushed to his room, which is filled with the kind of possessions so highly prized by American teen-agers plus special trophies he has picked up in our travels.

"David," I said breathlessly in Icelandic, which we always

use in talking to each other, "we're going to Timbuktu this summer!"

He raised his head from his book and murmured, "That's nice, Mommie." And then his eyes widened. *"Timbuktu?* You're kidding!"

"She certainly is not," Hal said in English over my shoulder. He had learned to understand Icelandic, in self-defense, as he put it, and so had been able to follow our conversation. "I want you to do some research on the country before we leave late in June."

David jumped up. He is as tall as I am; before long he will tower above both Hal and me. I don't know why it was that at that particular moment it suddenly dawned on me that our son was growing up and before long would be assuming a man's responsibilities in our world.

"I already know something about Timbuktu," he said.

"You do?"

I kept watching David. Through my mind ran fragments of memory like a motion picture montage—such as carrying him as an infant in a portable crib through the streets of Hong Kong, and the serious expression on his face when he had met Fulgencio Batista in Cuba. It was getting harder and harder for me to remember all his birthdays now.

The first one was easy—morning in Israel and afternoon in Rome; he had walked for the first time in shoes that I bought him in Rome. His second birthday came during Fidel Castro's attack on Moncada Barracks in Santiago. The third? That was when he fell down and broke a tooth just before his birthday in Brussels, Belgium. Fourth? Oh yes. What was that town in Japan—Karui-something? Ah yes—Karuizawa. How cute he had looked in his kimono and wooden sandals! On his fifth birthday, while traveling down the Congo River from Stanleyville to Leopoldville, we had brought out a big birthday cake we had ordered for him and kept in the ship's refrigerator until the day arrived. And the sixth had been spent in Honolulu while we were en route to the South Seas. The

rest of the birthdays were like a kaleidoscope—the seventh in
Istanbul on our way to the Soviet Union; the eighth in Lima,
Peru; the ninth in Liechtenstein; the tenth in the Kingdom
of Nepal; and the eleventh in Barcelona.

I had to smile as I remembered the look on people's faces
when we told them that David had celebrated his twelfth
birthday in no country at all! I remembered the party we had
made for him in the middle of the North Atlantic on the
Empress of Canada while we were going from Scotland to
Montreal. Where would he have his birthday this year?

I came back to the present with a start. David was saying,
"... and what's more, that's where they have the Touaregs,
who are fierce desert fighters. They used to give the French
Foreign Legion a bad time."

Hal smiled. "I can see that you're an expert on the subject.
Don't you think so, elskan-min?"

I gathered my wits together and nodded. "Of course, Hal-
minn."

And now here we were, months later, with our four-engine,
propeller-driven plane slanting down toward Bamako's airport. The cabin grew noticeably warmer. I glanced at Hal's
open briefcase on the seat between us. There were our three
airline tickets—our three tickets to Timbuktu. I smiled and
turned to look out of the window.

Below us I got a glimpse of mud huts surrounding an area
of rather uninspiring concrete buildings. Hal, seated next to
me, instinctively checked to see that my seat belt was fastened,
then glanced across the aisle at David, whose nose was pressed
against the window. The pilot throttled back the engines.
And then an unexpected updraft shot us skyward again. Full
power was applied and we started to climb once more and
again circle for a landing.

Although by this time I had had more hours in the air as
a passenger than many a military pilot on active duty, sudden
unexpected maneuvers such as this are still unsettling.

Hal, who can anticipate my every mood, wordlessly slipped

his hand over mine. "It's these rising currents, especially over hot lands like Mali, elskan-min." He had to raise his voice to make himself heard above the uneven drumming of the engines.

I nodded, feeling perfectly reassured. Our ability to communicate and understand one another's emotions without saying a word has grown with the passage of years.

The plane repeated its landing maneuver. This time the pilot maintained power. The air was still rough but we made a perfect landing.

Stepping out of the plane was like entering a blast furnace. While I knew that the interior of West Africa would not be the world's coolest spot in early July, I had not expected anything quite as wilting as this.

Although Bamako is more than two hundred miles from the coast and some distance from the heart of the desert, the rainy season had begun and the humidity made the heat even more oppressive.

We gathered together such equipment as we carried by hand and hurried into the shelter of the small airport terminal building. By the time we confronted the ebony-skinned, French-speaking Mali customs and immigration officials, we were wringing wet with perspiration.

Hal mopped his face and throat. "The folders say that Mali's mean summer temperature averages ninety degrees. All I can say is that it is *really* mean!

I managed a smile. "Well, Timbuktu has always been the promised land to me as a traveler. I'm going to like this country if it kills me!"

"Don't say that," Hal said with a grin. "It looks as though it's trying to do just that."

From the ground, the "European" part of Bamako—built by the French after they occupied the area in 1894—was more attractive than it had appeared from the air. The avenues were wide and lined with large shade trees. The buildings were mostly of two stories. Several were interestingly colonial.

The largest in the city was the towering Catholic Cathedral in the very center of town. Most of the others were somewhat severe architecturally and reminded us of fortresses, as though the French Foreign Legion David had mentioned actually had found it necessary to stand ready to defend itself, even in the heart of the city.

Since the French had been ousted by Mali in 1960, everything had been taken over by the new native government whose chief of state at the time of our visit was Mobido Keita. The authorities, all with leftist tendencies, had taken over all public services.

Although in some respects the only hotel, a two-story colonial structure called the Grand, was managed in rather haphazard fashion by government employees, the food, service and general sanitation were excellent. (A Frenchman was in charge of the cuisine.) That plus the fact that our window was equipped with an ancient and noisy but still functioning air-conditioner made Bamako's climate more nearly bearable. Later we were to find ourselves in accommodations in other parts of Mali that would make us look back on our stay in Bamako's Grand Hotel as days of pure luxury.

The people of Mali, an ethnic mélange of Bambara, Puuls, Markas, Songhais, Malinkes and Touaregs, had said "Allez" in no uncertain terms to the French. Still, the country had a predominantly Gallic atmosphere. Ironically, also, these people, who profess to despise their former rulers, buy 75 percent of their imported goods from the French. During our wandering through Bamako, we got some indication of their feelings when we filmed a large World War I memorial dedicated to the Askaris, the native soldiers of what was then French Sudan, who had served in Europe under the tricolor from 1914 to 1918. The statues of the charging African soldiers on the monument were still intact, as were the engraved names of battles they had engaged in that meant nothing to me as an Icelander but which Hal told me still live in people's memories all over Europe and America—the Marne,

Rheims, Château-Thierry, the Aisne and so on. But what struck us at once was the fact that the words of commendation and dedication that had been inscribed on the monument had all been carefully chiseled off and painted over with white paint!

Abdul Sow, the scholarly, lean, middle-aged director of the Office National du Tourisme Malien, obtained a Volkswagen Microbus for us, but our driver could communicate with us only in French, since very few English-speaking people can be found in Bamako.

Hal dug deep into his memory for the French he had learned in school twenty-five years before and did wonderfully well. He has a knack for languages and speaks five of them. By the time we had finished with our driver, the two of them were chattering away like a pair of Parisian boulevardiers.

Our first filming objective was the Central Market, which we had heard was quite picturesque. As we drove down a wide, tree-lined thoroughfare en route there, Hal spotted an impressive new building. It looked like an ideal setting to illustrate the recent architectural progress of the country.

While Hal used one of his movie cameras, I shot some stills with my Rolleiflex, and when we returned to our car Hal asked about the building we had just photographed.

Our guide hesitated and then shrugged. He blurted out something and Hal looked startled.

"What did he say, Hal-minn?"

My husband shook his head disgustedly. "Evidently we've just taken extensive movies and stills of the new headquarters of the Communist Party of Mali!"

For a moment our faces were red, a color appropriate to the occasion. Then we realized that this, too, was an important part of the story of Mali. As has been the case elsewhere in the world, the vacuum created by the departure of the Europeans had immediately been filled by die-hard leftists.

The Central Market is a block-long building that looks like

a fortress from which legionnaire *Beau Geste* characters might have sallied forth in some television motion pictures. Its interior is filled with noisy stalls in which clothing, foodstuffs (both familiar and exotic) and of all things women's wigs, were being sold.

Although the wearing of wigs is still a comparatively recent fad in the Western World, here in Mali native women have been using them for some time, we were told. Evidently most African women here cannot grow long tresses, and wigs are the answer. However, Mali wigs for the less-affluent women are made of dyed horsehair. I visualized wearing one of these horrors in that heat and had to shudder.

A profusion of fish, herbs and spices were being hawked by vendors, all of them women. Various types of moss and tree bark which we were told have aphrodisiac qualities seemed to be popular items.

That evening Abdul Sow arranged for us to attend a social soiree at a private home, and I was awestruck by the beautiful, flowing national costumes and the glittering silver and gold jewelry worn by prominent Mali matrons. Like their less-well-to-do sisters, they also wore wigs, but theirs were Paris imports and not horsehair specials from Bamako's Central Market.

As we grew more familiar with Bamako's byways, we grew increasingly aware that the Cold War was being actively waged here by the Russians. Just across the way from the Great Mosque of Bamako stood the Parliament Building, in the process of being completely rebuilt by Russian technicians with Russian trucks and construction equipment all marked SOCOTRA, for Soviet Commercial and Trade Commission.

In the European shopping areas we became aware that almost as many of the customers spoke Russian as conversed in French!

While there seemed to be no sign of any American visitors besides ourselves, except for the staff of the American Embassy of course, we learned that an American Industrial and Economic Exhibition had closed here just a few days before. It had been set up on the banks of the Niger, and off we went to see if any Americans were still there. On the way we passed the weather-beaten plaster building that had been used by the Chinese Communists for their own exhibit just before ours had opened. A tremendous sign over the entrance still read ÉXPOSITION SUR L'ÉDIFICATION ÉCONOMIQUE DE LA RÉPUBLIQUE POPULAIRE DU CHINE, with its Chinese equivalent alongside, and we wondered whether China's economic "progress" would be the model for that of Mali.

The United States exhibition was in the last stages of being dismantled. Two young Americans were in charge: Mr. Gayton, a red-bearded Oregonian, and a tall Texan named Miller. Both were extremely happy to see fellow Americans and were proud of their part in bringing tangible signs of America's industrial progress to remote corners of the world. Gayton told us how pleased he was that the American presentation had been so popular. Ghana had been their next previous exhibit area, and now they were heading for Vienna.

The building in the process of being dismantled was a geodetic domelike affair—a sort of igloo made of prefabricated steel triangles.

"This design was chosen primarily as a modern American development, but it sure came in handy for the storms we've had here." Miller smiled. "Have you met up with one of these Mali storms yet?"

Hal shook his head. "Are they bad?"

"Bad?" Miller looked serious. "They make some of our panhandle northers feel like a gentle April breeze! They pop out of nowhere, just like that"—he snapped his fingers—"one minute it's bright and sunny, and the next thing you know the sky has turned green and you see a low cloud on the horizon. And before you know it, winds of from eighty to a hundred miles an hour hit you. Boy! We sure learned whether these geodetic domes could take it. And let me tell you," he continued proudly, "they actually stood up to the wind better than any other kind of construction."

Hal pursed his lips. "Do they have these storms inland at Mopti and Timbuktu?"

Gayton glanced at Miller. "We haven't been in there ourselves but those who have say it gets even worse because they become sandstorms in the Sahara area and— Say, are you planning to visit Mopti and Timbuktu?"

We nodded.

"Well all I can say is—be careful. By the time you see a storm building up, it's almost too late to run. Just get under cover and sit tight till it blows past."

"But suppose there *is* no cover?" David spoke up, his eyes shining in fascination.

"Don't go where there's no solid shelter handy," Gayton answered.

"If you *are* caught in the open, cover your head with a sheet or blanket, turn your back to the wind, and hope for the best," said Miller.

It was a disturbing prospect. We returned to our hotel for a rest before going out to film the special Friday gathering of devout Moslems at the Great Mosque.

David was still absorbed by the description of the storms. "Do you know, Pabbi, I remember reading how Arabian camel caravans are sometimes caught in the Sahara by one of these storms and buried forever under sand!"

"Well, I'd be worried if we were going to travel by camel caravan to Mopti and Timbuktu," Hal answered, "but since we'll fly with airline pilots who know this area and its peculiar weather, I don't think we'll have any problems."

Much later he admitted to me that he had assumed an air of confidence for David's and my sakes. Inside he had been quite concerned and begun to turn over in his mind whether or not we should risk running into such a storm, particularly since this was the time of year they could be expected.

But our visit to the huge mosques, where we saw thousands

of Moslems kneel and prostrate themselves in prayer, all facing toward holy Mecca, drove thoughts of the fury of Sahara's wind from our minds.

Our driver was very nervous when he learned that we intended to film this weekly religious ceremony that takes place on a vast field surrounding the mosque. He spoke excitedly in French.

Hal shrugged and turned to me. "He is afraid the Moslems may strenuously object to being filmed. I've filmed similar ceremonies before without being molested. I don't anticipate trouble. However"—he smiled and substituted a long-range telephoto lens for the kind he uses for close-up shots—"since discretion is the better part of valor, I'll film from a safe distance without disturbing the worshipers."

As he began I looked about for our driver. He had quietly disappeared and he remained away until we had finished. The assemblage at the Great Mosque must have numbered nearly 10,000 people. Women and men occupied separate areas. When the muezzin chanted the summons to prayer, his voice was amplified by loudspeakers on the minaret towers. The effect was quite startling. Almost as one, the worshipers first bowed from the waist toward Mecca, then dropped to their knees and touched the earth with their foreheads while their arms remained outstretched before them. We had seen this impressive ceremony in other parts of the Moslem world from Morocco to Pakistan, and it varied but little.

Meanwhile the afternoon sun began to sink lower. Its rays slanted directly into my eyes and I moved to the shaded side of our vehicle. Kneeling in prayer not twenty feet away from me was a young woman who carried an infant slung over her back papoose fashion. She sat some distance away from the other women.

As she straightened up, I noted that her baby was sound asleep, oblivious to the reverberating, amplified chanting from the muezzin. But what caught my eye were the mother's hands. They bore unmistakable marks of the ravages of lep-

rosy, signs I had learned to recognize after our experience at
Aksum.

The woman turned her face toward me. It had once been
attractive; now it was a grotesque mask of misery. My heart
went out to the poor girl and her even more unfortunate infant, eventually doomed to contract the dread disease through
prolonged, intimate contact with its mother.

Hal finished his filming and came up to me. He noted my
look, glanced at the leper girl who fixedly watched us, and
grasped my arm. "Come, Halla-min, I know how you feel but
there's nothing we can do to help her. Leprosy is beginning
to disappear from the world. Perhaps in time medical science
will be able to sweep dark corners like Mali clean of dread
ailments like this."

He was right, of course, but it was a long time before the
picture of that young mother grew dim in my memory.

Saturday night is usually a time for relaxation and entertainment in most places, and we discovered that the tradition
prevails in Mali as well. Thanks to our sponsor at the Tourist
Office, we were invited to attend an intimate performance of
ancient music and dances by a local troupe that was being
welcomed back after having presented its unique style of
dancing throughout Europe. The auditorium where the performance was held was also used as the dancers' rehearsal hall
and held about a hundred spectators.

When we arrived the place was jammed with perspiring
humanity. The heat was overwhelming, but once the curtain
rose on the first dance, our discomforts were forgotten. The
music would have been startling enough in the open; indoors
it was a shattering, reverberating cacophony of sound. The
dances were intricate, with gyrations and contortions of body
and limbs that were difficult to follow at first. But as the performance progressed, an electric excitement began to build
up between the dancers, musicians and audience. Even my
Icelandic blood stirred as I found my body involuntarily
swaying to the pounding of primitive drums and the wailing

of native instruments. If the effect on me was electric, you can imagine how the Malians in the audience reacted.

The individual dance numbers frequently left little to the imagination. "Le Mandiana," performed by supple young girls, was actually a ritual of Manding tribespeople. The "Guele" was an athletic tour de force performed by dancers who represented all the ethnic strains of Mali. The "Sounou" was an ancient prayer for a good harvest, while the war dances of the Souba and the mystic ritual of Gomba could be followed, even without the assistance of the short program notes written in French that had been handed us before the performance.

When the music stopped between dances, I felt emotionally drained. David sat beside me, his mouth half open with incredulity. Hal had been filming the spectacle and sound-taping the music. He caught my eye and shook his head in amazement. His expression told me that the performance was making as profound an impression on him as it was on us and our Malian neighbors.

In most places intermission time is a signal for relaxation and discussion. Here it was different. Everyone leaned forward tensely, impatiently awaiting what was to follow. It seemed as though they knew what to expect. Hal left his camera mounted on its tripod and came over to us.

"If what the program says is true, the next number, the finale, should be a humdinger, elskan-min! It's supposed to show the punishment of members of a secret society who violate the rules."

The word "humdinger" hardly does justice to what followed. Amid a breathless silence, two huge drummers, their muscles rippling beneath gleaming dark skin, advanced to the front of the stage, Although their movements were slow and deliberate and their faces expressionless, they somehow reminded me of the deceptively languid lions that had taken over the abandoned buildings in Mozambique's Gorongoza Game Preserve.

The drummers seated themselves crosslegged, raised their powerful arms, and paused briefly. Then they began a slow, deliberate beat that had an almost physical impact. Other drummers appeared behind them. The drums began to echo one another in eerie counterpoint. The tempo slowly increased. When male and female dancers, waving their arms and singing and shouting, abruptly leaped upon the stage, we almost jumped from our seats. And then a nightmarish figure, the "witch-doctor," sprang among the dancers with incredible agility and began to cast a spell upon the secret society's betrayers.

The movements became a whirling maelstrom. The shouting, screaming and drumming grew almost more than eyes and ears could stand. The dancers, particularly the witch doctor, accomplished prodigious and incredibly graceful leaps and bounds that would have been worthy of Nuryeyev.

I saw Mali mothers snatch up their children and dash for the door before their offspring could start shrieking in fear.

The writhing, gleaming dancers moved faster and faster. The tempo quickened even more and the sound volume increased steadily.

At any moment I expected the roof to explode skyward and the walls to fly apart. And then—when I thought that surely they could not go on at such an inhuman pace any longer—they arrived at a thunderous climax that nearly reduced me (and many Malians in the audience) to a quivering nervous wreck!

Then it was finished. The dancers, their bodies running with perspiration, stood frozen in various poses; the drummers sat like statues. Only their heaving chests and straining muscles showed the punishment their bodies had sustained.

For a long moment everyone in the auditorium—performers and audience alike—remained locked in a rigid silence. And then applause exploded like a bursting bomb. The three of us were swept along with the cheering, hand-pounding Malians. I clapped so hard that my palms were bruised.

Although we had seen many native dances performed against authentic backgrounds, we had never before encountered anything remotely resembling what we had just experienced.

Later when we televised Hal's film of the dance, the audience reaction proved that the strange, almost supernatural, excitement of that Saturday evening in Bamako had literally reached out from their television sets and held people spellbound in their own living rooms.

Although neither Hal nor I pretend to be "show-biz" experts, we feel that the Mali dancers of Bamako could become a gold mine for any entrepreneur who brought them to the United States.

It was rather late when we returned to the hotel and we had packing to do for our early flight to Mopti the following morning, but Hal and I simply sat and talked about that amazing performance.

I said, "I don't see how you were able to concentrate on filming during that dance!"

He shrugged. "Frankly, neither do I. Guess it's habit. After all these years of watching war, people and places through the view-finder of a camera. I somehow instinctively keep my finger on the trigger."

There was a sudden reverberating rumble that seemed to shake the building.

Hal stood up. "Don't tell me those drummers have followed us!"

The noise came again, louder and closer. And then the night exploded with furious lightning, window-rattling thunder and a shrieking wind of near-hurricane velocity.

The electric lights dimmed, brightened, and dimmed again. We stared at one another and hurried to the window. Our room boys were already out on the balcony that extended completely around the house and were slamming the iron shutters that protected each window. Before those in our room were closed, we could see horizontal sheets of water pouring down and blotting out the world.

"I guess this is one of the storms Gayton and Miller warned us about," Hal muttered, urging us back from the windows, which seemed to bulge inward from the pressure. "Keep away from the glass. I don't want anyone to get cut by flying pieces if it breaks."

It took two hours for the storm to exhaust itself and then it ended as abruptly as it had begun. Although none of us said anything, I know we all had the same thought in mind when we finally bedded down for what remained of the night. What if we encountered such a storm while flying?

18

Masks of the Dogons

I T was not yet dawn when we checked out of the hotel in Bamako and headed for the airport for our 5:30 flight to Mopti. It had been painful to arouse ourselves after an hour or so of sleep, but we did not complain. The early flight time meant that the old DC-3 that was to take us to the inland city some 200 miles upriver would fly in comparatively cool, stable air.

Had the schedule called for a later departure, we would have met violent up-currents of air heated by the almost equatorial sun. And while none of us has ever been seriously air-sick, there could always be a first time.

We had expected to find a deserted terminal occupied by a handful of sleepy, yawning people like ourselves. Instead we found a line of Mali troops in dress uniform lined up in precise ranks. Behind them stood an enormous crowd for that time of day, half a dozen or so of Bamako's spectacularly uniformed, white-helmeted motorcycle police and a troop of shining-faced children, each holding a bouquet of flowers.

Still half asleep, we got out of the little Volkswagen bus and blinked at the soldiers, civilians and police. They blinked back. And then there were shouted commands. The band's

269

drum major moved his baton, and the brassy blare of a military march brought us wide awake.

And now we saw the reason for this predawn spectacle. Emerging from a four-engined transport that had Red Chinese markings came the honored guests—a group of Chinese Communists who had flown to Mali on an economic-aid mission. The soldiers fired a military salute.

"Shucks! And all the time I thought these people had turned out to see *us* off," Hal complained, with a grin.

He mounted his camera in time to film the children as they solemnly handed the floral offerings to the Chinese. The latter, spotting his camera, seemed to move with deliberately slow steps, to make sure we got good pictures. And then it dawned on me that they actually thought my husband was part of the official Mali reception!

When Hal had finished, we summoned porters for our baggage and pushed our way through the crowd, past the Red Chinese, who now looked perplexed, and finally settled ourselves in the DC-3.

Our venerable twin-engined transport followed the Niger, which separated into tributaries before reaching the cluster of sun-baked, mud-walled buildings that constitute Mopti. The airport was merely a dirt landing strip with a tiny nearby building that served as both control tower and terminal.

If anything, Mopti was hotter than Bamako and much more primitive. The "city" is divided into native and European areas, with the former sprawling along an embankment while the latter occupies the wide end of a peninsula jutting into the river. As we were driven to our "hotel" by another Volkswagen bus provided by the local authorities, we noticed that the approach to the European part of Mopti was quite narrow, barely wide enough for two cars abreast.

"The French probably kept the entrance narrow," Hal remarked. "In that way a handful of troops could hold it against the natives in case of attack."

Our headquarters turned out to be a run-down, one-story,

eight-room motel-like affair called *l'Encampement*. Originally it had been a special residence constructed by the French for occasional government visitors. Now it would have to do for us, since it was the only place resembling a hotel this side of Bamako.

We were assigned a room about the size of a modern prison cell. Three cots with mosquito netting filled it. The air was hot and close. By now the sun was directly overhead and the roof and walls intensified the merciless heat and funneled it in on us. A grinning houseboy stood by while the three of us examined our surroundings.

David spoke up. "Mama—what's that over there?" He pointed to a wall, extending only part way to the ceiling, that partially blocked the end of the room.

I went over to investigate. Behind this half wall were our toilet facilities consisting of a cracked, stained porcelain sink with rusty fixtures and a toilet with a seat encrusted with hardened excrement. Hal peered over my shoulder. He called the houseboy and in French instructed him to clean it. The boy looked puzzled, as though unable to understand why such a little thing as that should upset us.

I thought of the Grand Hotel in Bamako and sighed deeply as I returned to the outer room to check the bedding. If Mopti were indeed the threshold to Timbuktu, the fabled end of the world, what in heaven's name might we run into there?

My hunch about the bedding was right. The wrinkled sheets were obviously unchanged. Now I grew annoyed.

"Hal!" I called.

He turned from watching the houseboy trying to clean the bathroom. "What is it, elskan-min?"

I pointed to the wrinkled bedding.

Hal's face crimsoned. He went to the front door and called to the young native manager who was lounging outside. He, too, was a government employee, as were all hotel personnel. There ensued a heated discussion in French. Finally the manager walked away, shaking his head and muttering to himself.

"What's the verdict, Hal?"

My husband was still fuming. "Can you imagine his nerve? He tried to tell me that the sheets aren't really very dirty. He insisted that since a Frenchman had slept on them for only a few hours the other day, he couldn't afford to waste such almost clean linen. But we'll get new sheets now," Hal assured me.

The room was stifling. When another houseboy trotted in with reasonably fresh linen, Hal took him by the arm, pointed to an electric outlet on the wall, and asked a question.

The houseboy grinned. *"Oui, m'sieu, certainment!"* He left at a gallop.

"What did you tell him, Pabbi?" asked David.

"I asked him if he could dig up an electric fan. He's gone to fetch one."

A few moments later the houseboy returned, proudly carrying a tiny, battered fan with warped and nicked blades. As we watched, he placed it on the floor, and taking the bare cord in his hand, was about to insert it into the electrical outlet when Hal let out an exclamation and grabbed his wrists. The boy looked up inquiringly.

"Are you trying to kill yourself?" Hal asked. He held up the boy's hands. There was no plug at the end of the wires!

The houseboy's eyes went from Hal's face to mine. The reason for our concern finally dawned on him. He grinned and explained, in his halting French, that there was nothing to worry about.

"Regardez!" he said.

Hal and I *regardezed* with a certain amount of fear for his safety. He calmly inserted the naked ends of the wires into the outlet; the fan came to life. He removed the wires; the fan stopped. This shortcut took the place of a switch, since such luxuries were not available here.

"Comprenez, m'sieu ... m'dame?"

"Oui, nous comprenons," my husband answered slowly.

For the duration of our stay we poked the wires into the outlet to start the fan and pulled them out to stop it!

Mopti's native architecture is Sudanese. All the buildings are of reddish clay and resemble windowless fortresses, so that I could only assume that the past history of the area had taught the people to trust only themselves and to live in closed bastions. Dominating the native area was the strange-looking clay-walled mosque that boasted several hundred-foot towers. These somewhat reminded me of the giant anthills called *termitières* that we had seen in the Congo and Mozambique. But an added touch were the wooden poles protruding from the sides of the towers. Our guides could furnish no explanation for them other than that they made excellent perches for birds.

"Then the people here are bird-lovers?" I asked.

Our guide looked blank, and we dropped the subject.

The 2,600-mile-long Niger River, which is a navigable waterway most of the year, gives Mopti, a community of about 6,000, an unexpected maritime atmosphere. The stream is one of the longest in the world and meanders in a vast arc from the center of Africa to the Gulf of Guinea.

We were at Mopti during the dry season and the river was quite low. The only craft we saw that could navigate the river at this time of year were the narrow trading canoes used by the neighboring tribes.

While filming along the river bank, we saw women of the Puul tribe who still follow the custom of having their ear lobes pierced while still very young; they enlarge the holes each year. The ornaments they wear in these openings are gradually increased in size until, when they reach adulthood, they can wear tremendous gold earrings the size of a head of lettuce! Fortunately, these immense decorations are made of hollow gold and weigh "only" three or four pounds. Such ostentation, of course, is reserved for prosperous matrons whose glittering golden decorations advertise the fact that the wearer is married to a wealthy man. Most Puul women of means wear these enormous decorations in their ears and many also add tremendous gold necklaces from which are suspended gold baskets the size of a fist. These adornments are obviously status symbols.

Along the waterfront we filmed the daily chores of the average Mopti housewife as she washed the family's clothing and the children at the same time, all the while enjoying a good gossip with her neighbors.

I judged by their expressions that they were probably saying, "Look at that strange-looking foreign woman there with all that ridiculous clothing on. She'll probably get sick wearing so much. Oh well, you know how those white foreigners are."

At a group of huts along the water's edge I came upon some women sitting with their hands immersed in a gooey indigo-colored, molasseslike substance in metal pots. A closer inspection showed that they were dyeing cloth. I learned that these were the famous "indigo women" of Mali whose hand-dyed material is highly sought by the desert Touareg for robes. This cloth has been one of the most important articles of trade with those desert nomads since time immemorial, and the indigo women have apparently kept their secret formula to themselves through the ages. Their own hands and arms were stained a deep indigo right up to the elbows, since they always mix the dyes with their hands. But I learned that they proudly carry this mark of their unique skill for all to see, proclaiming to the world who they are.

It was here in Mopti that we heard of a mysterious tribe called the Dogons who live some seventy-five miles beyond Mopti, in the interior, toward Timbuktu. These people exist in a civilization that can best be described as Late Stone Age. Despite the fact that Berbers, Spaniards, Arabs, British and French have marched up and down the Sudan for more than a thousand years, the Dogons escaped the attention of the outside world until 1925 when Marcel Griaule, a French ethnologist, stumbled on them.

Hal's insatiable curiosity made him press for further details. He learned that the Dogons practice ancestor worship and bury their dead in caves carved out of the sides of cliffs. These tombs resemble the settlements of the Indians of the American Southwest. The Dogons indulge in pagan dances that feature grotesque masks adorned with swastikalike arms. Some of their headdresses are thirty feet high! When our guide Cisse also told us that an American missionary couple had built a church in Dogon territory and had even converted a few to Christianity, Hal turned to me, his eyes glowing.

Before he could utter a word, I said, "Yes, Hal, I know. When do we start for the Dogons?"

He smiled and squeezed my hand in thanks. We were preparing to start that very afternoon when our guide suddenly squinted at the sky, which had suddenly darkened.

"Mon Dieu!" Cisse muttered. *"Un vent du sable."*

"Sandstorm?" Hal echoed. He peered up into the sky. "Look, Halla-min, this is what those Americans in Bamako meant when they warned us about Sahara storms."

He pointed to the sky, which by then had become a sickly gray-green in color. I noticed an ominous black cloud hovering low upon the horizon and remembered Gayton's warning that by the time you spotted a storm it was already too late to run. I was on the verge of reminding Hal of Gayton's words when the storm hit with full fury.

Although we were only half a dozen yards from our room, the wind almost swept us from our feet. Sand cut into our flesh like thousands of red-hot needles. We could hardly breathe, and the gloom was so dense that the outlines of the encampment were almost invisible, although the door to our room was not much more than an arm's length away.

We somehow made it to the room and slammed the door behind us. Now we could breathe without filling our lungs with Sahara sand.

A howling wind shook the encampment. Dust sifted in through cracks around the door and windows. It began to grow murky even inside our room. I saw Hal reach for his camera and then go to the door.

"Where are you going, Hal-minn?"

"I've just *got* to get some footage of this! I've *got* to!"

"Wait!" I seized one of my large handkerchiefs and made a mask of it, tying it around his head to keep the sand out of his nostrils.

Looking like a masked bandit, he whirled, opened the door and slid out sideways. It took both David and me to push the door shut behind him. The room was filled with a fresh supply of sand. There was grit underfoot, as well as in our mouths, eyes and hair.

I went to the window and peered out. Hal was hanging onto a column of the porch with one hand while he worked the camera with the other. He took scene after scene. Then the wind whipped the kerchief from his face. He ducked his head, held the camera against his body, and rushed toward the door. I opened it and the three of us pushed it shut.

"I got it! I got it!" Hal croaked exultantly, hardly able to talk because of the sand in his throat.

Then we carefully began to clean the sand from the camera.

We postponed our start for the Dogon until early the following day. The storm had exhausted itself within an hour, but by the time the sky had cleared the sun was setting. Besides, it took us until dinnertime to shake the grime from our hair and wash the sand and dust from our bodies.

When we did set forth in Cisse's car—a Volkswagen bus although we would have preferred a Land Rover—I kept glancing uneasily at the cloudless sky. Although our guide told us that we probably wouldn't encounter another *"vent du sable"* for weeks, I had a hunch—call it premonition if you will—that it would be otherwise.

But as we lurched over the rutted dirt trail that wandered

along the river bank and passed one village after another filled with natives who seemed none the worse for having weathered the "wind of sand," I began to feel better.

In order to move freely among the Dogons and get them to dance for our camera, it was necessary first to visit the village of Sangha and get a special permit from the governor of the district. The Dogons were considered a national asset and were under government protection.

Sangha was distinguished from the other villages not so much by the Governor's Residence—larger than most but still a red-clay fortress—as by the eight-foot monument in the town square. This obelisk, which bore only an inscription in French, AUX MARTYRS DU COLONIALISME, eloquently proclaimed the strength of Mali's anti-French sentiments. It was ironic that this anti-French message could only be communicated to passers-by in the French language.

The governor, a tall rather handsome man whose aquiline features proclaimed his intermixture of Arabic blood, was at first rather cool to Hal's request for official permission to film the Dogons. But after he was introduced to David and me he softened noticeably. "How could anyone who traveled the world with his wife and young son do any harm to my Dogons?" his new attitude seemed to say—and permission to film was granted.

The nearest Dogon village was just a few miles farther along the road. Cisse had told us that it had skyscrapers, and we thought he was trying to be funny until we sighted the village and discovered that most of the Dogon houses were actually three stories high. From a short distance away, they did give the impression of a modern city's skyline.

The chief of the village was a slender, genial, middle-aged gentleman who wore a black fez and the long, flowing white robes of the Arabs. While his messenger went to summon the dancers, I wandered over to a nearby hut and watched the Dogon women cooking and baking over open ovens. We established an immediate rapport through sign language and got along famously.

One proud mother balanced a set of twin boys on her broad hips as she sauntered up to me. When I asked, by means of sign language, if I could hold one, she hesitated momentarily. The other women nodded and obviously told her to grant my request. So she relented, and as I held the little one it stared at my white Icelandic skin and blond hair, Hal raised his camera and began to film us. These were the first twins we had ever seen in any African village. Multiple births are usually considered bad omens by many African tribes, and the infants are permitted to die, lest they contaminate the tribe. With the Dogons, however, twins were apparently a good omen.

The insistent pounding of drums and weird chanting of male voices warned us of the approach of the Dogon dancers. I returned the baby to its mother as the performers, grotesque in their masks and strange headdresses that towered in the air like swaying antennae, assembled and began their gyrations.

Only males are permitted to execute these ritualistic religious dances. Since some of the routines tell stories involving women, however, men take female roles by wearing small gourds strapped to their chests.

All the dancers had their faces covered by masks, either of decorated seashells or of wood, with slits for the eyes. A few wore headdresses crested by arms which were shaped almost like swastikas. The most spectacularly costumed wore incredibly high, tapering spires on top of their headdresses. How these towering decorations stayed on during all the twirling and hopping is still a mystery to me. These antennae reached twenty or thirty feet above the dancers' heads.

During this unique performance Hal moved from place to place, searching for different camera angles, while David and I scurried about shooting still pictures in both black and white and color film with the two Rolleiflex cameras. We also helped by operating the sound recorder and capturing on tape the weird music and the shrill yipping sounds, like the bark of a dog, which the dancers emitted as they twisted and jumped.

When the performance was over, we were exhausted and limp from the broiling sun. It was almost noon. The thermos jug of water was now only half full, and we still had the long ride back in the heat of the day. Hal quickly evaluated our predicament and ordered Cisse to drive still farther away from Mopti in the direction of the American missionaries we had heard about.

Then he turned to me. "If I know Americans, they'll be tickled to death to see us and we can replenish our water supply there. We have enough now to get us home if all goes well, but not if we have a breakdown or run into a sandstorm. Let's not take a chance."

I smiled in full agreement.

We spotted the missionary headquarters while we were still more than a mile away. It was like seeing a bit of the United States magically placed in the middle of the Sahara Desert. The house resembled a spick-and-span Kansas farmhouse built of stone. Nearby stood the church, an imposing structure with a towering steeple. Like the house, it was also a bit of Midwestern America, solid and reassuring.

The missionary couple, the McKinneys, stepped out on their porch just as Cisse brought our car to a stop. They did not see us at first, but they knew our guide and greeted him in fluid Mali. From where we sat we could see that they were pleasant-looking people in their late fifties. Hal later described them as "American Gothic." But they were warm and friendly and in that respect not at all like the dour Midwestern farmer and his wife in Grant's famous painting.

When we got out of the car, they blinked in amazement. Mrs. McKinney came up to me and began to speak in French.

"We're Americans!" I exclaimed.

"For mercy sakes!" she gasped.

Her husband came forward, his eyes shining. "Where are you folks from?"

Their voices had an unmistakable Kansas twang. It was good to hear.

"From Los Angeles," Hal answered.

"California!" Mr. McKinney echoed. "Well now, we have a married daughter living there in Claremont. That's near Los Angeles, isn't it? But here—come on in out of the sun. And I'll bet this is your son." He chuckled and pumped David's hand.

Their porch was delightfully cool and spotless. We apologized for our intrusion. And of course they came right back and scolded us for even thinking that we could visit the Dogon area without stopping by to say hello. I explained that we had brought sandwiches with us from Mopti but were parched with thirst and wondered if we could replenish our supply of water.

"Heavens!" exclaimed Mrs. McKinney, "what'm I standing around for!"

She darted into the house and in a few minutes came back with a large tray that held a huge pitcher of ice-cold lemonade and glasses! I cannot remember any beverage ever tasting so refreshing.

As for our lunching on sandwiches—absolutely not! It was utterly fantastic. There we sat in the middle of Mali on the fringe of the Sahara, and to all intents and purposes we were seated in a cool Kansas kitchen at a large table covered with a checkered cloth, eating a bounteous midday dinner of delicious cold fried chicken, preserves and homemade bread that smelled heavenly and tasted even better. Afterward we literally had to loosen our belts as we sat and chatted. The McKinney's were intrigued by our way of living. And then, in response to our questioning, they casually told us of their life in the Dogon area.

As members of the Christian Missionary Alliance, they had come to Mali and settled here in 1932, seven years after Griaule had discovered, or perhaps "rediscovered," the unique tribe.

"We took things easy at first," Mr. McKinney explained. "For a couple of years we just tried to let the Dogons know that we wanted to be neighbors, that's all. We didn't pester them and they let us alone. But we were busy learning their language." He chuckled. "That and some French. Practically taught ourselves, didn't we, Mother?" He smiled at his wife affectionately. She nodded.

"That must have been some job," Hal said.

"Oh, learning the tongue wasn't so bad. The hard part was inventing a writing for it and then translating the Bible into the language!"

Just the thought of what these friendly, generous people had accomplished all by themselves was awe-inspiring.

"Once we got the Bible translated into their language, we started to teach school here. And when a few of 'em learned to read, we turned them loose on the Good Book!" Mr. McKinney paused. "I got some of the younger folk interested in becoming Christians; in fact, the flock helped us build the church."

"What about the headman and the rest of the Dogons? They're still pagans, aren't they?" I asked.

He nodded.

"Did the headman give you any trouble?" Hal asked.

Mr. McKinney grinned. His eyes twinkled behind his rimless glasses as he turned to his wife. "Oh, we had our ups and downs, didn't we, Ma?"

"Not as bad as with the local politicians though." Mrs. McKinney laughed. "They're always underfoot. We Americans who live and work in West Africa sometimes get exasperated by the impossibility of getting important things done. It's often like coming up against a stone wall, and then we have to give up. When that happens we just turn to each other and say, 'Well, WAWA.'"

"WAWA?" Hal echoed.

McKinney's grin widened. "Yes. It stands for West Africa Wins Again!"

"I'll have to remember that," Hal said, "if the going gets rough and I can't get anything done. WAWA. That's a good one."

"In the meantime would you like to see our church?" McKinney continued and the pride in his voice was obvious.

We all said yes in unison.

Then Hal continued. "We noticed it when we arrived. It's quite substantial."

The McKinneys told us how they had built the church with only native help, and we could not disguise our amazement at this accomplishment, since the church was quite large —about 150 feet long and at least 38 feet wide. It was constructed of large stones cemented together, and its corrugated-covered steeple towered almost three stories above the entrance.

"I suppose you're planning to film the Dogon City of the Dead and the Cave of the Dead before you go back, aren't you?" Mr. McKinney inquired as we left the church.

"Cave of the Dead and City of the Dead?" Hal's voice echoed with that tone of interest I knew so well. "No one told me such things were near here."

"Oh, they're quite a sight. Only about three or four miles up the road there's a huge cave and palisades. Your driver knows how to get there."

"I hope so. Cisse is with the Government Tourist Office."

"Well, let's ask him to take you there."

Cisse was asleep on the porch, enjoying a siesta after our unexpectedly heavy lunch. He obviously was reluctant to be disturbed. When Mr. McKinney spoke to him in the native tongue, he hesitated and then answered slowly and grudgingly.

The missionary turned to us. "He says he hasn't enough gas to get there and come back and still drive to Mopti, but I know he has plenty of fuel because the round trip is only six miles. Besides, you can get more gas on your way back at a town fifty miles this side of Mopti. I'll just have to make sure that it isn't WAWA today." He winked at us and started to put on his sun helmet. "Very well," he said loudly in French, "I guess I'll have to take you there myself in my own truck and then I'll drop a note to the director of the Tourist Office in Mopti explaining why you couldn't go in your own car and requesting that he repay me for the gasoline I used."

Cisse was on his feet in a flash. "Pardon, m'sieu," he said to Hal, "I have just remembered we have an extra can of petrol in the back of the bus. I will be most happy to take you to the cave myself."

Mr. McKinney slowly removed his sun helmet and calmly wiped the perspiration from its band with a large red bandanna as we entered our small bus. These stalwart people watched us smilingly as we waved good-bye.

Just as we pulled away, Mr. McKinney called out, "You see, it isn't *always* WAWA!"

Our little rear-engined vehicle navigated for a few minutes through ruts and around potholes, but all too soon we came to the end of the road and from there on we had to proceed on foot in the broiling sun for more than a mile. But the exertion and effort were well worthwhile—there, spread out on a vast cliff, was an entire Dogon city of three-story buildings. Immediately below gaped an immense cave.

Cisse shifted the camera case he was carrying and pointed to the buildings. "Those, m'sieu, are for the living. The dead reside beyond that cave. Come, I will show you."

When we plunged into the dark entrance to the cave, we could see at once that it was a natural archway obviously worn out eons ago by the strong current of some stream long dried up by the desert heat. The cave was almost a city block wide. A cool breeze flowing through it made us shiver after the heat of the tropical sun. When we came out at the far end, we found ourselves standing on the edge of a precipice. Far below us, tucked into cavelike recesses hewn out of the side of an enormous cliff, were the houses of the dead of the Dogon tribe, arranged in the form of a village. The similarity to the cliff dwellings of the Indians of New Mexico was startling.

It was thought-provoking to note that the houses of the dead seemed to be far superior to those occupied by the living!

Hal installed the long-range telephoto lens on one of his cameras and squinted through the view-finder at the City of the Dead below us. "I'll have to lean out over the edge if I am to get some good shots," he muttered.

"Not unless I hold you, elskan-min," I protested. And I took firm hold of his belt. Overhearing me, David came and took firm hold of me *and* the belt. He was strong and almost my height. Together we braced ourselves while Hal fixed his tripod as near the edge of the precipice as he could. My heart was in my mouth. Cisse, who could understand barely a word of English, had paid no attention to our conversation and had wandered off. Suddenly he turned and saw Hal leaning over the precipice, with David and me both holding onto his belt. He stood still, transfixed with astonishment.

But before he could utter a word Hal jubilantly exclaimed, "Got it!" and wriggled back to safety.

19
Timbuktu!

TIMBUKTU! The mecca of world adventurers! Our battered Air Mail DC-3 circled the fabled city. In the distance we could see the Niger River bending toward the southeast. From the air the town looked like a cluster of sun-baked clay boxes with an occasional beehive sticking up here and there.

The landing-gear wheels dropped into place; the wing flaps came down. The plane seemed to hesitate and then it swooped down to a feathery landing. We were the only white passengers aboard.

Now the ship taxied to the disembarking area. There was no terminal building although one was being built a short distance away. The few native passengers quickly descended the rickety ladder from the plane and were gone. We began to collect our gear at the baggage compartment. And then the pilot and copilot emerged from the cabin. They had already been on board when we entered the plane at Mopti, and we had not seen them during the hour-and-a-half flight.

Now they stopped to chat with us and we saw that they were gray-haired and elderly, as pilots go. Both were French but both spoke passable English. They wanted to know if we had enjoyed the flight. We had. They asked if we were on business or pleasure. Hal told them it was both. And with that they cheerily waved adieu to us and marched off. Later we learned that they had both reached the retirement age while piloting for a major transatlantic airline and had afterward found a sort of retirement job flying the old DC-3's on the run between Bamako, Mopti, a place called Goundam and Timbuktu.

Our informant ended by saying, "A touching story, don't you think? Those two old pilots and the old airplane—all three growing older together as the years go by!"

Hal managed to get the driver of a big truck to take us into town with our equipment, and there we found another *Encampement,* this one operated by a jovial proprietor named Abdul Jalil. The rooms here were as small as those of our cells at Mopti, with only a tiny opening near the ceiling for ventilation; there were no windows at all. It was gloomy but we learned that this type of construction had been borrowed from the desert Touaregs who had developed it as a way of coping with the fierce Sahara heat.

I was relieved to see that Mr. Jalil apparently believed in cleanliness. Our room was swept regularly and the sheets were changed like clockwork. Furthermore the bathroom facilities were clean. After Mopti, Jalil's hostelry was like a seventh heaven.

No sooner had we settled ourselves than our host knocked on the door. He spoke no English and French was our only means of communication.

"Since you're the only guests here, I've prepared a special luncheon." He beamed.

We were famished and lost no time in hurrying to the small dining room. Mr. Jalil doubled as a waiter. He proudly brought out a platter of what seemed to be some kind of fried cottage cheese.

"A native dish?" Hal asked.

"Ah oui, m'sieu. Delicieuse!" Jalil fluttered.

Hal and I simultaneously tasted the food. It was awful but Hal politely smiled and took another forkful. Somehow I managed to swallow my mouthful. David watched us brightly, his hands clasped in his lap. He hadn't started to eat. We were to be the king's tasters and he was the king.

Hal looked up at Jalil, who now wore a baffled expression.

"M'sieu Jalil," Hal began, "it's delicious, this repast you have prepared for us and whose identity I seem to have forgotten for the moment—"

"It is the *cerveille,* m'sieu." Jalil beamed again. "A specialty of the house."

"Ah, the *cerveille.*" Hal nodded. "Of course!" But he looked perplexed.

I suddenly realized that I knew the word. I had seen it in my collection of cook books at home.

I managed to gasp weakly, "Hal-minn, *cerveille* in French means brains. These are fried brains!"

Jalil read the expression on our faces. His smile faded.

Hal looked up at him. "It is an admirable and succulent dish. Of a certainty."

"Yes. Of a certainty," echoed our host.

My husband pursed his lips and gazed pensively at the table. Jalil looked as though he were on the verge of tears.

"Unfortunately, madame has a delicate stomach," Hal said.

"How tragic!" Jalil's dark eyes looked at me with compassion.

"She requires delicate food. Like scrambled eggs, perhaps?"

Jalil straightened up. "I understand. At once, m'sieu."

"But wait!" Hal exclaimed. Jalil paused. "Because we do not wish to make her feel ill at ease, our son and I always eat what she does. You understand, of course."

Jalil smiled. "It is a most sentimental thing, this. I, too, have a great tenderness for my wife!" He whipped away the plates and disappeared into the kitchen.

Hal covered his eyes. His shoulders began to shake.

I could only say, "Hal Linker, you should have been an actor!"

"I was merely being diplomatic, elskan-min. After all, I didn't graduate from the School of Foreign Service for nothing."

Jalil reappeared, this time with platters of scrambled eggs and bread. He served us with a magnificent flourish, wished us *bon appétit!* and then went back to the kitchen.

"You see," said Hal, "He's now our friend for life."

Mopti had been hot but Timbuktu was almost unbearable during daylight hours. Although the Touareg method of construction did help keep our room cooler than it was outdoors, the heat was still intense and dry. After luncheon we did the only sensible thing to do in such climates—we retired to our rooms to rest until the sun sank lower. To keep even halfway comfortable, we had to take turns under the shower and then cool off as best we could by letting the water evaporate from our bare skins in the dry air.

We finally managed to doze off, only to be awakened a short while later by the sound of distant bugles and military drums. Hal leaped up, slipped into light-weight cotton slacks and sandals, and hurried outside to investigate. He returned almost immediately. Jalil was standing outside and told Hal that by good fortune we had arrived during a local holiday.

"They're holding a military parade of some sort and I'd better film it, for our Timbuktu episode," Hal said.

I got up. "I'll help you."

"Me, too, Pabbi." David was already awake.

The three of us, burdened with our equipment, left the encampment and trudged toward the scene of all the activity a few hundred yards down the dirt road. There at a large soccer field we found what seemed to be most of Timbuktu's leading citizens and their wives, the men wearing long, voluminous, Arab-style robes while the women were resplendent in the national costume of Mali, which we had first seen at Bamako.

With nodded approval, the onlookers were watching three

platoons of barefooted, uniformed militiamen, who seemed to range in age from eight years to the early twenties. They all wore blue military shirts and shorts. The platoon leaders, obviously officers, wore steel helmets. The thought of the heat underneath those helmets made me wince. The rank and file at least had the benefit of more sensible headgear—perky, light-weight overseas caps. While most of them carried long-barreled rifles (some were as long as the boys shouldering them), at least several in each platoon were armed with wicked-looking submachine guns!

The band marched along with the militiamen. Comprised of equally young boys, the musicians were not exactly skillful. The din that came from the trumpeters made my head ache but I kept a straight face to avoid offending the watchers. And most of the people there, including tall, burnoosed Touaregs, kept staring at us.

After we had such footage of the parade as we needed, we dragged ourselves back to the encampment. Jalil met us with the suggestion that we should attend the special dances that night which would conclude the holiday festivities.

"When the sun goes down it becomes most pleasant out-of-doors," he added.

He proved to be quite right. When the sun finally dropped behind the horizon, it grew delightfully cool compared to the heat of the daylight hours. Through Jalil's efforts, we got a ride in a Land Rover to the edge of town where we found a small stage in the open facing rows of temporary seats that were already occupied by many important local personages including the Governor of Timbuktu, Ataher Ek Chegu, accompanied by his wife and child.

The dances were performed by children who presented in costume the various steps of their parents' tribes. The audience was interested but somewhat restrained, we thought. And then the entire group of youngsters, ranging in age from seven to the late teens, began to enact skits that were obviously humorous, judging from the reaction of the audience. We couldn't understand a word of what was said, since it was all spoken in the native language, but the meaning was obvious. Each skit was ridiculing the French, who were shown wearing their official uniforms and costumes as army officers and judges of the pre-independence days, all looking and acting quite stupid and pompous. The patriots brought to trial before the judges were always noble, and their impassioned speeches evoked thunderous applause and cheers from the hitherto lethargic spectators. This was what they had been waiting for all evening.

During a short intermission Hal was checking his equipment when an unmistakable American voice was heard. "Hello, folks," it said.

We turned.

A tall, broad shouldered man in his late twenties stood there, smiling. "I'm Dave Marshall," he introduced himself. "I live here with my brother Frank and our families. We're missionaries."

He looked more like a football player. We introduced ourselves and learned that he had heard through the Timbuktu grapevine that other Americans were in town and that he had hoped to run into us at this performance.

"Would you like to meet the Governor?"

We most certainly would. His Excellency Ataher Ek Chegu was quite friendly and in turn introduced his wife, an attractive woman but enormous in size. I wondered if West Africans, like the Samoans of Pago Pago, feel that a well-padded wife is a status symbol for her husband. Apparently unsuccessful husbands are not able to afford to stuff their wives that well! I remembered that during our travels in the South Seas I had several times been urged by Polynesian women with whom I had become friendly to "fatten up a bit so your husband can be proud of you."

The Governor's wife was charming, although we could not bridge the gulf of language for easy communication. She wore the glittering Mali costume and held in her lap her tiny baby girl, whose eyes were already outlined with the kohl that West African women use the way European women use mascara. Seeing this makeup on an infant was no longer as startling as it had been the first time I saw it years before in Tangier.

We promised to look the Marshalls up before we left Timbuktu, and then the three of us once again paid our respects to the Governor and his lady and returned to the encampment. Here we remained for a long time outside our cell, enjoying the cool night air. We marveled at the glittering expanse of what seemed to be billions of stars in the night sky over the Sahara Desert.

By now we were dead tired and when we reached our beds we practically collapsed with exhaustion—but not until I made everyone perform the nightly ritual of brushing his teeth! After all, Timbuktu or no Timbuktu, I couldn't let my family get cavities through neglect. For safety's sake, we always used boiled and filtered water, even for this simple act.

We've been awakened in many parts of the world by a multitude of sounds but our first reveille in Timbuktu consisted of the most ungodly snortings, gruntings and gurglings imaginable. We got up and opened the door. Confronting us was a camel. In fact several camels! Each was hobbled by having its doubled-up foreleg bound against the upper leg. The beasts had arrived in a caravan during the night and were drinking water from an oasis a few yards from our encampment. They were guarded by Touareg men whose eyes seemed to pierce us from over their faces veils.

Well, it was colorful and different. It was Timbuktu and I loved it.

After a breakfast of eggs (Hal pointed out that from now on we'd probably have to resign ourselves to that dish and tea), we were ready to explore and film the legendary city that had drawn us like a magnet from thousands of miles away.

Timbuktu has been alternately described as the "meeting

point of camel and canoe" or the "Port of the Sudan in the Sahara." The latter may be more appropriate during the rainy months because although it apparently never rains in Timbuktu, the Niger River which flows nearby becomes swollen by the deluges in the interior and is navigable for six months, by medium-sized steamers, almost up to the ancient city's doorstep.

Hal had read much about Timbuktu during the time when he was plotting to surprise me with the announcement of our trip here. As we wandered through the streets, he held both David and me spellbound with a brief résumé of Timbuktu's history.

The city had actually been founded by the nomadic Touaregs in the 11th century as a trade settlement. Just to the south a powerful Negro race known as the Songhai, who had originally migrated from the Nile Valley three centuries before, founded a city called Gao and became interested in the Touareg settlement of Timbuktu as an outlet for trade.

For quite a while the nomadic Touaregs, blood cousins of the fierce Berbers, seemed to get along well with the Songhai and to profit by the relationship. During the 12th and 13th centuries, Timbuktu's fame as a central point for trade with all the peoples of North and West Africa had spread even to Europe. Tales that gold and salt were plentiful in Timbuktu's marketplaces attracted adventurous souls from Spain and Italy.

"There's an old Catalan map dated 1373 A.D. that accurately shows Timbuktu, or Timboutch, as it was then called, located at the edge of the Sahara," Hal told us.

As the city's fame and wealth grew, so did the greed and ambitions of neighboring powers. In 1434, the Touaregs themselves, after having been pushed out of their own city, returned as invaders and captured Timbuktu. The Songhai, who had become Moslems themselves and were then at the zenith of their power, came back under King Sunni Ali thirty-five years later and drove the Touaregs back into the Sahara.

Under Ali's successor Askia, Timbuktu really blossomed. The great University of Sankore, founded at that time, became a center of Moslem culture and learning.

Of course Timbuktu's ascendancy was bound to act as a magnet for plunderers. The city was finally captured by an expedition sent by El Mansur, Sultan of Morocco, and led by an Andalusian Moor who succeeded in smashing the Songhai Empire.

Moroccan control brought about the downfall of Timbuktu. From a vast, flourishing city, it became a place of impoverished desolation. Legends of its former glories and tales of its remoteness still lingered in the folklore of Europeans during those centuries when it was thought of as a lost city, and led to the use of its name as a symbol of the remotest place one could think of—the farthest corner of the earth.

The Moslem conquerers had declared its area a forbidden city for infidels and no one dared break this taboo. No one, that is, until an English officer named Alexander Gordon Laing traveled through the Sahara from Tripoli to Timbuktu in 1826, only to be detected after a few days in spite of his Arab disguise, and murdered. Then the French explorer, René Caillié, managed to remain undetected during his visit to the city two years later.

Caillié's published account of that trip helped impel France into a program of colonial expansion that sixty-five years later was to give her possession not only of Timbuktu but other vast sections of West Africa. Had Major Laing survived, Timbuktu might well have become a British possession.

Walking along dirt roads through sections that had once been prosperous neighborhoods in the city's days of glory, I reflected on the fact that while France's name is unpopular in Mali today, actually Timbuktu had been able to struggle back into some semblance of stability only under the protection of French rule.

When that first tiny contingent of French soldiers had

"seized" the city (with the approval of its remaining citizens), Timbuktu was a vast ruin. By 1900, the French had effectively stopped Touareg raids and the people slowly began to rebuild their citadel.

Although it was not yet 9 in the morning, the hot Sahara sun gave baleful promise of what the day would hold. If we were to accomplish anything during the daylight hours, it would have to be squeezed into those few when the out-of-doors was livable for such Sahara tourists as the Linkers.

On all sides were interesting buildings constructed in Sudanese style of red earth and clay, each resembling a fortress. The portals of most houses were massive wooden doors reinforced with copper and brass in ornate designs.

The Great Mosque, which once stood near the center of Timbuktu, now finds itself at the western edge of the shrunken town, all that remains of the former metropolis. We could see the high tower of this mosque and that of the Mosque of Sidi Yahia from many parts of the town, and we used them to orient ourselves in our wanderings. I was awe-stricken when I learned that these high-walled edifices and their towers, built of red clay and mud, had withstood almost five centuries of wind and sand. Fortunately rain is practically unknown in Timbuktu, otherwise they would have long since been dissolved into nothingness.

The majority of passers-by on the dirt roads were men, most of them wearing flowing robes and turbans. Some were veiled Touaregs. We stopped and filmed several of these fierce, half-tamed desert warriors. They are always armed with a wicked dagger at least and most of them also carry their cross-hilted swords on their hips in soft leather scabbards. Many of them carry long spears as well. They are blood brothers of the Berbers of North Africa, and only the men are veiled. Their women never wear face coverings. The chests and arms of the men were covered with amulets to ward off evil, and I learned that their religion, while basically Moslem, still has vestiges of Christianity and even of Judaism!

I suddenly realized that we had not seen any Touareg women in the streets, and then the reason dawned on me. These men were on business trips from across the Sahara Desert. Like commercial travelers in the United States, they were not able to take their wives with them. My strongest memory of the Touaregs we met is the impact of their piercing eyes as they mysteriously watched my every move from behind their heavy face coverings.

While there are some local industries such as cotton weaving, leatherwork and embroidery which help support the permanent population of about 7,000, the main business activity in Timbuktu is still trade, as it has been for centuries. From March to June the population swells to about 25,000 as merchants and traders from all over the southern Sahara flock to this trading center. We saw caravans of plodding camels from the ancient desert salt mines of Taoudenni, some 375 miles away. Almost unbelievably large slabs of salt resembling tombstones were tied to the camels' humps. This product is still Timbuktu's main support in its struggle for continuing existence.

As we were filming in the narrow streets of the market area where colorfully robed native Negro women swarmed about, David stopped at a large, well-painted sign in French. His lips pursed as he tried to make it out. He had studied Spanish in school and speaks Icelandic, but he had never studied French.

"I can make out the word 'library' and the word 'dictionary,' " he said, "but what does the rest of it say?"

I looked up. The sign read:

LIBRAIRE ÉVANGÉLIQUE
DICTIONNAIRES
LIVRES SCOLAIRES
LIVRES RELIGIEUX
PAPETERIE
TA PAROLE EST UNE LAMPE A MES PIEDS ET UNE LUMIÈRE SUR MON SENTIER.

I translated the phrase at the bottom as: "Thy word is a lamp unto my feet and a light unto my path."

Then, just as Hal joined us, we heard a familiar booming voice from within the dark recesses of the shop.

"Well, I see you found us." David Marshall came out and greeted us jovially. "This is our mission's book shop and library. Say, Frank," he called out toward the interior of the establishment, "come on out and meet the American family I was telling you about."

In a moment, towering in the doorway stood another young American, almost a duplicate of his brother but a year or two older. Introductions were made all around.

"Well, I see you're busy filming," David Marshall said, "but if you have a chance why don't you drop over to visit us? Our wives and the youngsters would be delighted to meet you. Just ask anyone where the Americans live: they'll know." And with a friendly wave, the Marshalls went back to their customers.

The sign over the entrance to the old fort gave its name as CHEIK SIDI BEKAYE. It was garrisoned and is still in use. It looked so much like the Hollywood movie sets for films about the French Foreign Legion that I half expected to find Ronald Coleman or Charles Boyer in charge.

Hal anticipated filming problems because we had heard that the Army was rather jittery here. The cautious attitude of the military was due to the fact that the proud Touaregs, hearing of other small areas of Africa that had obtained their independence in recent years, now wanted their own Touareg nation! Obviously independence was fine when you were seeking it but not as desirable when others sought it from you. The Mali Government was resisting their demands.

"I'd better ask for permission before I even take a shot of the outside," Hal murmured and went over to talk to the armed sentry on duty at the gate. He had left his cameras with me and as I waited I noted that on each side of the entrance were two small but wicked-looking weapons. They resembled small cannons, each with several barrels. I had never seen guns like these.

David examined them at close range and then casually announced, "They are a type of Gatling gun. They were invented by an American named Gatling before the Civil War."

"Really?" I murmured. "What are they for?"

David looked at me with a My goodness! don't women know anything? kind of expression. "Well, they're the first type of machine gun. The barrels turn as the gun is fired and the movement brings each barrel into position in rotation. This one is a sort of cannon Gatling and must date from about 1880 or 1890."

"Interesting," I said politely.

At that moment Hal returned. "Well, armies are armies all over the world," he announced. "I'll have to make inquiries according to rank until I find an officer with authority to give me an okay. I'll be back as soon as I can. You'd better wait here." And off he trotted.

He returned almost an hour later, wringing wet with perspiration. Without a word, he took his camera and tripod from me and filmed the fort from several angles. I knew he would tell me what had happened as soon as he had finished filming.

He finally paused to wipe his brow. "As I was telling you, armies are armies all over the world," he began. "The sentry called the sergeant on duty. The sergeant took me to the lieutenant, who chatted with me for a while and then turned me over to the major. Finally I was taken in to the colonel, to whom I had to repeat the whole story as to why we were here, and then the colonel said, 'Why of course, Mr. Linker. You can take all the scenes you wish of the fort—but only from the outside, you understand.' "

As we wearily made our way back to the encampment, we heard children singing in the distance. I was almost too tired and hot really to care, but Hal stopped dead in his tracks and listened carefully.

"No, it can't be true!" he exclaimed.

"What can't be true, dear?" I asked.

"That song. It's 'Old Black Joe.' "

"Oh come now, you're imagining things," I scoffed, but I listened more carefully. It *was* "Old Black Joe." Coming around a corner was a group of about twenty young Negro schoolchildren with their native teacher, a young man in his twenties. They were singing the old southern song as they walked, but the words were in French. Hal lost no time requesting permission of the teacher to record the scene, and it was readily granted. Then Hal filmed them and I recorded their voices as the ebony-skinned youngsters sang the old song in French, except for the last words, which they clearly chanted as "Old *vieux* Joe."

Hal felt that we should renew the experience of riding a camel before we left Timbuktu, and so the next morning arrangements were made with Abdul Jalil for a camel with its Touareg owner to meet us at the Great Mosque so that again we could sail the ship of the desert as we had years before in Egypt. The time of rendezvous was set for 2 o'clock in the afternoon. This arrangement would allow us hours of sunlight and still be sufficiently late after the noon siesta to make it safe to venture out-of-doors.

In true West African style, Abdul said, "Yes, m'sieu" to every admonition that he must be sure that our camel was on time.

We were punctual. No camel. No Touareg. Two hours later he casually rode up. It was almost 4 o'clock. He was an impressive figure, a young man dressed in typical desert style with indigo robes which must have been dyed by the indigo women we had filmed at Mopti. He seemed to be handsome and probably had a haughty look on his face. I say "seemed to be" and "probably" because he was completely veiled from the bridge of his nose down, in the Touareg style. Only his piercing eyes gave any hint of emotion. Strapped to his left wrist was the traditional dagger; at his side was a Touareg sword; good-luck amulets covered his left arm.

"Well, two hours late. That's not too bad. It's WAWA again," Hal said with resignation. "We'd better start filming." At that moment he suddenly glanced up at the sky. As far as I could see it was perfectly clear. There wasn't a cloud above us. He pursed his lips and gazed at the horizon, then cried, "Let's get going, fast! We'll have about fifteen minutes of sunlight. You'll be the only one who can take a ride." He turned to the Touareg and tried to get the information to him. He was met with a blank stare. The Touareg spoke no French!

A group of passers-by had gathered to see the strange Americans, and now Hal appealed to them, asking if anyone spoke French. A young boy, obviously a student, volunteered to act as interpreter. But when Hal excitedly told him about the approaching storm and the short time left us before the sun would disappear, the boy looked up at the burning sun in the cloudless sky in amazement. Then, shrugging his shoulders, he passed the message on to the Touareg. There was an excited buzzing from all the spectators as they heard Hal's prediction, and I thought I detected a strange look in the Touareg's eyes, but he seemed unperturbed as he kicked his mount's flank with his heels to make it crouch so that he could dismount. The camel wheezed, grunted and gurgled its displeasure, but the Touareg, his eyes glinting, would not be denied. Finally the beast bent its front knees and knelt with a great sigh. Its rear end followed suit and the ship of the desert was ready for boarding.

The animal moaned and then slowly twisted its long neck and looked at me as though saying, "Well, let's get it over with, lady!"

It made all of us laugh. I approached the camel. Fortunately I was wearing slacks, but even so with the pommel of the saddle about two feet high, with triple-pointed prongs,

I almost fell over backward as I tried to lift my leg high enough to clear the vicious-looking obstacles and mount. Finally I managed to swing one leg over the ornate saddle horn with David's assistance.

The animal, urged by a guttural command accentuated by a firm kick from its owner, raised up on its forefeet, almost pitching me backward over its stern as it did so. As I pulled myself forward into position, the camel's rear deck soared skyward and I was almost thrown over its head! I escaped this fate only by holding onto the pommel like a shipwrecked sailor clutching a floating log. After all this pitching and tossing, I could well understand how camels became known as "ships of the desert." But, even so, the title fails to convey that the camel is a ship in a storm. It had been years since we had ridden in Egypt, and I had forgotten what happens when you board a camel.

Once we got under way the ride was fine. As I rocked and swayed my way through Timbuktu, Hal recorded the ride on film. The pace was so leisurely that he had no difficulty in keeping up with me and could in fact run on ahead to set up his equipment.

Finally he gave a signal to the Touareg to let me off. The latter had been walking alongside me and now, after a few well-placed kicks and barked commands, the camel retracted its rear landing gear. Once more I went through the spine-jarring, neck-snapping gyrations until the animal crouched again and I was able to dismount.

Just then the sun disappeared in a bank of clouds and the wind started to whistle. The Touareg stopped in the act of mounting and looked at the sky in astonishment. There was a buzz of excitement from the spectators who had been following our caravan through the streets. Those with wrist-watches looked at them excitedly. It had been exactly fifteen minutes since Hal had predicted that the sun would disappear within that time! My husband looked smug and self-satisfied.

"How in the world did you do it?" I asked as he hurried to pack his equipment before the storm hit us.

"It was easy this time," he replied. "I've gotten so used to judging light that I noticed a very slight haze. That made me examine the horizon carefully and I saw a low cloud away over there. Since the wind was blowing from that direction, I watched the cloud for a few seconds and saw that it was headed this way. It was a cinch to estimate how long it would take to reach here." He looked up at me and smiled. "Didn't do too bad this time, eh?"

Whatever reply I might have intended making was forgotten as a violent gust of wind hit us, sweeping up clouds of sand.

"No time to get back to the encampment!" Hal shouted. "I'll get that truck driver to take us to the Marshall's." He hailed a small truck that was passing and after a hurried conference signaled us to get aboard. The driver was heading for shelter, too, but the Marshalls were nearby and very little out of his way, he told Hal.

As we pulled up to the substantial-looking, one-story, walled-in residence, the truck driver shouted, *"Les Améri-caines! Les Américaines!"*

Frank Marshall came out to greet us. He had heard the clatter of our vehicle coming up the road. We thanked our driver and turned to Frank.

"Come on in before the sandstorm hits," he urged.

As we entered the door we were greeted by Dave Marshall, who introduced us to his wife Peggy and Frank's wife Barbara. Dave's two daughters, Diane, ten, and Sandra, twelve, could hardly restrain themselves until our David got rid of his camera bag and was ready for a visit with them. Frank Marshall's daughters then joined us, Bonnie, ten, and Pattie, only five. Frank explained that his son Peter, who was twelve, was away at school in Abidjan on the Ivory Coast.

"He and David would have had quite a time together," he said regretfully.

The roar of the wind rose even higher, and the sound of sand pelting against the window panes grew louder.

Frank cocked his head to listen, then began to give instructions to the girls. "Turn off the wind vane on the water pump, then close all the shutters quickly."

The girls obeyed with speed born of long practice, but sand still continued to sift through cracks and under doors so that there was a slight haze around the lights in the room.

"It's getting near dinnertime," Frank's wife called out from the kitchen, "and this storm will last for a while. Why don't you just eat with us tonight? I'll make up something special."

The wind howled. The lights, operated by a panting gasoline generator outside the house, flickered off and on. I remembered that scrambled eggs and tea waited for us at the encampment, even if we could make it, and gratefully accepted Mrs. Marshall's offer.

For the next half hour or so we exchanged anecdotes about Africa and our travels and learned that the Marshalls had set up their mission in Timbuktu in 1959. The children of missionary parents themselves, they had struck out on their own and initiated a unique method of bringing the Gospel to the area near the Niger River. During the Niger's flood season, they cruised the stream in a hand-built houseboat called the *Niger Gospel Boat*. From a photograph, we could see that it resembled the houseboat that had been our home during our sojourn in Kashmir. The Marshalls' craft was equipped with a galley and could accommodate seven passengers. It had been built and was operated under the auspices of the Evangelical Baptist Missions and was considered the property of about six hundred people who had contributed funds toward its construction. From it the Marshalls dispensed the Gospel message and whatever medical aid the local authorities permitted them to extend, which was unfortunately usually limited to prescribing aspirin, since none of them had a medical degree.

We were engrossed in this story when a voice from the

kitchen called out, "I hope you like this. It's all I could make quickly, and I'm sure you're all famished." Frank's wife came in with a tray stacked high with a dozen hamburgers on rolls. One of the girls brought in a pitcher of iced tea, and we dug in with cries of surprise and delight. In our travels throughout the world, we've dined at many famous restaurants but in none of them do I recall enjoying every morsel I ate as much as I did those American-style hamburgers on rolls during a raging sandstorm in Timbuktu.

Later that evening the storm slackened and David Marshall drove us back to the encampment. Our clothing, suitcases, and beds were covered with a thin layer of Sahara sand that had seeped into the room, even though it had no windows.

We were scheduled to leave Timbuktu the next morning at 9. When 10 o'clock came and then 11 and no word was heard from the plane, we began to worry. Hal paced back and forth, occasionally pausing to scan the sky and listen for the motors.

I could see that he was seriously disturbed.

I put my hand on his arm. "What is it, elskan-min?" I asked gently.

"I want to get us out of here," he said vehemently. "Since we've been in Mali we've weathered about four storms. That's one every three days."

"Can't we take the next plane if this one doesn't come today?" I asked.

"No, the next plane isn't due for three days and even then it is supposed to be one of those ridiculous little Antonev planes I've seen pictures of. It's a Russian-built single-engined biplane like those of thirty years ago and it carries ten passengers at a speed of about a hundred and ten miles an hour. Today's plane is scheduled to be a twin-engined American-made DC-3. They're old but they're safe and stable." He pounded his fist in his hand. "But what worries me most is starting out so late, even if the plane *does* come today. The thermals can be bad when it really heats up."

I recalled the thermals in Ethiopia and couldn't suppress a shudder. Hal reached over and put an arm around my shoulders and pressed me to him.

It was not until 2 o'clock in the afternoon that David was the first to hear the distant hum of the approaching plane. We hurriedly got our gear together and entered the half-ton truck Abdul Jalil had arranged for our transport to the field. In five minutes we were there. On the way Jalil informed us that they had just learned that the plane had been delayed at Goundam, a tiny town up the Niger, by the same storm we had encountered the previous night. Early in the morning the plane had continued on to its original destination at Niamey and was now arriving, five hours late, on the return trip.

As it taxied toward us I heard Hal gasp. He gazed in dismay at the transport. Then he said, "I'm sorry, Halla-min. That's an Ilyushin-14, not a DC-3."

Mention of that name brought back a flood of memories. Several years before when we were traveling through the Soviet Union, we had scheduled a flight from Odessa to Kiev. Our plane was an Ilyushin-14, a Russian-built imitation of the American twin-engined Convair. But the Russian version was different in several respects. It was not pressurized, as is the Convair, primarily because the Russian pilots liked to fly close to the ground and never needed pressurizing equipment. When we had entered the Ilyushin at Odessa, a frowsy-haired, middle-aged stewardess directed the passengers to drop their luggage on the floor alongside the entrance near the tail. And there the bundles and boxes and suitcases had remained, lying loose during the entire flight, sliding about during landings and takeoffs. Hal had been horrified to find that there were no seat belts on the plane, but the final straw had been the sound of the motors during the flight. I can only describe them as sounding like power-driven lawn mowers! As we seemed to skim along just over the treetops during that trip of several hundred miles, Hal had sworn that we would never ride in another Ilyushin-14 in Russia. And we continued our travels completely across that nation by means of trains until we reached Helsinki. Now here it was again—another Ilyushin-14.

Hal shook his head. "We'll just have to take it, elskan-min. We have no choice."

And we prepared to go aboard.

The pilots were Russians, we noted as they came off the plane to stretch their legs. When they saw Hal filming them and the plane, they quickly turned their heads away, but he had already taken the footage he wanted.

Inside the Air Mali plane, however, we were pleasantly surprised. Not only did it have a baggage compartment but there were seat belts for each passenger, apparently as a concession to world safety regulations.

Shortly after we took off and started to climb, we noticed that the plane had leveled off at an altitude of only about 2,000 feet.

"Well, the Russians *still* like to fly low. That's one thing that hasn't been changed," Hal remarked wryly. The seat-belt sign, in French, went off and the charming young Mali stewardess began to serve pineapple juice in paper cups. There were only three Europeans aboard, all men. We had noticed them at the airport where they were freely conversing in the native language with some of the Mali passengers. And from that and their general appearance—their sandals, white shorts and short-sleeved, open-collared shirts—we knew they must be Frenchmen who had lived in Central Africa for some time. About twenty Africans had also boarded the plane with us at Timbuktu, some in European dress and some in flowing desert robes. There were no women among them.

Hal was seated across the aisle from David and me, and I smiled at him because the juice was so nice and cold and tasted so good. I happened to glance at the Frenchman seated behind Hal and he looked ill at ease.

At that moment our plane seemed to hit an obstruction. There was a terrifying jar and we plunged downward as though our wings had fallen off. We twisted and vibrated, although a despairing glance out of the window assured me that the wings were still intact. Our gyrations were so violent that I wondered how long they could withstand the pressure.

I could hear the Frenchman moaning what sounded like *"Une orage! Une orage!"*

Hal caught the words and shouted across to me, "Hold on! Hold on! He says it's a desert storm." He reached for my hand across the aisle and missed. There was no chance to fasten our safety belts.

A familiar nauseating odor permeated the cabin. Every African in the plane was air-sick and vomiting. I remembered the scent all too well from our flights in Ethiopia.

Hal reached over again and this time grasped my hand. He gave me a reassuring look. With my other hand, I held onto David, who had looked inquiringly at me when the buffeting began and who now held onto his armrest with both hands. There was a slackening in the gyrations and we quickly fastened our seat belts.

David took this opportunity to try to ease my obvious tension. "Wasn't it funny, Mommie, the way those heads in front of us went popping up into the air all at once and the paper cups of pineapple juice all hit the ceiling?"

I managed a sickly smile.

Our reprieve ended. Once more the plane plummeted toward the ground, shaking and vibrating hideously.

I could hear Hal muttering, "Come on, Ivan, pull her out of it! Pull her out of it!"

And then the movements of the plane again began to smooth out and we were once more on an even keel.

I looked down. We were only a few hundred feet above the ground. The weather was clear; there was not a cloud in the sky. We started to climb again, and this time we leveled off several thousand feet higher than we had been flying at the time the gyrations began. But I still couldn't relax. My nerves were taut. I knew that one more violent thrust of movement would make me burst into tears.

"What happened, Hal-minn?" I tried to sound calm.

"We must have flown through the beginning of a desert storm," he said thoughtfully. "There was probably an abrupt temperature change accompanied by violent winds, and we plowed into the invisible trap at full cruising speed. I've been reading about it in the States lately. It's called 'clear-air turbulence.' It was rough all right. I'm sorry I got you and David into it."

"Don't ever say that, elskan-min," I replied. "My place is where you and David are—no matter where."

Our son, completely relaxed, entered the conversation. "Say, Pabbi, now that we've been to Timbuktu, is there any other faraway place we can visit someday?"

"How about Shangri-la?" I suggested, managing a smile.

"Shangri-la, eh?" Hal repeated musingly. "That's the mysterious place where people never grow old, isn't it?"

I nodded.

"I think we've been there already," my husband continued thoughtfully.

"We have?"

Hal gave me a broad smile. "We *must* have been there, elskan-min, because I swear you don't look a day older than when you married me. In fact, you look younger and much prettier!"

Is it any wonder that I consider myself the luckiest woman alive?

The engines sounded strong and powerful now. I sat back, perfectly relaxed, wonderfully happy again. Those mighty engines were taking us home—home from Timbuktu.